LEE SVITAK DEAN

COME ONE,

With over 150 recipes from the *Star Tribune* Taste section

COME ONE, COME ALL

COME ALL

EASY ENTERTAINING
WITH
SEASONAL MENUS

MINNESOTA HISTORICAL SOCIETY PRESS

www.mhspress.org

The Minnesota Historical Society Press is a member of the
Association of American University Presses.

Manufactured in the United States of America

10 9 8 7 6 5 4 3 2 1

♾ The paper used in this publication meets the minimum requirements of the American National Standard for Information Sciences—Permanence for Printed Library Materials, ANSI Z39.48-1984.

International Standard Book Number
ISBN-13: 978-0-87351-619-8 (cloth)
ISBN-10: 0-87351-619-2 (cloth)

Library of Congress Cataloging-in-Publication Data

Dean, Lee Svitak
Come one, come all : easy entertaining with seasonal menus : with over 150 recipes from the Star tribune taste section / Lee Svitak Dean.
p. cm.
Includes index.
ISBN-13: 978-0-87351-619-8 (cloth : alk. paper)
ISBN-10: 0-87351-619-2 (cloth : alk. paper)
1. Entertaining. 2. Cookery, American—Midwestern style. 3. Menus. I. Star tribune. II. Title.
TX731.D4334 2009
642'.4—dc22
2008023362

For my mother

CONTENTS

Come One, Come All

All people are made alike.
They are made of bones, flesh, and dinners.
Only the dinners are different.

....

GERTRUDE LOUISE CHENEY

Preface

MOST OF THESE MENUS first appeared on the pages of the Taste section of the *Star Tribune* newspaper in Minneapolis, where I have been food editor since 1994. They were part of a series of seasonal menus that reflected restaurant trends that could be adapted for the home kitchen. But these are not restaurant recipes. Those too often require hard-to-find ingredients, a staff to prepare them, and a dishwasher for cleanup (I'm talking about a human one, in addition to the machine). That's why we go to restaurants: to get food we don't normally have at our own dinner table.

The recipes in this book are for the home cook who has a taste for vibrant flavors and intriguing food combinations, but who is short of time. I like flavors that pop and these recipes reflect that preference. They also are easy to prepare. You don't need to be a culinary student to make them work. I lean toward recipes that don't require serious concentration because, as likely as not, in the midst of measuring or sautéing, someone—or something—is likely to distract me. You are safe with these recipes. It is helpful if you know your way around the supermarket but, if not, I'll tell you where to find certain ingredients. In fact, I'll take you step-by-step through anything that seems a little tricky.

Cooking isn't hard. At its most basic, it is simply following directions. Once you are comfortable with some classic dishes and techniques, you can experiment. That's what chefs do at restaurants. They take a traditional recipe and make it their own. Their spin may push the limits. Yours doesn't have to. Guests aren't expecting a restaurant experience when they gather at your table. They are looking for the comfort of friendly faces while their hunger is being met. If the meal tastes good, so much the better.

As I have preached for years, it doesn't take any longer to make good food than it does to make bad food—so you might as well make good food. My daughter, recently married, called home to report on the success of one of these recipes, a favorite of hers. "I had no idea it was so easy," she said. Yes, indeed. When cooks respond to a compliment and say, "There was nothing to it," they're not just being modest.

When compiling the menus for this book from the newspaper archives, it became apparent that, over the years, I had overlooked some seasonal foods or cooking techniques, or overused others that clearly were favorites of mine (who knew I was so fond of caramelized onions, feta, and mushrooms?). So I refigured some menus, created new ones to replace others, tweaked and updated recipes to match our current tastes. Some recipes published a decade ago called for ingredients that were novel at the time, but today are mainstream. (How quickly roasted red peppers have become part of our culinary vocabulary and pantry.) What you find here are recipes that have withstood the test of time—and our lack thereof. Let's call them the New Classics.

The menus on these pages make the most of our seasons and acknowledge the time constraints we face daily. You won't need fancy equipment or a sous-chef (the second in command in the restaurant kitchen) to help you cook. All you need is a sense of adventure and a love of the kitchen. And, yes, a dishwasher helps.

INTRODUCTION

I BLAME MY MOTHER.

Dinner parties would have been a whole lot easier had she not shown me, over the years, what to do.

My mother made it look simple. She always had a plan—and a recipe. The good dishes and glassware were sparkling, the silver polished, and the linen tablecloth ironed. She made sure the kitchen was spick-and-span by the time guests arrived. And the house smelled good, too, like she had spent the whole day cooking, which, of course, she had.

I recall the momentous occasions in my family by what we ate and how it was served. For the first Thanksgiving after I left for college, my mother had planned to hold a gathering on my return. "We have a lot to celebrate," she said with a lingering smile that made clear I had been missed. Then an elderly relative offered to host the meal. Mom reluctantly agreed and, on that Thursday afternoon, the five of us emptied out of the old Pontiac station wagon into the house where the feast would be. But there wasn't any. The tip-off was the smell of cleaning supplies. This being a Scandinavian household, the eau de cologne was Pine-Sol. No turkey fragrance wafted through the foyer. No scent of cinnamon, cloves, and ginger from the pumpkin pie lingered in the kitchen. In fact, there were no good smells at all. Nor were the windows fogged from the steam of boiling potatoes and rutabagas.

"Surprise," said Great Aunt Esther. "We're going to a restaurant."

That was not how to throw a party. We grumbled for years about that Thanksgiving meal.

That wasn't the only gathering I remember. For the dinner celebrating my church confirmation, my mother worked on the menu for weeks, settling on a dessert of ice cream balls rolled in different textured treats: finely chopped nuts, shredded coconut, and a variety of colorful sprinkles. Even the ice cream came in different flavors, creating a kaleidoscope of hues that she presented in a clear glass bowl. In 1968, it was stunning. Even today it would be. Given the number of people at the meal, she had decided to use paper plates, a decision she rued for years. "I should have used the good dishes," she would mutter whenever the meal was discussed. "You should never use paper plates."

Well, this was the 1960s, after all, and paper plates weren't all that common even though few cooks had dishwashers. Her words still echoed when I planned a recent gathering for a lot of people: "Hmm, paper plates? Are you sure?" So I didn't. I borrowed the rest from a neighbor who very thoughtfully has on hand thirty-plus white plates that she keeps in storage for just such occasions. Fortunately she's happy to share. I do have seventy-five champagne flutes in my own storage (don't even ask why), so together we're set for any grand, or even not-so-grand, occasion.

Holidays, birthdays, reunions, picnics. There always seemed to be reasons to get together in my family, though the occasion seemed to matter less than the food itself, all carefully plotted out in menu form. Would there be a roast or a ham? Pheasant, chicken, or walleye? Curry, spaghetti, or sandwich loaf? By today's standards, nothing was exotic or upscale, though there was an effort to be fashionable. But we were a meat-and-potatoes kind of family and any side trips off the beaten path generally were not too far from the highway.

Though my mother's menu was never ahead of its time, that didn't matter to those gathered around the table, and it wasn't simply because of the era. Hers was a good gathering because she made it so. The food was plentiful and the table looked beautiful, its colors and accoutrements changing with the season. Every guest shared that opinion, even the youngest waiting for the cherries jubilee to be lit. Dinner was drama and this was the place to be.

And it wasn't just dinner. My mother was known for her parties, especially the interactive ones. Consider the year of the desert isle. She and a neighbor wrote invitations in rhyme on pieces of brown paper bags, which they then rolled and stuffed into bottles. These were hung on front door railings (and in one instance a basketball hoop), unannounced, late in the evening. Then she rang the doorbell and ran. (My mother, the delinquent! Wonder where my sense of adventure comes from?)

Meanwhile, our basement became a desert isle. Murals depicting an island with grass huts were painted on the concrete block walls by my mother's sister. My father built a wooden slide down the full length of basement stairs for the guests to "escape" from their shipwreck onto the island. A mattress at the bottom softened their landing. My two siblings and I could not believe it. ("Our parents built an escape route *into* the basement," we would whisper after sneaking a ride down the slide.) This was circa *Gilligan's Island*, four decades before *Pirates of the Caribbean* and Johnny Depp. Let's just say Mom was ahead of the curve on that occasion.

For another party, my mother created a mini-speakeasy in the basement, and the guests dressed as though they were from the Roaring Twenties. Our toys were tucked away while a roulette wheel and blackjack and dice table took center stage, and peanut shells were strewn across the floor. Never

mind we were Lutherans who tended to be a bit more straight-laced than such a party reflected. I later borrowed her ideas, with her blessing, for church youth gatherings. Then there were the Super Bowl parties where she constructed a mini-football field on the dining room table. Or the party where the focus was to look like a song, and she wore a maternity dress. The lyrics she embodied? "I've Got You Under My Skin." (Clearly, my birthright as firstborn was silliness. I was born to laugh.)

"People don't throw parties like we used to," she sighed recently. "Now it's just wine and cheese."

Yes, I have a lot to live up to.

My mother knew the ingredients of a good party, though I don't think she thought of them as anything but the general rules of the kitchen: plan ahead, make lists, do as much as possible in advance, clean up after yourself as you work, and don't leave all the mess to the end. And have fun. Yes, indeed, she had a lot of fun.

The key, she knew, was the menu. Not that it had to be unusual or overly impressive. But the components had to work together.

For fifteen years, as I planned the Christmas Day menu for the Dean clan, I asked myself the same question she did for one gathering after another: Does the menu work? Then I considered what my mother never mentioned, but which she clearly understood: What can be done ahead? That meant shopping, of course. But it also meant all the details that didn't have to wait until the last minute: Vegetables to be precooked. Pies to be baked in advance. Bits and pieces of the whole menu that could just as well be done now rather than later to free up the host during the party. That's how she did it and, sure as I was in the kitchen, that was how I would do it, too.

We all have gatherings to plan, some of them with more enthusiasm than others. The toughest part of the planning may well be the preparation of the menu. What's new? What's doable? How can I shave time off this recipe to make a gathering possible? Today few of us have all day to cook in the kitchen. Yet we want to get together with others, and what better way to spend time than around the dinner table?

This book will help you set the menu for just about any occasion. These menus are defined by the seasons—by the events that often occur during specific times of the year and by the foods available during those months. Produce in season is at its peak of flavor, especially when sourced from local farmers' markets or other outlets. It's less costly than buying out-of-season foodstuffs and, most important, it tastes better. (A strawberry in February? Oh, please. A tomato in January? Might as well be eating a tennis ball.) Not so incidentally, seasonal food often needs less prep because it is fresh.

Food in season also just seems right. The reason Thanksgiving menus vary so little is that they are dependent on the flavors of the harvest. In other words,

the foods are part of the season. That's true throughout the year. Who eats a cold soup in January? Or a heavy stew in May? Or, during the summer when everything is fresh and abundant, who calls out for a pot of chili or a root vegetable?

The menus in this book are set up for three levels of cooks: those with a lot of time who don't flinch at making everything from scratch, those who need to work ahead in order to ease party prep into a busy week, and those who prefer to use shortcuts, substituting some store-bought options in a menu where only a few items need be home-cooked.

Whichever option you choose, it's okay. Even my mother says so.

After years of being a homemaker and cooking up parties, she headed to the workplace when her three children were in college. When Thanksgiving rolled around, my mother had something to tell her daughters: "This year it's going to be different. I can't do it all."

Yes, we all need a little help in the kitchen. These menus will show you how.

GENERAL RULES OF THE KITCHEN
- Plan ahead.
- Make lists.
- Do as much as possible in advance.
- Clean up after yourself as you work.
- Don't leave all the mess until the end.
- Have fun!

All You Need to Know to Throw a Party

AS I WAS PREPARING each of these menus, what struck me long before anything was ready to nibble was how fragrant the ingredients were. They bathed my kitchen in the most wonderful perfume: Fresh tarragon and mint, thyme, dill, and sage. Strawberries and asparagus. Salmon and blue cheese. Mushrooms and onions. Peaches and pecans. Apples and pears. And that was before the cooking began. The heady aromas were simply raw ingredients in their prime.

HIGH-QUALITY INGREDIENTS

That's the real secret to a dinner party: quality ingredients. Your meal is only as good as what you put into it. That doesn't mean that expensive ingredients are necessarily better than the cheap variety. It does mean that you should carefully choose the pieces that make up the whole. Those dried-up carrots in the refrigerator? Toss them—or give them to a rabbit. The wine that's been open for a month? Empty it in the sink. If it's not good enough to sip, don't use it as a cooking ingredient. And the chocolate for the cake? Skip the discount version and go for the serious stuff, which, yes, costs more—the Ghirardelli, Valrhona, Guittard, Scharffen Berger and the like. I assure you, after one taste, there will be no going back, at least not for special occasions.

In most of my life, I am a frugal shopper. (There are those who would say that's a generous description. Tightwad is the term that more frequently pops up.) But when it comes to food, I don't hesitate to spend freely. Good food is worth it. And these days it's not hard to find. Nor is it necessarily high priced. Americans pay less of their income, proportionately, for food than anywhere else in the world. Consider splurging on good ingredients as a national service in support of U.S. growers and producers.

When I shop for food, I first look for freshness. In the summer, that's easy. I search for fruits and vegetables at their peak, that bowl me over with their fragrance, whether I pick them from my garden, buy them from farmers' markets or small roadside stands, or gather them from the produce aisle at the supermarket. For the rest of the year, I shop carefully, hunting through the produce and adjusting my menu accordingly, avoiding the peppers if they look wrinkled, passing by the cauliflower with brown flecks on its edges. Nor does my quest for freshness stop with the produce. Dry seasonings need to be at their peak, too. If you don't know the age of your herbs and spices, they are probably too old. Keep track by writing their purchase date on the exterior of the bottle when you buy them. If they are more than a year old, they've lost much of their flavor.

In fact, for all food, good flavor goes hand in hand with freshness. That's where the seasons come in—and good menu planning. Produce in season tastes like it belongs. It pairs with other fruits and vegetables grown during the same months. That's why apples taste so good in the fall with squash, why corn on the cob pairs well with slices of fresh tomatoes. I also look for flavor beyond the produce aisle, in the olive oil, honey, or cheese I choose, the slab of beef or fresh turkey that's destined for my table. Those are the products of growers who put their heart and soul—and a lot of skill—into what appears on our tables. There's no substitute for that kind of care in our food supply—all of which translates into the Holy Grail of good flavor. This means I buy "real" food and check ingredient labels: Real maple syrup, not imitation. Butter, not margarine. Parmesan in a chunk, not the powder in the green box.

MENU PLANNING, PREPARATION, AND PRESENTATION

When I plan a gathering, I start with the menu and, if there are new recipes to try, I sometimes preview them, depending on who is coming to dinner (some guests are more flexible than others with experiments). My menus tend to follow a certain path. I often serve both soup and salad, at least in the colder months, because I think they are good starters. Research backs me up. A little soup keeps us from overindulging (and it's a surefire way to impress guests who don't know it's so easy to make). As for a salad, that bite of vinaigrette gets the juices flowing. If I'm not hungry when the meal starts, a salad gets me ready. The menus here reflect those preferences.

Whatever you choose for the menu, plan ahead. Don't leave all the work to the last minute or you'll be in the kitchen during the dinner party instead of with your guests. That means getting organized. Read the recipes in their entirety when you're still preparing the menu so you will know if something has to be done in advance—or if you've double-booked your oven. Buy the ingredients at least the day before the event, earlier if something has to ripen or thaw. Dinner parties aren't difficult, but they do require some advance thought and logistical consideration.

When it comes to cooking for a dinner party, I don't pretend to be Martha Stewart. I know I don't have time to make everything myself—and I don't have to because there are plenty of skilled artisans who do a single task better than I ever can. I have no problem serving a crusty baguette that comes from

THE KEY TO COOKING

Cooking is an art as well as a science. Consider the kitchen to be your canvas. What amazing creation can you make today? Whether you are preparing food for yourself or for guests, remember these elements:

- Use food at its freshest. Buy it in season.
- Choose flavorful, high-quality food.
- Read through the recipe in advance.
- Don't leave all the work to the end. Plan ahead.
- Use recipes as guidelines. Once you're comfortable, experiment to make the recipe meet your preferences.
- Consider your time. You don't have to make everything yourself. There are many good-quality prepared foods that you can share with guests.
- Have fun. Now say that again. Gathering friends and family around the dinner table should be pleasurable—and so should the cooking. If you're not having fun, you need to rethink the process.

someone else's oven or a fancy layered dessert that I didn't make because, after all, guests don't really care who prepares a food. They simply want it to taste good.

After years of talking with readers of the Taste section, I offer this advice: loosen up in the kitchen. Recipes should be viewed as guidelines, not commandments. This is especially true with the amounts of ingredients. A little more of this or less of that won't make a difference in most dishes. If you only can find a 15.5-ounce can of beans and the recipe calls for a 16-ounce can, don't fret. If the recipe specifies a cup of chopped onion for a stew and your large onion clearly offers more, it's okay to add the extra, provided you like onions. Don't waste ingredients, especially not fresh, flavorful ones. Think of seasonings as suggested guidelines, too. If you're uncertain about the flavor of thyme in a recipe where it is specified, use less and then taste the result. Add more thyme slowly, always sampling between additions until you are satisfied, keeping in mind that even small additions of herbs can have a big impact.

Baking is the exception to this advice on variable ingredients, because chemistry is crucial in the process. If a recipe calls for a half teaspoon or a quarter cup, stick to the specifications to ensure the recipe will work. When you bake, you're essentially working with formulas, and you can't tinker with them willy-nilly and get predictable results.

For a sit-down dinner party, I prefer to serve my meal in courses with plated food—arranged on a plate as a restaurant does—rather than family style on a platter to pass. The effort takes only a few moments (and practice definitely makes it faster), and the payoff is big. A salad composed on a plate gets more *oohs* and *aahs* than a bowl of greens passed around the table. (And truth be told, all of us cooks

aim for those verbal high-fives, though frankly, it's not that hard to impress your guests. They are simply happy that they're not cooking dinner themselves.)

I plate entrees if I want them to look a particular way—the braised short ribs and polenta in the fall menus, for example, look more presentable when artfully arranged instead of plopped in a bowl or on a platter. You can make those plates look even better with sprinkles of herbs or drizzles of the sauce (use a plastic squeeze bottle to do so). Another tip from restaurants: wipe off any stray drips or smudges on the plate. It only takes a second with a clean towel.

For impact, I often serve soup in very small portions—espresso cups or shot glasses are particularly dramatic—just like some restaurants do. For the final course, I not only plate it but also often make or buy it in individual portions. Never mind that a slice of strawberry pie tastes the same as an individual strawberry tart (see the spring menus, beginning on page 14). For presentation, single servings impress, whether it's a goblet of mousse or individual mini-tarts. And it's no more work for the cook. (Well, nothing significant, says this busy cook.)

The exception to plating for me is any informal gathering, such as one with pizza or with burgers outdoors, or a large gathering where it's not practical. Keep in mind that these are my preferences, not rules for the kitchen. Do whatever makes you comfortable with your guests.

Ready to break out the invitations? Whether you're a longtime host or someone new to the kitchen, it's time to expand your repertoire. Cooking is an adventure. Forget the notion that you should be working yourself to exhaustion—or cooking for a week in advance. Having dinner with friends and family ought to be considered one of our basic human needs. Because, in our hearts, we know it is.

RECOMMENDED INGREDIENTS

large eggs
all-purpose flour
freshly squeezed lemon and lime juice
freshly cracked black pepper
coarse salt instead of iodized salt, when indicated
    (kosher salt is one variety; there are other
    coarse sea salts available)

HELPFUL EQUIPMENT

baking pan (9 x 13 inches)
blender (either immersion or counter) or food
    processor for puréeing
double boiler (or metal bowl to place in pot as
    substitute)
candy and meat thermometers
cookie sheet
electric mixer
graters, in a variety of sizes (for citrus zest,
    cheese, etc.)
grill
jelly roll pan
loaf pan (9 x 5 inches)
mandoline or other device for fine shredding
meat mallet
mini-muffin pan and regular-size muffin pans

mini-tartlet pans
pasta pot with colander
pastry bag or substitute
pepper grinder
pie pan (9-inch)
popover pan
potato ricer or spaetzle maker
ramekins (small ovenproof bowls)
roasting pan
round baking dish (5-inch)
round cake pans (9-inch)
sieve, strainer, or colander
slow cooker or Dutch oven
springform baking pan (9- or 10-inch)
steamer for vegetables
tube cake pan or Bundt pan

SPRING

MENUS

Elegant Spring Dinner 16
Watercress and Oyster Soup
Spring Greens with Mustard-Tarragon Vinaigrette
Stuffed Leg of Lamb with Spinach and Goat Cheese
New Potatoes with Parsley
Fresh Strawberry Tartlets

Spring Luncheon 22
Sparkling Wine with Chambord
Vegetable Spreads with Crackers
    Lentil and Black Olive Spread
    Carrots, Curry, and Cumin Spread
    Eggplant and Roasted Red Pepper Spread
Broiled Salmon with Spring Greens and Chermoula
Strawberry Mousse with White Chocolate–Dipped
    Strawberries

Afternoon Tea 30
Earl Grey Tea
Chicken Salad Mini-Cups
Blueberry-Banana Mini-Muffins
Toast Points with Smoked Salmon Spread
Cucumbers with Blue Cheese Mousse
Coconut Macaroons

Fresh Vegetarian Flavors 38
Asparagus Soup
Spring Greens with Mustard-Peppercorn Vinaigrette
Wild Mushrooms in Phyllo with Fresh Herb Sauce
Maple Mousse

Celebration Buffet 48
Sparkling Fruit Punch

Spicy Beef Brisket Sandwiches
Spring Vegetable Platter with Sun-Dried Tomato Dip
White Bean Salad with Feta and Basil
Roasted New Potatoes with Sweet Onions and Olives
Marinated Olives
Carrot Cake with Cream Cheese Sauce
Fresh Strawberries

Brunch for a Bunch 58
Sparkling Wine or Mimosa
Variety of Juices
Mushroom and Onion Quiche
Chicken and Ham Roulades with Asparagus
    and Dijon Mustard Sauce
Fruit and Yogurt Parfaits or Fruit Platter
Cheese Platter
Fish Platter
Bread Basket
Almond Pound Cake with Strawberry-Rhubarb Sauce

Salad Sampler Luncheon 66
Asparagus and Greens with Pesto Quenelle
Spicy Chicken with Angel Hair Pasta and Watercress
Spring Berries with Vanilla Sauce

Grad Party 101 74
Margarita Punch without the Punch
Chicken Fajitas on the Grill
Make-Your-Own Tacos
Nacho Cheese Sauce and Chips
Guacamole for a Crowd
Pico de Gallo
Cinnamon-Fudge Bars

SPRING

RECIPES BY COURSE

Make Ahead

UP TO A DAY IN ADVANCE

Prepare soup.

Make vinaigrette.

Prepare tartlet pie crusts.

UP TO 8 HOURS IN ADVANCE

Make stuffing for leg of lamb and prepare meat.

UP TO 3 HOURS IN ADVANCE

Roast lamb.

UP TO 2 HOURS IN ADVANCE

Make tartlet filling and assemble tartlets.

LAST-MINUTE PREP

Steam potatoes.

Reheat soup and add oysters.

Assemble salad.

Shortcut Savvy

Buy prepared fish stock.

Use prewashed, packaged salad greens.

Buy bottled vinaigrette.

Use prewashed spinach.

Buy precooked new potatoes (available in packages in the refrigerator section of the supermarket).

Use premade pie crust or purchase dessert.

ELEGANT SPRING DINNER

For 8

Watercress and Oyster Soup
Spring Greens with Mustard-Tarragon Vinaigrette
Stuffed Leg of Lamb with Spinach and Goat Cheese
New Potatoes with Parsley
Fresh Strawberry Tartlets

TIME TO DUST OFF the good dishes to celebrate the arrival of a new season. Never mind that the out-of-doors may still be a bit dingy. Let's keep the early springtime in perspective: the days are longer, the snow melts quickly, and the crocuses will soon be out of hiding. That's reason enough to celebrate. For cooks this welcome change of season is cause to replenish their dinner staples. Tiny new potatoes, spinach, watercress, and strawberries offer winter-weary diners a tasteful respite. This elegant menu is easy and quick to prepare, practically foolproof for even the novice cook. It also offers in abundance the most welcome of springtime sights: the color green, in many splendid shades.

Watercress and Oyster Soup

SERVES 8 TO 10 (ABOUT 10 CUPS)

2 tablespoons oil

1 large onion, chopped (about 1 cup)

3 medium potatoes, peeled and chopped (about 3 cups)

1 cup dry white wine

3 cups fish stock (see Note)

2 carrots, chopped (about 1 cup)

2 cups milk

Dash cayenne pepper

Salt and white pepper

1 to 2 pints shucked oysters, chopped, and the liquid reserved

2 (1-ounce) packages (or one small bunch) watercress, stems removed
(reserve 8 to 10 sprigs for garnish)

In a large, heavy pot, heat oil over medium-high heat and sauté onion a few minutes until it is translucent. Add potatoes, wine, stock, and carrots. Bring to a boil; then reduce heat and simmer, covered, for about 15 to 20 minutes or until vegetables are soft.

In small batches, purée vegetables and liquid coarsely in a blender or food processor, leaving some small chunks. Return purée to the pot and stir in milk and cayenne pepper; season to taste with salt and white pepper. (Can be made in advance up to this point.)

Immediately before serving, gently reheat soup. Add oysters, their liquid, and watercress; simmer about 3 to 4 minutes, until oysters are cooked through and their edges are curled. Garnish with a sprig of watercress. Serve immediately.

Note: *Fish stock, sometimes called seafood stock, is available in many supermarkets, usually in aseptic packaging, the box-like containers that juice comes in for children. Some restaurant kitchens will sell their stock, if asked. For a recipe for fish stock, see page 266. If you're making the fish stock yourself, plan ahead and allow for prep time. If you prefer not to cook with wine, substitute additional fish stock in the soup.*

Beverage

As an aperitif, serve chenin blanc or fumé blanc. The leg of lamb calls for a pinot noir.

COOK'S NOTES

Lovely as it is flavorful, the oyster soup gets both color and a peppery zing from the watercress. The amount of oysters used in the recipe can be adjusted according to your guests' tastes, as well as your budget. The soup calls for fish stock, which can be either homemade or purchased.

Spring Greens with Mustard-Tarragon Vinaigrette

SERVES 8

2 teaspoons Dijon mustard
2 tablespoons white wine vinegar or tarragon vinegar
1 tablespoon minced fresh tarragon or 1 teaspoon
    dried and crushed
¼ cup extra-virgin olive oil
Salt and freshly ground black pepper
4 cups mixed greens (see Note)

In a small bowl, whisk mustard, vinegar, and tarragon. Slowly add olive oil, whisking constantly. Season to taste with salt and pepper. Arrange greens on individual plates and drizzle with 1 tablespoon vinaigrette over each salad. Serve immediately.

Variation: Add asparagus spears to the salad. Steam 3 or 4 spears per person until slightly tender, but still firm, about 4 minutes. Plunge the cooked asparagus into icy water immediately. Drain and refrigerate, covered, until ready to serve. Bring to room temperature before placing on top of greens and serving.

> Note: *A variety of greens makes this course more interesting: curly red and green leaf lettuces, radicchio or escarole, perhaps some Belgian endive— all will look pretty on the salad plate.*

Stuffed Leg of Lamb
with Spinach and Goat Cheese
SERVES 8

Stuffed leg of lamb is a spectacular main course in appearance and flavor and—pay attention now, this is the best part—it requires only a modest effort on the part of the cook. Tart goat cheese or chèvre (SHEHV), spinach, and lots of garlic are rolled up jelly-roll fashion in a leg of lamb, which can be bought deboned (the leg is then said to be "butterflied"). All that's left for the cook is to roast the lamb for a few hours.

2 tablespoons freshly minced garlic, plus 2 slivered garlic cloves, divided
12 ounces goat cheese (chèvre)
2 cups chopped fresh spinach (about 12 ounces)
Salt and freshly ground black pepper
1 (5 to 6 pound) boneless leg of lamb
Coarse salt
3 tablespoons or more minced fresh rosemary leaves

Preheat oven to 350° F.

In a bowl, mix minced garlic, goat cheese, and spinach; season to taste with salt and pepper.

Flatten out lamb and spread spinach mixture evenly over the top of it. Roll meat up lengthwise and tie in several spots with kitchen string. Make small slits in roast and insert slivers of garlic. Sprinkle roast with coarse salt, pepper, and rosemary.

Place lamb in a shallow roasting pan and roast, uncovered, 25 to 30 minutes per pound for rare meat (140° F on a meat thermometer inserted in the thickest part); 30 to 35 minutes per pound for medium (about 160° F on a meat thermometer). Let lamb rest for 15 minutes before carving. Cut into ½-inch-thick slices, and serve.

COOK'S NOTES

Not sure your guests will like the tang of goat cheese? You can substitute cream cheese. Bring it to room temperature and beat it with a mixer until it is easy to spread. This lamb is a wonderful change from the more traditional ham that appears on spring tables.

New Potatoes with Parsley
SERVES 8

24 to 32 small new potatoes, unpeeled, and halved or quartered, depending on size of potato
4 tablespoons (½ stick) butter
⅛ to ¼ cup chopped flat-leaf parsley

Steam or boil potatoes until tender, about 15 to 20 minutes, depending on size. Drain water thoroughly from pot and toss potatoes with butter and parsley.

Fresh Strawberry Tartlets
MAKES 8

CRUST
3 cups flour
1 cup sugar
1 cup (2 sticks) cold butter, cut into 1-inch pieces
2 eggs, slightly beaten
1 egg white, slightly beaten

STRAWBERRY GLAZE
1 pint (2 cups) fresh strawberries, rinsed and hulled
¾ cup sugar
½ cup water
2 tablespoons cornstarch
Dash salt

FILLING
2 pints (4 cups) fresh strawberries, rinsed and hulled
1 to 2 teaspoons kirsch (cherry brandy; optional)
Whipped cream, for garnish
Fresh mint leaves, for garnish

FOR CRUST

In a large mixing bowl, mix flour, sugar, and butter. Beat at medium speed, scraping bowl often until mixture is crumbly, 2 to 3 minutes (if you've got some hard-to-break lumps of butter, use a fork to finish them off). Make a well in the center of flour mixture and pour in 2 beaten eggs. (Egg white will be used later). Blend with fork until incorporated thoroughly. Mixture will be very dry.

Press dough to ¼-inch thickness on bottom and sides of tartlet pans. Chill for 30 minutes to prevent shrinkage.

Preheat oven to 400° F. Brush crust with beaten egg white and bake 10 to 15 minutes or until golden brown. Cool.

FOR STRAWBERRY GLAZE

In a medium saucepan, mash berries slightly; then add sugar and water. Bring to a boil, reduce heat, and simmer for 5 minutes. Remove from heat and strain mixture, reserving syrup. Return syrup to pan and whisk in cornstarch and salt. Simmer until mixture thickens and is clear, whisking constantly. (If glaze gets too thick, thin with a little water.) Remove from heat. Strain, if desired, and cool. Spread about 1 tablespoon of glaze on each tartlet shell.

FOR FILLING

If berries are small, use them whole; if large, slice them. Toss berries in kirsch, if using. Distribute berries among tartlet shells. For sliced berries, overlap slices around the perimeter of the tart. Refrigerate and serve within a couple hours of assembling. Remove from refrigerator about 10 minutes before serving. To serve, remove tart from tin. (Push up on the bottom of the tart. Slip the tart shell off the bottom of the tin, if possible, or leave it on when you serve it.) Top each tart with dollop of whipped cream and garnish with fresh mint, if desired.

Variation: When serving a different entrée (one that doesn't have cheese for the filling as this lamb dish does), the strawberry tartlets can have a layer of cream cheese filling under the berries. To do so, beat together 8 ounces softened cream cheese, ⅓ cup sour cream, and ¼ cup sugar until smooth. Spread evenly over baked crust before adding the glaze and berries.

Make spreads.

Cook potatoes for salad.

Slice radishes for salad and store in water (drain thoroughly before using).

Make chermoula.

Prepare dipped strawberries (up to 12 hours in advance).

UP TO 8 HOURS IN ADVANCE

Prepare mousse.

Wash lettuce and watercress.

LAST-MINUTE PREP

Bring spreads to room temperature if made in advance.

Reheat potatoes if cooked in advance.

Broil salmon.

Add liqueur to sparkling wine.

Shortcut Savvy

Buy commercially made spreads, such as hummus and baba ghanoush.

Buy precooked new potatoes (available in packages in the refrigerator section of the supermarket).

Use prewashed, packaged salad greens.

For dessert, skip the mousse and serve only a platter of dipped strawberries.

SPRING LUNCHEON

For 6

Sparkling Wine with Chambord
Vegetable Spreads with Crackers:
    Lentil and Black Olive Spread
    Carrot, Curry, and Cumin Spread
    Eggplant and Roasted Red Pepper Spread
Broiled Salmon with Spring Greens and Chermoula
Strawberry Mousse with White Chocolate–Dipped Strawberries

SPRING MEANS FRESH PRODUCE as surely as it does crocuses and tulips in bloom. After a long winter of relying on root vegetables and canned goods, our ancestors must have been flush with relief at the sight of fresh vegetables poking through the ground.

The produce market has changed since then, of course. Fresh strawberries and asparagus are available while we're still knee-deep in snow—if we're willing to pay the price and don't mind the woody taste. But we lose more than dollars by eating out of season. We lose the luster of anticipation, of tasting flavors anew that have been set aside for months. Strawberries year-round? That's like a candy dish that is never empty. Or noticed.

The Spring Luncheon menu offers the cook a bounty of produce worthy of the new season and, yes, a few standard vegetables outside the season. The key is that they are all fresh: radishes, green onions, carrots, spring greens, new potatoes, lemons, eggplant, and strawberries. Health guide-lines suggest we all could benefit from five or more servings of produce a day. You'll get most of them in this single meal. Highlighted with fresh salmon and accented with such herbs as watercress, flat-leaf parsley, chives, and mint, this meal will refresh the palate in need of spring's renewal. The salmon is topped with chermoula (cher-MOO-lah), a North African marinade used with fish and seafood.

This menu is particularly well suited to what used to be called "ladies' luncheons." I've prepared it for baby and wedding showers (substituting sparkling apple cider for the wine for the mother-to-be), and it invariably draws *oohs* and *aahs*, in great part because of the vegetable spreads that add just the right touch of novelty. Well, that and the white-chocolate dipped strawberries.

Beverage

What's the difference between champagne and sparkling wine? Its origin. Only sparkling wine from the Champagne region in northeastern France can use that name. In Italy sparkling wine is called *proscecco* or *spumante*, in Spain it's *cava*. Chambord, a raspberry liqueur, gives this a lovely pink color and a not-too-sweet flavor. The amount of Chambord will vary according to the size of the glasses. Pomegranate juice or a raspberry-flavored syrup or soda are inexpensive substitutes.

COOK'S NOTES

Your blender or food processor will get a good workout from this menu, which begins with puréed vegetables in the form of spreads. That may seem an unlikely food for anyone but infants. But consider the Middle Eastern hummus, which is mashed chickpeas. What differentiates these spreads here from a jar of Gerber is the seasonings that give them zing.

If you haven't time to prepare the spreads, similar Middle Eastern ones are available at many supermarkets. Hummus is similar in texture to the lentil spread on this menu. The eggplant spread here is similar to baba ghanoush (bah-bah gha-NOOSH)—puréed eggplant with tahini and seasonings. All three spreads can be made a day in advance and refrigerated, though they should be brought to room temperature before serving.

These three recipes for spreads are not the most attractive of dishes. They are, after all, puréed vegetables, and they look like it. Garnishes make them more presentable, but only to a certain degree. They are to be used as a replacement for butter or cheese on thin crackers, such as water crackers, and served at the same time as the salmon.

Sparkling Wine with Chambord
SERVES 6

Chambord (raspberry-flavored liqueur)
1 or 2 bottles of sparkling wine (see Note)

Pour 1 to 1½ teaspoons Chambord into each glass. Add sparkling wine and serve immediately.

> **Note:** *Depending on the size of the glass you use, a bottle of sparkling wine yields 5 or 6 glasses. Plan accordingly.*

GUIDELINES FOR TASTY SPREADS

If possible, use extra-virgin olive oil for these spreads because it is more flavorful than other olive oil designations. The extra-virgin comes from the first pressing of the olives, giving its flavor and fragrance more oomph.

The black olives used in the lentil spread will add more flavor if they are one of the many varieties of Mediterranean-style olives rather than the blander, common ripe olives available in a can.

Stick with plain crackers to showcase the flavor of the spreads.

Lentil and Black Olive Spread
MAKES ABOUT 1 CUP

½ cup uncooked lentils (see Note)
1¾ cups water
1 garlic clove, chopped
2 teaspoons balsamic or red wine vinegar
¼ cup extra-virgin olive oil
2 tablespoons chopped, fresh flat-leaf parsley
¼ cup brine-cured Mediterranean-style black olives, pitted and chopped
Additional flat-leaf parsley or black olives, for garnish

To cook lentils, bring water to a boil and add lentils and garlic. Simmer for about 25 minutes, or until lentils are barely done. Pour the cooked lentils, along with any extra cooking water, into a food processor or blender; add garlic and vinegar and purée the mixture. Add olive oil and blend thoroughly. Transfer to a bowl and fold in parsley and black olives. Garnish the serving dish with additional parsley and olives. Serve with crackers.

> **Note:** *Lentils come in different colors, though the brown ones are most available; for this recipe, any version will work.*

Carrot, Curry, and Cumin Spread

MAKES ABOUT 1 CUP

2 carrots, sliced (about 1 cup)

3 green onions, chopped (about ¼ cup)

1 garlic clove, chopped

4 tablespoons extra-virgin olive oil, divided

1 teaspoon curry powder

½ teaspoon ground cumin

½ cup canned white beans, such as navy beans or Great Northern beans, rinsed and drained (see Note)

¼ teaspoon salt

1 teaspoon white vinegar

Boil carrots in water to cover until tender, about 5 to 10 minutes, depending on size of slices; drain.

In a skillet, mix onion, garlic, and 2 tablespoons olive oil; cook over medium-low heat until golden. Add curry powder and cumin, and cook 1 minute longer.

In a blender or food processor, purée onion mixture with carrots and white beans. Add the remaining 2 tablespoons olive oil and season to taste with salt and vinegar; blend thoroughly. Put through a fine strainer for better texture, if desired. Transfer to a bowl and serve with crackers.

Note: *The small amount of beans added to the puréed carrots gives the spread a different texture than if it were simply puréed carrots. Save any extra beans for your next meal—or make a triple batch of the spread. You can always freeze the extra for another lunch or snack.*

Eggplant and Roasted Red Pepper Spread
MAKES ABOUT 1 CUP

Roasted red pepper gives a richer flavor and softer texture to the spread than does a crisp, fresh red bell pepper, though a fresh one can certainly be used. The roasted version is available in a jar or can.

¼ cup plus 1 teaspoon extra-virgin olive oil, divided
1 pound eggplant, peeled, cut into ½-inch slices
1 garlic clove, chopped
1 teaspoon fresh lemon juice
¼ cup chopped, roasted red pepper (about half of a pepper)
1 tablespoon chopped fresh flat-leaf parsley
Salt

Preheat oven to 400° F. Use ¼ cup olive oil to brush on eggplant slices. Arrange on a rack (such as a broiling rack) and bake for 20 minutes per side, or until browned. Cool eggplant.

Sauté garlic in 1 teaspoon olive oil for 1 minute; do not let brown.

In a blender or food processor, purée eggplant, garlic, and lemon juice. Transfer to a bowl, and stir in roasted red pepper and parsley; season to taste with salt. Serve with crackers.

Broiled Salmon with Spring Greens and Chermoula
SERVES 6

Warm salads have never caught on in quite the same way that cold salads have. Oh, there's the occasional wilted spinach salad with hot bacon dressing, or a hot German potato salad. But few beyond those two are found in the repertoire of many cooks. Still, there's something very satisfying about a warm meal, and when paired with tangy salad ingredients, this is a winner.

For some extra zip to the salad, watercress has been added to the lettuce. This member of the mustard family has a pungent, peppery flavor. Radishes add another springtime burst of flavor and color to the salad, or try thin slices of red onion.

2 heads of curly or red leaf lettuce
1 small package (about 1 ounce) watercress, stems removed
6 radishes
Chermoula (see recipe)
12 tiny new potatoes, unpeeled (1- to 1½-inch diameter; see Notes)
Salt and pepper
1¼ to 2¼ pounds salmon fillets, skinned (see Notes)
Fresh chives

Rinse and dry lettuce and watercress. Thinly slice radishes. Prepare chermoula.

Steam new potatoes or cook in boiling water to which a little salt has been added. Cook until barely done, about 20 minutes, depending on the size of potatoes. When done, a fork should pierce easily through potato.

Preheat oven to broil.

Season the salmon to taste with salt and pepper. Set aside 2 tablespoons chermoula and brush onto salmon (since the fish is raw, do not dip the used brush directly into the remaining chermoula, which will be used on the cooked fish). Place salmon under broiler for about 8 to 10 minutes, or until fish separates easily into flakes when pulled at with a fork. Watch carefully as fish is easily overcooked. The fish does not need to be turned over. (Time will vary depending on thickness of salmon. If using several pieces of fish, try to have them all the same thickness.)

To serve, arrange lettuce and watercress on individual plates. In center of lettuce, add individual portions of broiled salmon, slightly broken apart, and radishes. Slice warm potatoes and place atop lettuce. Garnish with chives and drizzle each serving with about 2 tablespoons chermoula. Serve immediately.

Variation: During the summer when the barbecue is nearby, grill the fish instead of broiling it. For bigger eaters, use individual salmon steaks instead of fillets.

Variation: Serve a layer of couscous under the salmon and atop the greens. If doing so, skip the potatoes. Couscous, a light and fluffy grain-like pasta, should be made according to package directions (it only takes 5 to 10 minutes to prepare).

Continued on page 28.

Notes:

- *When you buy the salmon fillets, you can ask the butcher to skin them, or you can do it yourself. To remove the skin before it is cooked, make a slight cut between skin and flesh and insert a sharp knife. Hold salmon firmly with one hand and move the knife along the skin in one smooth stroke.*

- *The new potatoes can be prepared in advance and reheated slightly before serving by steaming or microwaving, or they can cook while you're preparing the salmon. The potatoes don't necessarily need to be hot for the salad; warm will do.*

CHERMOULA

Makes about ¾ cup

1 teaspoon ground cumin
½ teaspoon paprika
1 garlic clove, minced
¼ cup fresh lemon juice (1 lemon)
⅓ cup extra-virgin olive oil
¼ cup chopped fresh cilantro
Salt and pepper

Mix together the cumin, paprika, and garlic. Whisk in the lemon juice, olive oil, and cilantro. Season to taste with salt and pepper.

Strawberry Mousse with White Chocolate–Dipped Strawberries
MAKES 6 (½-CUP) SERVINGS

A tart berry mousse provides a light finish to this spring meal. Note that only half of a package of unflavored gelatin is used in this recipe. Depending on the size of your dessert dishes, you may want to make a double batch. If that's the case and you're using a blender, you'll need to do a single batch twice because a double recipe won't fit in the blender container.

2 tablespoons orange juice
1 teaspoon (½ envelope) unflavored gelatin
1 pint strawberries
¼ cup sugar
1 cup sour cream
Fresh mint leaves, for garnish
White-Chocolate Dipped Strawberries (see recipe)

Put orange juice in a very small saucepan and sprinkle gelatin over it.

Wash strawberries and remove stems and leaves. Set aside 2 or 3 strawberries for the garnish.

Heat orange juice–gelatin mixture until the gelatin has melted and the juice is clear. Add strawberries and sugar to the container of a food processor or blender. (In the blender, you'll need to squish the strawberries a bit by hand or with a utensil so that there is some juice at the bottom for the blender to use for processing.)

Purée strawberries, then add dissolved gelatin and continue to process until it is well blended. Add sour cream and blend again. More sugar can be added if the mixture is too tart.

Pour the mousse into 6 individual dishes, such as soufflé dishes, custard cups, or stemmed wine glasses. Refrigerate for at least 3 hours before serving. Garnish with mint leaves and thin slices of the reserved strawberries fanned out on top of the mousse.

Serve with strawberries dipped in white chocolate.

WHITE CHOCOLATE-DIPPED STRAWBERRIES

Makes 1 pint

1 pint fresh strawberries, with green leafy tops
1 cup (6 ounces) white chocolate in either chips or a large chunk

Wash and dry berries. Cover a baking sheet with aluminum foil or parchment paper.

If using a chunk of white chocolate, finely chop it. Melt white chocolate in saucepan over very low heat, stirring constantly. (Or use a microwave or double boiler. Don't get any water into the mixture, or it will harden into an unusable lump.)

Dip a strawberry halfway into melted white chocolate and gently shake off the excess. Place dipped strawberry on the baking sheet and repeat with remaining berries. If white chocolate begins to harden in the pan, warm up slightly before continuing.

Store dipped berries in the refrigerator if not using them immediately. The coated strawberries should be used within 12 hours.

WHITE CHOCOLATE

Despite the rather misleading name, white chocolate is not a paler version of chocolate. Nor can it be legally called "white chocolate" on its packaging. White chocolate is often flavored with vanilla, and is marketed under a variety of names that may suggest whiteness and chocolate, such as white dessert coating, vanilla milk chips, and Alpine white. Some white coatings do not contain cocoa butter, such as summer or confectionery coating—and they are not considered to be white chocolate. (Though they could be used for dipping strawberries, their flavor would be a little different.) For the best flavor, stay away from the artificially flavored varieties and those that use partially hydrogenated oil (check the ingredient label).

Though strawberries are more often dipped in chocolate, the soft color and sweet vanilla flavor of white chocolate better fit this spring menu. Use only perfect ripe strawberries— neither overripe nor under-ripe berries will look or taste good with the coating. They will only look good if eaten the same day they are prepared.

For 6

Earl Grey Tea
Chicken Salad Mini-Cups
Blueberry-Banana Mini-Muffins
Toast Points with Smoked Salmon Spread
Cucumbers with Blue Cheese Mousse
Coconut Macaroons

MOM AND AFTERNOON TEA go together as surely as a cup and saucer, even if Mom is a coffee drinker. At least that's so when "tea" refers to the supremely civilized British tradition of an afternoon break, restful as it is pleasurable.

Therein lies the magic: it's elegant. The emphasis on details—lovely little pieces that make up an even lovelier whole—give the occasion a charming sense of grace and dignity, both of which are in short supply these days. The pause in the day is reason enough to celebrate, but the plentiful treats and bracing cup of tea make such an occasion truly delightful. Though the style may be all-British, the tradition is welcome on the prairie, judging by the afternoon teas that have popped up at hotels and specialty tea shops.

Spring foods, with their lightness, especially fit teatime, so this menu for an afternoon tea—which also could be served as a morning brunch-style tea—is particularly well-suited to Mother's Day. This menu includes two midwestern favorites: chicken salad, served in mini-tart shells, and blueberry muffins. Here the muffin is crossed with another favorite, banana bread, and adapted to teatime by miniaturization. The coconut macaroon serves as the traditional teatime sweet.

A typical tea includes small sandwiches, usually with a spread that is based on cream cheese or mayonnaise. For this menu, Neufchâtel cheese is used; it's a lower-fat version of cream cheese, sometimes marketed as light cream cheese. Neufchâtel is named after the town in the Normandy region of France where it originated. In this menu it is used as a base for a smoked salmon spread that is delicious any time of day. (Try leftovers with your breakfast toast.)

Cucumber sandwiches are typical of a British tea. For this menu, cucumber slices take the place of the "sandwich" itself; the slices are topped with a spread of blue cheese thinned with cream.

Beverage

Earl Grey tea is a blend that originated in the eighteenth century. Its distinctive fragrance comes from oil of bergamot, a type of Mediterranean orange.

To make a good pot of tea, use fresh cold water and bring to a boil in a kettle. Just before the water boils, pour some of it into the teapot to warm the pot, then discard that water and add the tea leaves, about 1 teaspoon per serving, or to taste. (If you prefer that no tea leaves escape the pot and land in the tea cup, place the leaves in an infuser or strainer before putting them in the pot. Note, however, that the Brits would be scandalized by this.)

When the water in the kettle boils, pour it immediately into the teapot, and let the tea steep for 3 to 5 minutes. Additional hot water can be added, if needed, to dilute the strength of the tea. Offer a choice of sugar, cream, or lemon slices on the side.

COOK'S NOTES

These foods should be served all at once, presented on lovely plates from which the diners can pick and choose their pleasure. If you have fancy linens, fine china, or silverware, this is the occasion to use them.

Chicken Salad Mini-Cups

MAKES 15

1 prepared rotisserie chicken from the deli (3½ to 4 cups chopped)
½ cup mayonnaise
3 tablespoons sherry vinegar or red wine vinegar
¼ cup sour cream
1 tablespoon soy sauce
4 or more green onions, with green tops, chopped (about ½ cup), or
    several minced fresh chives
Salt and freshly cracked pepper
½ cup chopped mixed spring greens
1 (15-count) box of mini-phyllo shells (see Notes)

Discard the chicken skin and pull apart the meat with your fingers. Chop the meat into bite-size pieces.

To make dressing, whisk mayonnaise, vinegar, sour cream, and soy sauce in a medium mixing bowl. Stir in chopped onions or chives and season to taste with salt and pepper. Add chicken and toss to coat with dressing. Refrigerate, covered, for at least a few hours to allow the flavors to meld. (Can be made in advance to this point.)

Just before serving, add the chopped greens and mix thoroughly. Spoon the chicken mixture into the mini-shells.

Notes:

- *For this menu, the chicken salad recipe makes more than is needed to fill the mini-cups, but the extra salad makes great leftovers.*
- *Phyllo shells (also spelled "filo") can be found at most supermarkets in the freezer case with puff pastry, phyllo sheets, and the like. The shells don't need to be thawed in advance because they defrost quickly.*

Blueberry-Banana Mini-Muffins

MAKES 24

4 tablespoons (½ stick) butter, at room temperature
½ cup sugar
1 egg
½ cup mashed banana (from 1 ripe banana)
¼ cup milk
1 cup flour
1 teaspoon baking powder
¼ teaspoon ground cinnamon
1 cup fresh, frozen, or dried blueberries

Preheat oven to 375° F. Grease mini-muffin tins or use paper muffin cups; set aside.

In a medium bowl with an electric mixer, cream the butter and sugar. Add egg. Mix in bananas and milk.

In another mixing bowl, mix flour, baking powder, and cinnamon. Carefully fold in blueberries. If you are using frozen blueberries, fold them while they are still frozen or they will turn the batter purple. Dried blueberries do not need to be reconstituted before they are added.

Fold banana mixture into blueberry mixture carefully, only until the batter is moist. Do not overmix.

Spoon the batter into the muffins cups, filling the cups to the top. Bake for 15 to 20 minutes, or until muffins are golden brown.

Let cool for 5 minutes in the tins; then transfer to a cooling rack. (Can be made 8 hours in advance or earlier, if frozen.)

Note: *If you like your muffins big, double this recipe and use full-size muffin tins. The mini-version, however, makes an attractive, bite-size snack for tea. The mini-pans are inexpensive.*

Toast Points with Smoked Salmon Spread

MAKES 12 LARGE OR 24 SMALL TOASTS

To make this teatime snack most attractive, use two or more colors of bread and types of garnishes. Pair slices from a sandwich loaf with those from thin, German-style cocktail bread, for example. If you intend for this to be a substantial meal, you may want to double the recipe.

4 ounces smoked salmon, cut up (plus additional salmon for garnish)
4 ounces Neufchâtel cheese (light cream cheese), at room temperature
    (see Notes)
2 to 3 teaspoons horseradish (optional)
1 tablespoon chopped green onion
1 teaspoon lemon juice
Dash salt
2 tablespoons or more capers (optional; see Notes)
6 slices (¼- to ½-inch thick) bread, lightly toasted
Thin slices of radish, diced salmon, or sprigs of fresh dill or watercress,
    for garnish

Remove any skin from the salmon and discard. With an electric mixer or by hand, mix together salmon, Neufchâtel cheese, horseradish, green onion, lemon juice, and salt. Set aside. (Can be made ahead and refrigerated overnight.) Stir in capers, if using.

To serve, carefully slice crusts off the bread and cut each slice into 2 or 4 triangles, depending on how big you want the toasts to be. Spread the salmon mixture on the toast (the British prefer to spread it all the way to the edges). Top each toast point with one of a variety of garnishes, such as slices of radish, diced smoked salmon, or sprigs of fresh dill or watercress.

Variation: On another occasion, serve the spread in mini-phyllo cups. (You're already using the cups in this menu with the chicken salad mini-cups.)

Variation: Add a thin slice of cucumber on top of the toast before adding the spread.

Notes:

• *Softened cream cheese can be substituted for the Neufchâtel, but you may need to add a little cream to make it more spreadable.*

• *Capers are small green berries that are traditionally served with smoked salmon. They offer a nice tang; they can be found in supermarkets near the canned olives.*

Cucumbers with Blue Cheese Mousse
MAKES ABOUT 40

6 ounces (¾ cup) crumbled blue cheese; if desired, reserve 2 tablespoons
    for garnish
2 to 4 tablespoons cream or milk
1 large cucumber (about 12 inches)

In a bowl, mix blue cheese and enough cream or milk to make a smooth, spreadable paste that can go through a pastry bag; do not make it too watery or it will not mound up properly. Mix thoroughly by hand or with an electric mixer. (Can be prepared a day in advance and refrigerated.)

If the cucumber is waxed, scrub it well with a vegetable brush. For decoration, the peel can be removed in long strips at even intervals along the length of the cucumber. Do this by scraping the cucumber with either the tines of a fork or a zester, the small grating tool that removes zest from citrus fruit. (You may want to cut the cucumber in half to make the length easier to work with).

Cut cucumber into ¼-inch slices. If desired, scoop out seeds from each slice, being careful not to go all the way through. (This is a nice touch, but it's not necessary to remove the seeds.)

Put cheese mixture in a pastry bag. If you do not have a pastry bag, use a sandwich bag and snip off a corner to make a hole about ⅛ inch across. Right before serving, pipe a small mound of the cheese mixture (about 1 teaspoon) onto each cucumber slice. If a garnish is desired, add crumbles of blue cheese on top of the mousse.

Variation: If your spring vegetable preferences run more toward sugar snap peas (those with the edible pods), pipe the mousse into them instead of on the cucumbers. First blanch the pea pods in boiling water for 1 minute, then plunge into cold water. Drain and cut one side open and pipe in the mousse as a filling.

Coconut Macaroons
MAKES 2 TO 3 DOZEN

These macaroons are the best you will ever have, from Michelle Gayer, a Minneapolis pastry chef.

6⅔ cups unsweetened, desiccated coconut (see Note)
1¼ cups water
4 cups sugar
½ cup light corn syrup
1 teaspoon salt
3 egg whites
1 ounce cream cheese, at room temperature
Vanilla bean, cut in half lengthwise

Preheat oven to 350° F. Line two baking sheets with parchment paper. Place coconut in bowl of electric mixer fitted with a paddle attachment and set aside.

In a large saucepan over medium-high heat, stir water, sugar, corn syrup, and salt, bringing mixture to a boil. Pour hot liquid over coconut and mix on medium speed until cool, about 5 minutes.

Add egg whites, cream cheese, and vanilla bean and mix another 5 minutes. Remove vanilla bean and discard; refrigerate dough, covered, at least 30 minutes.

Roll dough into 1½- to 2-inch balls (or use a small scoop, these don't have to be perfectly shaped) and place on the parchment-paper-lined baking sheets (these cookies don't spread). Bake for 10 to 15 minutes or until golden brown, rotating baking sheets once during baking. Remove from the oven and cool on the baking sheets until ready to serve. If baking ahead of time, store cooled macaroons in a single layer in an airtight container for up to 3 days.

Note: *Unsweetened, desiccated coconut—smaller, finer, and drier than the usual fluffy, sweetened coconut—is available at many natural food stores.*

*What was paradise but a garden full
of vegetables and herbs and pleasures.
Nothing there but delights.*

....

WILLIAM LAWSON

Make vegetable broth; store
in refrigerator up to a week or
freeze for longer time period.

Make phyllo turnovers to
freeze; or make day before and
keep in the refrigerator. Allow
time for phyllo leaves to thaw
in advance.

UP TO A DAY IN ADVANCE

Start mousse.

UP TO 8 HOURS IN ADVANCE

Make soup. Blanch asparagus
tips saved for garnish.

Make Fresh Herb Sauce for
the phyllo turnovers.

Finish maple mousse.

LAST-MINUTE PREP

Finish Fresh Herb Sauce if
prepared ahead.

Bake turnovers.

Shortcut Savvy

Use commercial vegetable
broth.

Use prewashed, packaged
salad greens.

Make phyllo in a 9 x 13-inch
pan instead of in individual
triangles.

FRESH VEGETARIAN FLAVORS

For 6

Asparagus Soup
Spring Greens with Mustard-Peppercorn Vinaigrette
Wild Mushrooms in Phyllo with Fresh Herb Sauce
Maple Mousse

MAYBE IT'S JUST ME, or maybe it's the nature of life in the Upper Midwest, but when spring rolls around I feel my senses awaken as surely as those perennials that poke up from my garden. A little warmth and a little sun do wonders for what has been dulled by underuse—or frozen into disuse—for too many months.

So let's turn to a meal that zaps the senses with flavor and fragrance: slim stalks of asparagus, fresh aromatic herbs, wild mushrooms in all sorts of shapes and sizes, and a tonic of maple-flavored cream.

This menu makes the most of the first early harvest with a meatless meal that should satisfy nonvegetarians, as well, with its intensely flavored, earthy courses. Afterward, it's perfectly acceptable for guests to shed their shoes and head to the garden. But keep the guests at the table until dessert.

The meal begins with a purée of asparagus soup, served in all its glorious green with tender asparagus tips as a garnish. This vegetable seems to shout spring with every bite, not so much because of its flavor, but because of its very welcome color, which is so like new grass. Unlike that short green carpet, however, this short-lived treat must be enjoyed during its brief season, before it disappears for another year.

Because this is a vegetarian meal, the soup base is made from vegetable stock rather than chicken broth, though the latter could be substituted if preferred. Vegetable stock is very mild flavored. It is available commercially, or it can be made ahead and frozen to shorten the cooking process on the actual day of presentation. Once the stock is made, the soup takes little time to prepare: about ten minutes to chop the vegetables, another ten minutes to simmer. To keep the soup at its best color, it should be made the day it is used. The lovely green gets quite dark when refrigerated overnight—though it's still tasty, its color becomes drab.

The menu is intended for an elegant lunch or lighter meal; for a more substantial dinner, the portions could be increased (two mushroom turnovers per person instead of one, for example).

Beverage

Sip on sauvignon blanc for the main course and finish with strong coffee, preferably espresso. If you don't have an espresso machine, adapt it to a drip coffee maker by using finely ground espresso beans or by using 2½ to 3 times the usual amount of ground coffee.

Asparagus Soup
SERVES 6

Many asparagus soups call for the addition of cream. I left it out of this recipe because it seemed like a lot of unnecessary calories. See the Variation if you would prefer to add cream. Use a nonreactive pan (not aluminum) for the soup preparation. The pan should have a stainless or ceramic interior.

1 large onion, chopped (about 1 cup)
1 tablespoon butter
2 pounds (2 bundles) asparagus
2 medium potatoes, peeled and cubed (about 2 cups)
About 5 sprigs flat-leaf parsley
5 cups vegetable stock (see recipe) or chicken broth
1 tablespoon fresh lemon juice
Salt and pepper

In a soup pot, sauté onion in butter until translucent; do not brown.

Break off woody ends of asparagus and discard. Cut off tips of asparagus and reserve. Cut remaining asparagus in 2-inch pieces. Add asparagus, potatoes, parsley, stock, and lemon juice to the pot with onion. Simmer until vegetables are cooked through, about 10 minutes.

Let broth cool slightly. Purée the soup in either a food mill, food processor, or blender. If you prefer the soup completely smooth, put it through a fine strainer; however, a few small bits of vegetable in the purée add some nice texture. Return the purée to the pot to rewarm; season to taste with salt and pepper.

For garnish, slice the reserved asparagus tips in half lengthwise (this makes them lighter so they won't sink into the soup). Drop the asparagus tips in a pot of boiling water for 1½ minutes or until just tender. Drain. To serve, ladle soup into bowls and garnish with asparagus tips.

Variation: Add ½ cup or more of cream to the soup before serving.

Vegetable Stock

MAKES ABOUT 7 CUPS

Vegetable stock isn't pretty when done, but no matter since this recipe calls for it to be added to a beautiful Asparagus Soup. Try adding a stalk or two of asparagus to the stock for some extra flavor. This recipe will make enough stock for both this soup and the herb sauce for Wild Mushrooms in Phyllo.

14 cups water
3 ribs celery, with greens, coarsely chopped
3 to 4 medium carrots, cut in chunks
Handful of flat-leaf parsley
2 bay leaves
2 large onions, quartered
6 or more black peppercorns
3 garlic cloves, chopped
Trimmings from fresh mushrooms used in the phyllo turnovers
2 teaspoons salt

2 asparagus stalks (optional)

In a large pot, add water, celery, carrots, parsley, bay leaves, onions, peppercorns, garlic, any trimmings from mushrooms, salt, and asparagus. Bring liquid to a boil and simmer uncovered for about an hour, or until the liquid reduces by half. Strain stock and refrigerate until ready to use.

If the stock stands for any length of time, it will accrue a dark cloud of sediment at the bottom. It's easy to eliminate that by pouring the stock into a pot, being careful not to stir up the sediment, which can then be discarded. Or the stock can be poured through cheesecloth or a fine strainer to eliminate the sediment.

Spring Greens with Mustard-Peppercorn Vinaigrette
SERVES 6 (MAKES ABOUT ¾ CUP VINAIGRETTE)

1 tablespoon black peppercorns (see Notes)
2 tablespoons Dijon mustard
½ cup olive oil
3 tablespoons white wine vinegar
1 tablespoon or more water
About 6 cups mixed greens (see Notes)

Grind the peppercorns in a blender or pepper grinder.

In a blender, thoroughly mix the mustard, olive oil, and vinegar with the ground peppercorns. Stir in the water until vinaigrette is of desired thickness. Toss greens with as much vinaigrette as desired. You will probably have extra vinaigrette. In addition to dressing salads, the leftovers make a terrific sandwich spread.

Notes:

- *Ground peppercorns give this dressing some bite. If you are hesitant about the spice, prepare the dressing first and add the ground pepper gradually, or leave it out completely.*
- *A 5- to 7-ounce package that includes romaine with radicchio, red oak, frisée, and other baby lettuces works well (the weight of packages varies, depending on the type of lettuce). One package of mixed greens should be enough to serve six people, unless they're really hungry, in which case buy two to be prepared.*

Wild Mushrooms in Phyllo with Fresh Herb Sauce
SERVES 6

These phyllo turnovers with their distinctive triangular shape resemble spanakopita (span-uh-KOH-pih-tuh), the classic Greek dish traditionally stuffed with spinach and feta cheese. These, however, are large enough for a single meal and call for a bounty of wild mushrooms. The Fresh Herb Sauce is a variation on a classic French sauce called a beurre blanc (burr-BLAHNGK), or "white butter." Either vegetable or chicken stock could be used as a base for the sauce, but only real butter will do—not margarine or any of the butter-margarine blends. If you've never cooked with fresh herbs, this sauce is a good place to start. Take a deep breath of the earthy fragrance of the sage and you'll see why the dried version is no substitute.

MUSHROOM FILLING
8 cups diced mushrooms, such as portobello, chanterelle, shiitake,
    cremini, or morels (16 to 24 ounces, depending on mushroom variety)
3 garlic cloves, minced
1 medium onion, chopped (about ¾ cup)
¼ cup olive oil
1 cup plain bread crumbs
1 cup freshly grated Parmesan cheese

PHYLLO
9 phyllo sheets, defrosted (see Phyllo Notes)
1 cup (2 sticks) butter, melted

FRESH HERB SAUCE (makes about 1 cup)
5 to 6 tablespoons cold butter, divided
3 shallots (about ⅓ cup), sliced (see Sauce Notes)
¾ cup dry white wine
2 cups vegetable or chicken stock
½ cup loosely packed fresh sage with stems removed (about 1½ packages
    at ¼ ounce each)
2 tablespoons fresh chives, chopped
Salt and pepper

GARNISH
1 tomato, seeded and finely diced (see Phyllo Notes)
Fresh chervil and chives

Continued on page 44.

Phyllo Notes:

- *Phyllo sheets are found in the freezer section at the supermarket, usually near the frozen pie crusts. The package takes awhile to defrost—either overnight or several hours in the refrigerator—so you need to plan ahead. Once defrosted, remove the sheets you need and refreeze the package (or use it for another purpose). A 1-pound package of phyllo holds about 30 sheets, each about 12 x 17 inches.*

- *The phyllo turnovers can be made ahead and frozen, or refrigerated for a day.*

- *To seed tomatoes, slice them in half, then gently squeeze to remove some seeds and juice. With your fingers, remove any remaining seeds. This will keep the garnish from being too juicy.*

FOR MUSHROOM FILLING

In a very large pan, sauté mushrooms, garlic, and onions in olive oil. Cook mushrooms until all moisture is gone. (You'll start out with no liquid in the pan; then some will accumulate from the mushrooms as they lose their moisture. That extra moisture must be evaporated to avoid soggy phyllo.) Remove mushrooms from heat; add breadcrumbs and cheese.

FOR PHYLLO TURNOVER ASSEMBLY

Place 9 sheets of phyllo on a flat surface and cut in half lengthwise to make 18 sheets. Return remaining phyllo to refrigerator or freezer.

Brush melted butter on one side of each of 3 sheets of phyllo; then stack the 3 sheets on top of each other. Place ⅙ of Mushroom Filling (about 5 to 6 tablespoons) at bottom of the lower right (short side) of phyllo. Fold that right corner over to the left, covering the filling to make a partial triangle. Then take the left side and fold over to the right, repeat, alternating from left to right as you would fold a flag. Fold over the top edges to complete the triangle, now shaped like a turnover. Brush the finished turnover on the top with melted butter and place on a lightly greased baking sheet. Repeat the process with remaining phyllo leaves to make 6 triangles. (Can be made to this point and frozen or refrigerated for one day.)

Bake at 375° F for 20 to 25 minutes or until golden brown. If frozen, they should be baked frozen; add an extra 10 to 15 minutes to the baking time. If refrigerated, add about 5 minutes for baking.

Once baked, serve the phyllo turnovers with Fresh Herb Sauce drizzled on top or in a pool underneath. Garnish with tomatoes and fresh herbs, such as chives and chervil, if desired.

Variation: If you don't want to shape individual phyllo triangles, the dish can be made in a 9 x 13-inch pan; then cut into individual portions.

To do so, cut the phyllo to fit the pan. Brush melted butter on the top of each of 6 sheets and stack them in a lightly greased pan; top with half the mushroom mixture. Brush butter on 6 more sheets and stack them on top of the mushrooms; top with remaining mushrooms. Brush 6 more sheets with butter and stack on top of mushrooms. Cover the top layer of phyllo with melted butter. Bake at 375° F about 30 minutes, or until the top is nicely browned.

FOR FRESH HERB SAUCE

Melt 2 tablespoons butter and sauté shallots until translucent. Add the wine and stock and simmer until the mixture has reduced by two-thirds, about 15 minutes. Add sage and heat for about 1 minute, until herb is limp.

Remove from heat and cool slightly (so it will not "explode" in the blender; see Cook's Notes on page 40, or use an immersion blender). Purée mixture in blender. (If making in advance, refrigerate sauce at this point until ready to use.)

Return sauce to heat. Add remaining 3 to 4 tablespoons of cold butter, 1 tablespoon at a time, whisking constantly (see Sauce Notes). Add chives; season to taste with salt and pepper. Drizzle on or under the baked turnovers.

COOK'S NOTES

Unless you're a mycologist—and a cautious one at that—you'll have to do your mushroom hunting in the supermarket produce aisle. The variety of mushrooms in the marketplace has grown tremendously. While the common button mushroom would work in these phyllo packages and costs less, its flavor is rather bland compared many other mushrooms.

Among the many wild mushrooms popping up in the produce aisle are the morel, portobello, chanterelle, shiitake, and cremini, all flavorful fungi that would work well in this recipe, whether in dried or fresh form. The package label for the mushrooms usually indicates how they can be used. Wild mushrooms can be pricey. For this recipe, choose a variety of mushrooms that fits your budget, using some button mushrooms to keep the cost down. As for these being "wild," it's a term that doesn't necessarily reflect where the mushrooms come from. When the mushrooms are exotic—as in non-button mushrooms—they tend to be called "wild." Morels are the exception, truly from the wild and found fresh in the springtime only. To clean them, soak the mushrooms and pat dry.

Sauce Notes:

- *Shallots look like small onions and have a mild onion-garlic flavor. They are usually sold in small packages that include two or three. Because they become bitter when browned, be careful when sautéing them. Mild onion could be substituted, but use less than you would for shallots; the intent is for a hint of onion flavor, not onion breath.*

- *Whisking in cold butter gives the sauce a thick, smooth texture; warm butter will make a thinner sauce. If you're trying to limit butter intake, simply eliminate the last of 3 to 4 tablespoons butter; the sauce will not be as thick, but it will still taste wonderful.*

Maple Mousse
MAKES AT LEAST 6 GENEROUS SERVINGS

When fall rolls around, so do the maple recipes. But that's a bit odd given that the maple season takes place in the spring when sap is collected, one of the treasures of this time of year. So this maple mousse is absolutely in season for a spring menu. The amber syrup gives only a hint of color but a depth of unexpected flavor that is very refreshing. Because of the richness of this dessert, with all its heavy cream, the best beverage is strong coffee, preferably espresso.

7 egg yolks
1 cup real maple syrup
Dash salt
2 cups heavy cream
Fancy cookie, for garnish

In a double boiler (see Note)—but not on the burner yet—whisk egg yolks lightly. Gradually whisk in maple syrup and salt. Put double boiler on burner over medium heat. Cook maple syrup mixture until it has thickened and lightened in color, about 20 minutes, whisking frequently. Do not increase the heat or flecks of cooked egg will appear in the mixture (and you don't want that in the finished product).

When syrup mixture has thickened, remove the pot from the heat and cool mixture, either by transferring it to a bowl and refrigerating it, or by putting the pan on top of a bowlful of ice cubes. As the mixture cools, stir occasionally to cool it faster. The syrup needs to be entirely cool before it is mixed with the whipped cream. (Can make a day in advance to this point.)

Whip the cream until very stiff, and fold the cooled maple mixture into the whipped cream. Portion the finished mousse into serving dishes, cover with plastic wrap, and refrigerate until ready to serve. The dessert will hold at least 8 hours in the refrigerator. Garnish with a small cookie.

Note: *Double boilers consist of two pots that fit together. The lower pot holds simmering water that gently heats the food in the upper pot. If you don't have a double boiler, a good substitute is a metal bowl in a larger pot of simmering water.*

Bake carrot cake and freeze.

UP TO TWO DAYS IN ADVANCE

Or bake carrot cake and
refrigerate.

Make cream cheese sauce.

Marinate olives.

UP TO A DAY IN ADVANCE

Make ice ring, if using.

Roast meat.

Wash green onions and
radishes.

Make bean salad.

Make sun-dried tomato dip.

UP TO 8 HOURS IN ADVANCE

Thaw juice.

Blanch asparagus and peas, and
slice squash.

UP TO 2 HOURS IN ADVANCE

Arrange vegetables on platter;
keep refrigerated.

Bring marinated olives and cake
to room temperature.

Prepare and roast potatoes.

LAST-MINUTE PREP

Make punch.

Finish bean salad with tomato,
extra basil, and feta.

Reheat meat.

CELEBRATION BUFFET

For 25

Sparkling Fruit Punch
Spicy Beef Brisket Sandwiches
Spring Vegetable Platter with Sun-Dried Tomato Dip
White Bean Salad with Feta and Basil
Roasted New Potatoes with Sweet Onions and Olives
Marinated Olives
Carrot Cake with Cream Cheese Sauce
Fresh Strawberries

IT'S THAT TIME OF YEAR when celebrations abound, when graduations, anniversaries, and retirements call for a smile, a gift, and, yes, a buffet.

This menu offers a meal that will leave cooks time to do some celebrating themselves. Most of the preparation can be done prior to the party. All that's left for the countdown is to reheat the meat, roast the potatoes, slice up any fresh vegetables, and bring out the punch—all done in less than an hour in the kitchen.

Workable? You bet. And flavorful. This meal's lively flavors wake up taste buds grown dull over the winter months.

As we move into the summer months, this menu can be adapted to other purposes, for it makes the most of the season's bounty. Each of the recipes would make a welcome addition to a potluck summer picnic.

Although the menu is written to feed twenty-five guests, the recipes that follow generally make about ten servings. This makes the recipes suitable for smaller gatherings. Each recipe easily can be doubled or tripled to feed larger crowds (and each indicates how to do so for twenty-five guests).

Shortcut Savvy

Use packaged cooked new potatoes.

Buy marinated olives.

Use bottled Greek vinaigrette.

Purchase carrot cake.

Sparkling Fruit Punch

MAKES ABOUT 16 CUPS, OR 32 (½-CUP) SERVINGS

For 25 people, double the recipe (or triple if the weather is hot).

Every buffet needs a punch. This tart sparkler is a sure pleaser, both for the guests and for the cook, who simply adds sparkling water to three juice concentrates. These include orange, grapefruit, and a sweeter juice concentrate to counteract the tartness of the citrus flavor, such as a pineapple-passion fruit–banana concentrate blend or other similar juice. If this is a gathering for adults, spike the punch with vodka.

1 (12-ounce) can frozen orange juice concentrate (undiluted), thawed
1 (12-ounce) can frozen tropical fruit juice concentrate (undiluted), such as
    pineapple-passion fruit–banana juice, thawed
1 (6-ounce) can frozen grapefruit juice concentrate (undiluted), thawed
3 liters chilled sparking water or club soda
Thin slices of orange and lemon, for garnish (see Notes)
Fresh mint leaves, for garnish
Ice ring (optional; see Notes)

About 20 minutes before serving, add juice concentrate to punch bowl and mix together. Slowly add sparkling water. The punch will foam up from the carbonated water and take about 20 minutes to settle down. Once it is clear, add the ice ring, if using, and garnish with mint leaves and slices of orange and lemon, if desired.

Notes:
- *The recipe makes about a gallon of punch, so be sure the punch bowl is big enough. Test in advance by measuring the amount of water the bowl holds.*
- *Slices of blood oranges, with their bright red flesh, look particularly pretty floating in the punch.*
- *To make ice ring, fill a ring mold with water, add orange and lemon slices, and freeze. The punch is tart enough that melting ice won't dilute it significantly; however, you could skip the ice ring and serve ice cubes from an ice bucket near the punch bowl.*

Spicy Beef Brisket Sandwiches

MAKES 10 TO 12 SERVINGS OR MORE

For 25 people, double the recipe and plan, similarly, for 3 to 4 dozen rolls.

1 tablespoon coarse salt
1 to 2 teaspoon coarsely cracked black pepper
2 teaspoons sweet Hungarian paprika
½ teaspoon cayenne pepper (optional)
½ teaspoon ground cumin
3- to 4-pound brisket of beef (half a brisket)
1½ to 2 dozen assorted rolls
Mustard (preferably a variety) and horseradish, as condiment

Preheat oven to 275° to 300° F.

Mix salt, black pepper, paprika, cayenne, and cumin in a small bowl. Rub all over meat. Place meat in covered pan and bake for about 4 hours (meat should be tender enough to come apart easily). If using immediately, cool slightly and slice meat thinly to serve. (An electric knife makes that easier.)

If cooked a day in advance, store meat uncut (to preserve moisture) in the refrigerator. To reheat, preheat oven to 300° to 350° F. Place meat in pan and add about ¼ inch water to prevent the meat from drying out. Heat, covered, for 30 to 45 minutes; then slice. The meat will be so tender that very little actual slicing is necessary.

Serve meat with a variety of rolls, and several mustards and horseradish as condiments. If serving buffet-style, keep meat warm in a chafing dish or slow cooker with a little water to keep it moist.

COOK'S NOTES

Often overlooked, beef brisket makes an ideal entree for a large group. Like ham, it takes little effort to prepare. Unlike ham, this meat has a certain novelty that offers a nice change of flavor for a buffet. The lean, boneless cut has little waste and goes a long way when served.

Briskets come in either half or whole sizes. The meat usually is trimmed of fat; if not, ask the butcher to trim it, or cut off the excess fat yourself. Don't confuse beef brisket with a corned beef brisket, which is made from the same cut. Because of the meat's leanness, it must be cooked very slowly, at low heat, for a very long time (at least 4 hours). This will make the meat so tender that it easily falls apart, which makes for a great sandwich.

Spring Vegetable Platter with Sun-Dried Tomato Dip

MAKES 10 TO 12 SERVINGS OR MORE

For 25 people, double recipe.

3 pounds asparagus, washed
8 ounces sugar snap peas, washed
3 bunches green onions, washed
2 bunches radishes, washed, green removed (about 12 ounces)
1 pound baby yellow squash or zucchini, washed and unpeeled

To prepare asparagus, bend each stalk from the bottom end until it snaps, discarding the end part that breaks off.

To prepare snap peas (unless they are stringless), snap each stem end off, breaking toward the inside curve of the pea; then continue pulling down the inside curve to remove the long string attached to the stem. (Snap peas taste better without the string.)

The asparagus and peas should be blanched to bring out their flavor and keep their color bright. To do so, drop them separately in pots of boiling water; bring to a second boil and continue for about 2 minutes for the asparagus and 1 minute for the peas. Drain and plunge immediately into cold water to stop the cooking process. Drain when cool. Do not overcook or the colors will fade and the vegetables will become mushy.

The green onions, radishes, and squash simply need to be cleaned and trimmed. The day of the party, slice the squash or cut in julienne strips. A few hours before serving, arrange all the vegetables on a platter. Refrigerate, covered, until ready to serve with Sun-Dried Tomato Dip (see recipe).

SUN-DRIED TOMATO DIP

Makes about 2¼ cups
For 25 people, double this recipe.

Sun-dried tomatoes add a pleasing zing and texture to this dip. This dip also makes a great topping for baked potatoes.

8 oil-packed sun-dried tomato halves, cut up coarsely
¼ cup fresh flat-leaf parsley
¼ teaspoon or more minced garlic
1 tablespoon chopped fresh chives, or 2 green onions, chopped
Salt and white pepper
¾ cup plain nonfat yogurt
¾ cup sour cream

Use a blender or food processor to purée tomatoes, parsley, garlic, and chives; season to taste with salt and pepper. Transfer to a bowl and stir in yogurt and sour cream. Cover and refrigerate for several hours or overnight. Can be made a day in advance; stir well before serving.

White Bean Salad with Feta and Basil
MAKES ABOUT 10 SERVINGS
For 25 people, double or triple this recipe, depending on your guests.

3 (15½-ounce) cans Great Northern beans, rinsed and drained
1 yellow or red bell pepper, sliced in thin strips
1 medium red onion, chopped
3 tablespoons chopped fresh basil, plus more for garnish
¼ cup olive oil
2 tablespoons red wine vinegar
¼ cup plus 2 tablespoons crumbled feta cheese, divided
Salt and white pepper
1 tomato, chopped

Continued on page 54.

COOK'S NOTES
Buffets and picnics this time of year often include a marinated bean salad. This version offers a twist. Instead of the three predictable types of beans, this recipe calls for the large, white, mild-flavored Great Northern, which is grown in the Midwest. This salad can be made from the canned variety, which makes preparation fast. Feta, the tangy Greek cheese, adds some unexpected zing to the dish. If you're really in a hurry, use bottled vinaigrette instead of making your own dressing. Stick with fresh basil rather than dried for more flavor.

For the Spanish, a blend
of potatoes and olives
seems a natural mix. For
Americans, the combina-
tion offers a different
take on a warm potato
salad that pleases the palate at any temperature.

For an open house,
pop the potatoes in the
oven before company
arrives and have the dish
roasting while the meat
for the Spicy Beef Brisket
Sandwiches reheats.
The house will smell
wonderful.

Begin the buffet with
the potatoes hot from
the oven; as they cool to
room temperature they
will still taste good. Once
again, fresh herbs are
preferable to dried.

Note: *If you're simultane-
ously roasting the brisket and
the potatoes for a crowd this
large—and doing so all in one
oven—it will take longer for
the food to be done because
the oven will be crowded.*

Mix beans, bell pepper, onion, and basil in a large bowl.

In a blender, purée olive oil, red wine vinegar, and 2 tablespoons feta; season to taste with salt and white pepper.

Drizzle vinaigrette over bean mixture and toss. Refrigerate for several hours or overnight. Just before serving, add chopped tomato and additional basil and toss; sprinkle with the remaining ¼ cup feta.

Variation: For a traditional Italian salad, toss in a 6-ounce can of drained tuna and skip the feta used as garnish. Use chopped parsley instead of basil.

Roasted New Potatoes with Sweet Onions and Olives

SERVES 10 OR MORE

For 25 people, double the recipe (see Note).

1 to 2 large onions (preferably sweet spring onions, such as Vidalia or Oso), sliced (about 2 to 3 cups)
1 tablespoon olive oil, plus more to coat potatoes
5 pounds new red potatoes, unpeeled
1 cup coarsely sliced black olives, Mediterranean-style or marinated (see recipe)
3 tablespoons chopped fresh rosemary sprigs, or 1 tablespoon dried
Salt and freshly cracked black pepper

Preheat oven to 350° F. Sauté the onions in 1 tablespoon olive oil until they turn nicely brown. (This step makes for richer flavor. If short of time, it can be eliminated.) Remove onions from heat.

Cut potatoes into quarters (or more) to make bite-size pieces. In a roasting pan or large baking dish, toss potatoes with onions, olives, rosemary, and enough olive oil to coat lightly. Season to taste with salt and pepper.

Roast potatoes uncovered, stirring occasionally, for about an hour or until fork tender. Toss again before serving. (Potatoes should not be made a day in advance, as they will become a little mushy and unsightly—still delicious, but not really for presentation to guests).

Marinated Olives

MAKES 2 POUNDS (ENOUGH FOR 25 PEOPLE)

2 pounds Mediterranean olives, such as kalamata or niçoise (2 or 3
    different sizes of olives make an interesting presentation)
6 garlic cloves, chopped
Sprigs of fresh rosemary
About 2 cups extra-virgin olive oil

Drain olives. Place olives, garlic, and rosemary in a crock or jar with enough olive oil to cover. If needed, divide the ingredients between two containers.

Cover and refrigerate immediately for several days to allow the flavors to mingle. Olives can be stored in the refrigerator for up to three weeks; then they should be discarded (see Note). The olive oil will congeal in the refrigerator. Allow time for the olives to get to room temperature.

Note: *The University of Minnesota Extension Service, which delivers educational programs and information throughout the state, advises that marinated olives be kept refrigerated for no longer than three weeks to avoid the risk of botulism. This is because the thickness of olive oil prevents oxygen from being present and sets up an environment where botulism can grow if it is introduced by another substance, such as the olives or the herbs. Marinated olives contain no acid, nor are they processed under heat, which would kill bacteria.*

Many cookbooks give incorrect information on marinated olives, according to the Extension Service, which urges adherence to the three-week time limit for storing the olives in the refrigerator. To use the olives, take out only what is needed and keep the remainder in the refrigerator. Leftovers from the buffet table should be discarded rather than returned to the refrigerator.

COOK'S NOTES

These olives are simply fabulous, whether used with the roasted potatoes or served alone on the buffet table. To keep them as safe as they are delicious, pay attention to the cautions in the recipe.

Use good-quality Mediterranean-style olives that are available at deli counters. The canned variety of olives won't improve much with the marinade. Fresh herbs are preferred over dried for the best results in fragrance and flavor.

The recipe is pricey: the per-pound cost of olives can rival that of some meat; extra-virgin olive oil, which offers a fruity flavor, costs more than regular; and you have the cost of fresh herbs. If you have extra to spend on this buffet, however, the olives are a worthy addition. Serve them on the side, as well as in the potatoes.

Carrot Cake with Cream Cheese Sauce

MAKES 1 LOAF CAKE WITH ABOUT 18 (½-INCH) SLICES

For 25 people, double or triple the recipe.

COOK'S NOTES

What's a buffet without a couple of desserts? For the health-minded, offer a big bowl of fresh strawberries, which makes a lovely seasonal addition to the table.

For lovers of sweets, serve a version of a cake that has been a favorite at buffets for generations. This carrot cake, fragrant with cinnamon and nutmeg, seems closer to a pumpkin or spice cake in flavor. Very dense and moist, it slices nicely, which is particularly helpful at a buffet table. Served here in very thin slices, the cake is topped with a luscious cream cheese sauce that also can be used as a dip for the strawberries. The cake can be made in advance. Since it's mixed by hand in a single bowl, be sure to use a large one to accommodate the bulk. The recipe is adapted from *The Fannie Farmer Baking Book* by Marion Cunningham.

6 tablespoons (¾ stick) butter
2 eggs
1 cup milk
1 cup dark brown sugar
1½ cups flour
2 teaspoons baking powder
1 teaspoon baking soda
½ teaspoon salt
2 teaspoons cinnamon
2 teaspoons nutmeg
1¼ cups grated raw carrots
Cream Cheese Sauce (see recipe)

Preheat oven to 350° F. Melt butter and set aside to cool to room temperature. Grease and flour a 9 x 5-inch loaf pan.

Break the eggs into a large bowl and gently beat by hand. Stir a little of the egg into the cooled, melted butter, stirring continuously. (If butter is not cooled enough, the eggs will cook.) Pour butter mixture into the remaining eggs and stir thoroughly.

Add milk to butter mixture and beat with a fork until well mixed. Add the sugar and beat well. In a separate bowl, stir together the flour, baking powder, baking soda, salt, cinnamon, and nutmeg. Add flour mixture to butter mixture and beat by hand until just blended. Stir in the carrots.

Spread batter evenly in the prepared pan. Bake 55 to 60 minutes, or until a toothpick inserted in the center of the cake comes out clean. Remove from the oven and let cool in the pan for 10 minutes. Run a knife around the edge of the pan, and turn cake out onto a rack to cool completely. Immediately before serving, drizzle slices of cake with Cream Cheese Sauce.

Note: *This cake freezes nicely, or it can be made a day or two in advance and stored in refrigerator, covered tightly in plastic wrap. Because it's so moist, it lasts a long time. Bring to room temperature before serving.*

CREAM CHEESE SAUCE

Makes about 2½ cups

For 25 people, make one recipe.

1 (8-ounce) package cream cheese, at room temperature

½ cup sugar

1 teaspoon vanilla

1 cup sour cream

About ½ cup half-and-half, cream, or milk

With an electric mixer, blend cream cheese and sugar together until smooth. Add vanilla, sour cream, and enough half-and-half to make sauce the consistency you want. Serve on top of cake or French toast or waffles, or use as a dip for fresh fruit.

COOK'S NOTES

Have you ever made cheesecake and dipped your finger into its luscious batter to taste it? This recipe was inspired by those flavors, in a variation of the cream cheese frosting that usually appears on carrot cake. This sauce oozes with flavor, whether drizzled across a slice of carrot cake or used as a dipping sauce for the strawberries. Save the extra sauce to top French toast the next morning, with a few strawberries scattered on top for a perfect brunch dish. The sauce can be prepared days in advance and refrigerated.

Make Ahead

UP TO A WEEK OR MORE IN ADVANCE

Bake cake and freeze.

UP TO 2 DAYS IN ADVANCE

Make strawberry-rhubarb sauce.

Sauté mushrooms and onions for quiche.

UP TO A DAY IN ADVANCE

Bake cake, if not done earlier.

Prepare chicken and asparagus for roulades.

Make mustard sauce.

UP TO 8 HOURS IN ADVANCE

Thaw juice, if frozen.

Prepare fruit and yogurt parfaits, if using.

Assemble platters of fruit, cheese, and fish, if using.

Prepare bread basket.

Mix together quiche ingredients.

UP TO 2 HOURS IN ADVANCE

Assemble chicken roulades.

LAST-MINUTE PREP

Bake quiche.

Bake chicken roulades.

Bring extra asparagus to room temperature.

BRUNCH FOR A BUNCH

For 10

Sparkling Wine or Mimosa
Variety of Juices
Mushroom and Onion Quiche
Chicken and Ham Roulades with Asparagus and Dijon Mustard Sauce
Fruit and Yogurt Parfaits or Fruit Platter
Cheese Platter
Fish Platter
Bread Basket
Almond Pound Cake with Strawberry-Rhubarb Sauce

BUFFET AND ABUNDANCE go hand in hand. Or perhaps it's "plate by plate." At the overflowing table we find a bit of the child in all of us: the sense of delight at the prospect of all those choices, the sheer wonder at the sight of more food than one could comfortably eat. Such tables are rarely seen in homes today because so many people think they are too busy to fill those tables properly.

Not true. Here's a little secret that's spreading from kitchen to kitchen everywhere: good food doesn't have to be made from scratch; it doesn't even have to be homemade. Good food is available from many sources, and the busy cook who likes to entertain puts those sources to good use. Indeed, a car may be an enterprising cook's most useful piece of equipment.

To meet the entertaining demands of a hectic spring season that includes Easter, Mother's Day, graduation open houses, and bridal showers, set up a brunch buffet for the easiest of meals to accommodate crowds of any size.

Keep the time in the kitchen to a minimum by incorporating platters of ready-made food, from cheese and fish platters to entrees and desserts that may or may not be homemade. The most modest of offerings shed their humble wraps when multiplied tenfold.

This is the key to a pleasing effect: abundance. Never mind who makes the food. Your guests won't care. They'll be smiling to themselves as they head back to the buffet table for seconds. Or thirds.

This menu is a brunch for ten, though it can easily be adjusted for groups of any size, as well as modified to meet the needs of the cook. If time is short, store-bought entrees or desserts can be substituted.

The biggest constraint is with food safety. The standard measure is that foods shouldn't be out of refrigeration for more than two hours—and that includes the preparation time. Leftovers should be discarded.

Shortcut Savvy

Substitute a ham to replace the chicken roulades.

Buy fruit already cut up, or already assembled on a tray.

Buy ready-made cheese tray.

Buy ready-made fish platter.

Buy ready-made quiche to warm up in the oven.

Buy prepared cake.

Beverage

For an aperitif, break out the sparkling wine, or for those not sipping something alcoholic, offer a choice of juices. Choose your favorite flavors—or have fun with new ones. Whichever you pick, keep them colorful (pastel is especially appropriate) to set off the springtime flowers you'll want on the buffet table. An option of two or more juices will make the choice more engaging for your guests. Either pitchers or individual glasses of juice are appropriate. Or have sparkling water available to add to the juice to make fruit spritzers.

COOK'S NOTES

Much of this brunch menu can be prepared in advance. If you're not buying ready-made food platters, allow time to assemble the platters immediately before serving. A spare set of hands would be useful, though not necessary; one person can handle the last-minute details. For garnishes, turn to the edible flowers and fresh herbs that are readily available and that give the table the look of spring.

FRUIT AND YOGURT PARFAITS OR A FRUIT PLATTER: Either prepare mini-parfaits with layers of vanilla yogurt, fresh fruit, and granola, or serve a platter of fresh fruit. For either, color is the key to making this look luscious; choose a mixture of fruit that appeals to your palate and budget, making sure it's fruit that can sit out for awhile. Keep the season in mind and incorporate fresh berries. A combination of kiwi, berries, and pineapple is lovely.

CHEESE PLATTER: Again, the object is to offer multiple choices for the guests. When shopping, look for distinctly different flavors (keeping in mind there is Gruyère in the quiche); only a small amount of each cheese will be needed for a platter. If you're expecting some very young guests, be sure to include a traditional cheese such as cheddar. For the adults, let them broaden their tastes.

Some options: Gouda, a soft cheese such as brie or goat cheese (chèvre), and a blue cheese. Whether it's sliced, cubed, or left whole is up to the cook; a variety of methods makes a more interesting display. Add a few nuts or olives to the platter to dress it up, with some crackers on the side.

FISH PLATTER: If your guests aren't fond of fish, by all means skip this dish. But for many, this is a special treat that comes only once or twice a year. Three varieties give the platter balance, but even a single bowl of pickled herring is sufficient. Possibilities include smoked salmon, smoked trout, or another smoked white fish, all of which are readily available at supermarkets. Include some crackers on which to spread the fish.

BREAD BASKET: Let loose in the bakery or freezer section of the supermarket to fill your bread basket. Stock up on bagels, croissants, muffins, and French breads. The choices are endless; only your budget will keep you in line. Mini-versions of bakery goodies are preferred because they allow guests to indulge in several pieces.

MIMOSA: Mix sparkling wine half-and-half with orange juice—preferably freshly squeezed—or mix it one part orange juice to two parts sparkling wine, depending on the crowd.

Mushroom and Onion Quiche

MAKES 10 TO 12 SERVINGS

This quiche does not have a crust. If you prefer one, roll out two prepared pie crusts and bake according to directions. Then add the egg mixture and bake as directed below. A white cheese is used in this recipe because its color blends better with the egg mixture. The more finely shredded the cheese is, the more it will melt into the eggs. Other vegetables or bacon could be substituted or added to the egg mixture. To make the most of the season, use morel mushrooms, which usually appear outdoors—and in the stores—in May.

6 to 8 ounces mushrooms, sliced
1 medium onion, sliced (¾ cup)
2 tablespoons butter, plus more to grease pan
8 eggs
1½ cups half-and-half or milk
4 ounces (1 cup) finely shredded Gruyére or white cheddar cheese
1 teaspoon salt
Dash white pepper
2 tablespoons chopped chives, plus more for garnish (optional)

Preheat oven to 350° F.

Sauté mushrooms and onions in a saucepan with butter until soft. Set aside. (If preparing in advance, refrigerate mixture until ready to use.)

Crack eggs into large bowl; whisk until egg whites and yolks are thoroughly blended. Add half-and-half or milk, cheese, salt, pepper, and chives; whisk thoroughly. Add mushroom mixture and stir.

With butter, lightly grease a 9 x 13-inch pan (glass or ceramic will look nicer than metal for serving) or two 9-inch pie pans. Pour egg mixture into pan(s). Bake until golden, about 20 to 25 minutes. Serve hot or at room temperature, with additional chives sprinkled on top for garnish.

Chicken and Ham Roulades with Asparagus and Dijon Mustard Sauce

MAKES 12 ROULADES AND ABOUT 1 CUP SAUCE

The roulades are the most time-consuming dish to prepare on this menu, but the time is not excessive. Their interesting appearance will make them a hit with your guests. They can be partially prepared a day in advance by readying the asparagus and by pounding the chicken breasts. The assembly requires about 30 minutes of attention from the cook, and can be done about 2 hours in advance. Then the roulades get about a half hour of baking. The only special equipment needed is some kitchen string and a meat mallet.

12 stalks of asparagus for roulades
1 pound asparagus for side dish (optional)
12 chicken breast halves (about 2½ pounds), skinless and boneless
    (see Notes)
12 pieces of very thinly sliced (deli-style) ham (about 12 ounces) or
    prosciutto (Italian thin-sliced ham)
Salt and white pepper
2 to 3 tablespoons butter
1 cup mayonnaise
1½ tablespoons Dijon mustard
Bottled vinaigrette, to drizzle over asparagus as a side dish

Cook asparagus for roulades and for side dish separately. For roulades, steam asparagus for 1 minute over boiling water, then plunge immediately into cold water; drain thoroughly. Repeat for asparagus as side dish, if desired, except steam until crisp-tender (about 10 minutes). Refrigerate asparagus until ready to use.

Flatten chicken breasts with meat mallet, pounding out until very thin and uniform in size. Sprinkle lightly with salt and white pepper. (Can be done in advance to this point.)

Preheat oven to 350° F.

For each chicken breast, top with single piece of ham or prosciutto and asparagus stalk. Roll up chicken breast and close by tying chicken with kitchen string on either end of roll-up.

Melt butter in frying pan over medium heat and brown roulades. Place in ovenproof dish and bake for 20 to 30 minutes, or until chicken is thoroughly cooked (time will depend on thickness of chicken).

Meanwhile, if serving asparagus on the side, bring to room temperature. Prepare Dijon mustard sauce in a small bowl by stirring Dijon mustard into mayonnaise. (Cautious cooks may want to begin with 1 tablespoon of mustard and gradually increase the amount to taste.)

Remove the string from the roulades and place them on a serving dish. Present sauce and additional asparagus in separate dishes, drizzling a little vinaigrette on the asparagus.

Notes

- *You need to be able to roll up these chicken breasts so they must be thin. Avoid the oversized thick chicken breasts that come pre-frozen in a sodium solution.*
- *To estimate how many roulades are needed, figure one per person, then add a few more for the occasional guest who will want extra (there always is one or two). If you have guests with smaller appetites, consider cutting each roulade into two to four pieces for more manageable portions.*

Almond Pound Cake with Strawberry-Rhubarb Sauce

MAKES 1 TUBE CAKE (24 SERVINGS)

1 cup (2 sticks) butter or margarine, at room temperature
2 cups sugar
6 eggs, separated
1½ cups flour
½ teaspoon salt
2 teaspoons baking powder
¼ cup plus 2 tablespoons milk
½ teaspoon almond extract
Strawberry-Rhubarb Sauce (see recipe)

Preheat oven to 350° F.

Cream butter thoroughly. Add sugar slowly and continue beating until light and fluffy. Beat in egg yolks one at a time.

In a separate bowl, sift flour, salt, and baking powder together. In a cup or small bowl, combine milk and almond extract. Add one-third of the flour mixture to the butter mixture and stir gently but thoroughly; add one-third of the milk mixture and stir gently but thoroughly. Continue to add flour mixture and milk alternately until all has been incorporated into the batter.

Beat egg whites until stiff but not dry; fold into batter thoroughly. Spoon into well-greased, 10-cup tube pan (an angel food cake pan or Bundt pan). Bake for about 50 to 55 minutes, or until cake tests done. Cool in pan for 10 minutes.

Loosen cake gently around rim and tube. Cool completely before removing from pan. Can be sliced very thin, if desired, or in larger pieces. Serve with Strawberry-Rhubarb Sauce.

Variation: Add the zest of 1 lemon (about 1 tablespoon) to the batter at the end.

STRAWBERRY-RHUBARB SAUCE

Makes about 2 cups

2 cups (1 pint) fresh strawberries, hulled and sliced

¼ cup sugar

2 cups chopped (½-inch pieces) rhubarb (2 large stalks)

Juice and zest from 1 orange (about ¼ cup orange juice and 1 tablespoon orange zest)

In a medium bowl, toss sliced strawberries with sugar; set aside.

In a medium pot combine rhubarb and orange juice and, over low heat, bring to a simmer. Cook rhubarb until it is barely soft, about 5 minutes. Set aside to cool slightly.

Add cooled rhubarb to strawberries and toss with orange zest. (Can be made 2 days ahead and refrigerated.) Serve over cake or ice cream.

COOK'S NOTES

This recipe calls for zest, which is the colored part of the skin on citrus fruit (not the white pith, which is bitter). Its aromatic oils add flavor. To remove zest from fruit, carefully use a grater so that only the colored part is removed; or use a vegetable peeler or a zester (a small kitchen tool with tiny cutting holes that scrapes off the peel in threadlike pieces).

SALAD SAMPLER LUNCHEON

For 6

Asparagus and Greens with Pesto Quenelle
Spicy Chicken with Angel Hair Pasta and Watercress
Spring Berries with Vanilla Sauce

NEVER BEFORE HAVE SO MANY PEOPLE ordered so many salads. It's an epidemic of sorts—albeit a healthy one—as leafy greens rival burgers, and pasta competes with potatoes in what may one day be called the Salad Revolution.

Once the purview only of dieters, salads have gone mainstream, from fast food to deli, school lunch to haute cuisine. No longer just the beginning of the meal, salads have cropped up at the middle, end, and everywhere in between, as they do here in this menu of salads.

Think of it as a salad sampler of spring flavors, to be served course by course, each one artfully presented for the lighter luncheons that appear as regularly as robins this time of year.

Should you need to adapt this luncheon to heavier mealtime needs, the servings of chicken can be increased and the meal filled out with popovers, muffins, or loaves of bread. The recipes serve six but can easily be adapted.

Asparagus and Greens with Pesto Quenelle

SERVES 6

For the first course on this menu, spring is at its essence in the form of asparagus. Take away the embellishments of this dish and it's simply a green salad. But gather a bouquet of asparagus and Belgian endive, garnish it with an honest-to-goodness flower, and this green salad becomes a springtime showstopper—proof edible that we "eat" with our eyes.

Traditionally, a quenelle (kuh-NEHL) is an oval-shaped dumpling made of minced fish or meat. Here it's made of cilantro pesto for an unconventional presentation and flavor for that ubiquitous Italian sauce, which most often finds its place atop pasta.

36 thin stalks (about 2 to 2½ pounds) asparagus
Cilantro Pesto (see recipe)
Simple Vinaigrette (see recipe; see Notes)
18 Belgian endive leaves
3 cups mixed baby greens (see Notes)
6 edible flowers, for garnish (see Notes)
Pine nuts, for garnish
Lemon zest, for garnish

Steam asparagus for about 3 to 4 minutes, or until crisp-tender, then plunge into cold water; drain. If making in advance, store in refrigerator until an hour before serving; then set it out to reach room temperature.

Prepare Cilantro Pesto and Simple Vinaigrette.

On each serving plate, fan out three Belgian endive leaves and place two stalks of asparagus in each of the leaves. Add about ½ cup baby greens at base of endive on each plate and garnish with an edible flower.

Prepare a quenelle by using two spoons to shape about 1 to 1½ tablespoons pesto into an oval shape. Place the quenelle next to the endive on plate.

Drizzle 1 tablespoon of vinaigrette across asparagus and greens. Top salad with sprinkle of pine nuts and some lemon zest, if desired. Serve immediately.

Notes:

- *Though any greens can be used for this salad, the baby variety offers a pleasingly delicate appearance; usually it comes packaged in a mix of several varieties.*

- *Edible flowers that are grown specifically to be eaten can be found in the produce department of the supermarket. Do not use flowering plants from the nursery because they may have been sprayed with pesticides. And don't pluck any old flower from your garden for nibbling purposes; some experts say that unless a seed is intended—and labeled— for growing edible flowers, it may have been treated with pesticides.*

Cilantro Pesto

MAKES ABOUT ¾ CUP

This pesto recipe is thicker than usual so that it can be shaped into quenelles. To use the pesto as a sauce, gradually add additional olive oil (2 tablespoons to ¼ cup) and process until it's the desired consistency. Basil can be used instead of cilantro if preferred. Leftover pesto can be tossed with pasta or used as a sandwich spread. To remove leaves from cilantro, simply pluck them off in a bunch; if a few stems get caught in the mix, it won't matter since they will be puréed.

1 cup firmly packed fresh cilantro leaves, stems removed
½ cup freshly grated Parmesan cheese
3 tablespoons olive oil
2 tablespoons pine nuts
2 garlic cloves

Using a blender or food processor, purée cilantro, Parmesan, olive oil, pine nuts, and garlic into a smooth paste. The finer the paste, the more successful the shaping of the quenelles will be.

Simple Vinaigrette

MAKES ABOUT ⅔ CUP

⅓ cup olive or vegetable oil
½ cup white wine vinegar
Salt and white pepper

Whisk together olive oil and vinegar; season to taste with salt and pepper.

Note: *Any simple vinaigrette, including a commercially bottled one, can be substituted for the recipe, but use a mild-flavored one because of the many flavors on the salad plate.*

Spicy Chicken with
Angel Hair Pasta and Watercress
SERVES 6

Like the first course for this seasonal menu, the presentation of the main-course salad is carefully composed. The spicy chicken salad could just as easily be served family-style on a big platter to be passed—and the family wouldn't mind a bit. But for company, let's have some fun with it. Radic-chio (rad-DEE-kee-oh), a red-leafed salad green with a slightly bitter flavor, makes a lovely "cup" from which this Asian-flavored salad spills out onto individual plates. The ginger, garlic, and red pepper flakes offer the distinct zing to this dish; amounts can be cut back slightly (or in the case of the red pepper flakes, omitted) if you have a table of people prone to heartburn.

DRESSING
2 tablespoons rice wine vinegar
1 tablespoon soy sauce
1 tablespoon vegetable oil
1 tablespoon sesame oil
1 teaspoon sherry or dry white wine
1 medium onion, thinly sliced (about ¾ cup)
Salt and pepper

PASTA
About 12 ounces angel hair pasta

SPICY CHICKEN
2 tablespoons vegetable oil
1½ tablespoons finely chopped garlic
1 tablespoon finely chopped fresh ginger root
¼ teaspoon red pepper flakes
5 or 6 chicken breast halves, boned and skinned (about 1¼ pounds)
6 green onions, chopped finely
1 cup watercress leaves, densely packed (about 1 ounce)
12 whole radicchio leaves (2 heads of radicchio)

GARNISH
Black sesame seeds

FOR DRESSING
Prepare dressing in a small bowl by whisking together rice wine vinegar, soy sauce, 1 tablespoon vegetable oil, sesame oil, sherry, and onion; season to taste with salt and pepper. Set aside.

FOR PASTA
Heat water to cook pasta; cook according to package directions. (If preparing in advance, cook until almost done, drain, and toss with a few drops of sesame oil; finish by dropping into boiling water for a minute before serving.) Drain pasta. If serving right away, toss pasta with the rice wine vinegar dressing.

FOR SPICY CHICKEN
Heat sauté pan with 2 tablespoons vegetable oil; add garlic, ginger, and pepper flakes. Add chicken breasts and green onions, and season to taste with salt and pepper. Cook chicken until done, about 3 to 4 minutes per side.

FOR SALAD ASSEMBLY AND GARNISH
Add watercress leaves to the dressed pasta. Place a scoop of pasta in 1 or 2 radicchio cups for each plate. Slice each chicken breast into several thin pieces and fan out onto pasta. Top with black sesame seeds, if desired. Serve immediately.

Spring Berries with Vanilla Sauce
SERVES 6

For those who adore sweets, fruit salad as dessert might seem a hard sell. But this recipe may change their minds. Berries tossed with crème de cassis, a black currant liqueur, are drizzled with a rich vanilla sauce so melt-in-your-mouth your guests will want to beg for more. (They won't, of course, because this is a civilized luncheon.)

Without the whipped cream that's added to the vanilla sauce, the thin custard would be called crème anglaise (krehm ahn-GLAYZ), which traditionally is used as a topping for cake or fruit. Add the whipped calories to the crème anglaise, and the French call it mousseline (moos-LEEN). Others might call it heavenly. But be careful while cooking the sauce, or you'll be calling it scrambled eggs.

VANILLA SAUCE (see Notes)
4 egg yolks
½ cup sugar
1 teaspoon cornstarch
1¼ cups milk
1 tablespoon vanilla
⅔ cup heavy cream

FRUIT BASE
6 cups berries: strawberries, red or yellow raspberries, blackberries or
    blueberries (a variety of colors is most attractive; see Notes)
¼ cup crème de cassis (black currant liqueur; optional)
Sprigs of fresh mint, for garnish

FOR VANILLA SAUCE
Place egg yolks in a medium pot and gradually beat sugar into them, using a hand mixer. Continue beating for 2 to 3 minutes until the mixture is pale yellow and thickens slightly. Beat in cornstarch.

In a small pot, heat milk almost to scalding. While constantly whisking the egg mixture, gradually add hot milk in a thin stream of droplets, so that eggs are slowly warmed and do not curdle.

Heat egg-milk mixture over moderate heat, stirring slowly and continuously with a wooden spoon, until the sauce thickens just enough to coat the spoon with a light, creamy layer, about 10 minutes (about 160° F on a candy thermometer). Do not let custard simmer or reach a temperature higher than 165° F or it will curdle.

Remove sauce from heat. Using a wooden spoon, stir for a minute or two to cool; then add vanilla and stir. Refrigerate until cool; then cover.

Within 2 hours of serving, strain sauce to remove any lumps. Whip heavy cream to medium peaks; continue beating on low while adding vanilla sauce to whipped cream.

To serve, toss berries lightly with crème de cassis. In serving dish (a stemmed dish, such as a goblet, is particularly nice), place a pool of sauce, then berries, and top with sauce and sprig of mint, if desired. Serve immediately.

Notes:

- *The vanilla sauce tastes and looks very much like a premium vanilla ice cream that has melted. If you're short of time, you could melt some good-quality ice cream and use it as a very untraditional substitute for the vanilla sauce. (In this case, you would omit the additional whipped cream.)*
- *You'll end up with much more sauce than you will need for a small luncheon; only about ¼ cup of sauce is needed per serving as you want to embellish the berries, not drown them.*
- *Unless you're deep into berry season, raspberries and blackberries may be costly. But you don't need many to dress up the bowl of berries. To keep the price down, use mostly strawberries.*

This menu involves some serious chopping on the part of the cook. If you don't have time to do it all yourself, enlist that graduate who is ready to party. Also keep in mind that you'll need to buy avocadoes enough in advance that they will be ripe for the party.

UP TO A WEEK OR MORE IN ADVANCE

Buy avocados.

Bake fudge bars and freeze.

UP TO 2 DAYS IN ADVANCE

Cook vegetables for nacho cheese sauce.

UP TO A DAY IN ADVANCE

Chop vegetables for fajitas and tacos.

Cut up chicken for fajitas.

Cook taco filling.

Make fudge bars, if not done earlier.

Make the ice ring, if using.

UP TO 8 HOURS IN ADVANCE

Cut up onions and chile for salsa.

UP TO TWO HOURS IN ADVANCE

Finish nacho cheese sauce and place in slow cooker to heat.

Finish salsa with tomatoes.

Make guacamole.

GRAD PARTY 101

For any size crowd

Margarita Punch without the Punch
Chicken Fajitas on the Grill
Make-Your-Own Tacos
Nacho Cheese Sauce and Chips
Guacamole for a Crowd
Pico de Gallo
Cinnamon-Fudge Bars

ATTENTION, STUDENTS. You know who you are: the graying bunch seated in the back, the folks squished into desks. (Are the desks too small or are you too big? I'll reserve judgment.) Please move to the front of the room so I don't have to speak too loudly.

Parents, we're here today to talk about graduation parties. Not yours. Theirs. The distinction is crucial.

Let me give my credentials. I have three graduation celebrations behind me. In the past few years, I've eaten at graduation parties galore. You might say I have a graduate degree in cooking. So here's my advice:

Lesson 1: It might feel like your big moment. But it's not. It's theirs.

I know, I know. It's been 52 report cards and 26 teacher conferences, 360 soccer games and 255 basketball games, 60 sleepovers, 240 piano lessons,

3 years of religious instruction, $2,700 in school lunches—and 2 minivans. It may feel like you've done the work—but you haven't. You've been the observer (and the one who paid for it). There's a difference.

Lesson 2: Plan the menu with the graduate in mind. If you want to satisfy the hunger of students, look to their taste buds for reference. Choose foods that delight them. Nothing new, nothing odd, nothing that will make them stand out too much in a crowded field of graduation parties (never mind the tattoos, piercings, and neon-colored hair—graduates want to fit in with their crowd, not yours).

Consider the graduate's daily diet. Then consider the graduate's snack foods. If these are one and the same, your graduate is the norm—and plan the menu accordingly. Of course, there are a few who follow the surgeon general's dietary recommendations. Those graduates will be celebrating in the back room at the local health-food store. The ones I know—and cook

NO GRADUATES?

Spring and summer are celebration enough. This menu is an informal party pleaser for anyone, especially for large gatherings, such as family reunions. Keep in mind you'll need a way to keep the taco filling and nacho cheese sauce hot. Either a slow cooker or a chafing dish will work.

To make your shopping list, plan on one corn taco shell (for tacos) and one flour tortilla (for fajitas) per person. You're likely to use half that amount (guests will usually have one or the other), but it will be hard to figure out who is having which. This way you're prepared and leftovers won't be a problem. For the flour tortillas, stick with the smaller ones as your guests likely will want only a taste of your menu.

UP TO 1 HOUR IN ADVANCE

Marinate chicken.

LAST-MINUTE PREP

Make punch.

Reheat taco filling.

Preheat grill. Cook chicken and vegetables for fajitas as needed for guests.

Shortcut Savvy

Buy prechopped onions (in the freezer case of the supermarket).

Buy preshredded cheese, available in economy-size packages.

Buy prepared guacamole.

Buy prepared salsa.

Buy prepared nacho cheese sauce, or make the classic one with 1 pound of Velveeta or other processed cheese food, chopped in chunks, and melted with a 10-ounce can of diced tomatoes with green chiles.

Buy bakery-made bars or other assorted mini-desserts.

Beverage

For those under twenty-one, keep the punch nonalcoholic, as is the case with the Margarita Punch Without the Punch. If you've got only adults in the crowd, add tequila.

for—have other food in mind. I'm assuming that's the case with yours. My graduate likes Tex-Mex food. So do her friends. Her parents do, too, but that is beside the point. We serve what she likes.

Lesson 3: The guest list is likely to be long. For my first graduation party, I thought we would invite relatives and a few friends of the graduate, just like when I was a high-school senior. Foolish me. I expected to invite 30 guests tops. But the final count was 80, which included former teachers. Naturally, I planned food for a crowd that big. But I ended up with leftovers for an army. Which brings me to the next consideration.

Lesson 4: Think little bites. Less is more. The phrase "hungry teenager" is almost redundant, except at graduation parties when the graduate flits from one happy gathering to another, to another, and maybe even another, all in a single afternoon. Graduation parties will be fast and furious, as your graduate visits as many as possible in the last gasp of high-school friendship.

Your youthful guests aren't going to eat a whole lot while they visit. They'll nibble here and nibble there before heading out to nibble elsewhere. You will not need as much food as you would normally serve at a buffet. But it's fun to offer a wide variety of foods. This is a party, after all.

Lesson 5: Make-your-own food keeps the guests busy. Not a bad idea for a party where Aunt Nora will be chatting with the friends of your son or daughter. Give your guests and the non-primary cook in the family (whether it's Dad, Mom, or a sibling) something to do by staging the meal at the grill.

Lesson 6: Skip the cake. It's tradition, I know, and a silly one. Judging by the number of intact sheet cakes I have observed, no one eats a piece of cake at graduation, so why bother? Instead, make mini-versions of your graduate's favorite dessert. Better yet, make a variety of them, a buffet's worth of desserts: cookies, bars, mini-cheesecakes. Not surprisingly, these small treats will be devoured, even by teens who insist they aren't hungry at all.

Lesson 7: Stick around for the party. Yes, it's their celebration, but you need to supervise. You may even have some fun on the occasion, though your fun is not the goal.

Class dismissed.

FOOD SAFETY

For this menu, you'll be handling a lot of raw chicken and uncooked vegetables. Be careful not to cross-contaminate cutting boards. The best way to handle this is by using separate cutting boards and knives. Clean the counter and boards thoroughly after the chicken has been sliced.

Remember also to keep hot food hot, and cold food cold, especially when serving a crowd and particularly if the weather is warm. Don't put all the portions of food on the table at the same time. It is far better to replenish bowls than it is to have all the food sitting out for hours. Remember the two-hour rule for food safety: don't leave food out for more than two hours—and that time begins when the food is taken from the refrigerator or off the heat.

Margarita Punch
without the Punch
MAKES 22 (4-OUNCE) SERVINGS

This calls for an orange-flavored syrup, often used with coffee, which is available at some coffeehouses and at kitchen specialty stores. This refreshing beverage is simply a variation on limeade.

1 (12-ounce) can frozen limeade, thawed
2 liters sparkling water, chilled
1 cup orange-flavored syrup, such as Fontana (Valencia flavor) or Torani
Ice ring (optional)

Shortly before serving, mix together limeade, sparkling water, and orange flavoring in a punch bowl. Add an ice ring with slices of lime and orange, if desired, to keep the punch chilled.

Variation: For an adult version of the punch, add 1½ to 2 cups tequila to the punch and substitute an orange-flavored liqueur for the syrup, such as Triple Sec, Grand Marnier, or Cointreau. For a special treat, use fresh lime juice (about 12 limes for 12 ounces) and add the sparkling water to your taste.

Chicken Fajitas on the Grill
MAKES 15 SERVINGS

The grill gives the fajitas a smoky flavor and offers the sizzle appeal the dish has in restaurants. The fajitas are made to order, similar to an omelet station at a brunch. Let the guests decide which ingredients to add. Keep the chicken cold for the gathering by storing in a bowl or pan that is kept on ice in a cooler for easy access by the cook.

2 (1¼-pound) packages boneless chicken breasts, cut in ¼-inch-thick slices
⅔ cup bottled Italian vinaigrette or lime-based vinaigrette (see Note)
2 green peppers, seeded and sliced
1 red or yellow pepper, seeded and sliced
2 large onions, sliced (about 2 cups)
Vegetable oil
15 (6- to 8-inch) flour tortillas

TOPPINGS (OPTIONAL)
Sour cream
Guacamole
Chopped onions or sliced green onions
Diced and seeded tomatoes
Shredded lettuce
Shredded cheddar cheese
Pico de gallo

Toss chicken slices with vinaigrette and refrigerate for not more than an hour. (Chicken doesn't need much time in a marinade.)

Bring coals to medium heat (you should be able to hold your hand over the coals for 3 to 5 seconds). Place a large, heavy skillet on the grate (the handle must be able to withstand heat).

Drizzle some oil in the pan and spread it around with a spatula. Add enough peppers and onions for several servings and cook for a minute or two, until vegetables start to soften, stirring constantly. Add chicken slices for several servings and cook through, stirring often.

Using tongs, place chicken, peppers, and onions in each flour tortilla. Serve immediately with toppings.

Note: *To make your own vinaigrette for the marinade, here's a recipe scaled for this amount of chicken fajitas: Whisk together ½ cup lime juice, 3 minced garlic cloves, ¼ cup vegetable oil, and several grinds of black pepper.*

Make-Your-Own Tacos
MAKES 30

¼ cup vegetable oil

3 medium onions, minced (about 2¼ cups)

3 pounds ground beef

6 garlic cloves, minced

3 tablespoons chili powder

2 tablespoons ground cumin

1½ teaspoons salt, or to taste

1 (28-ounce) can tomato sauce (about 3 ½ cups)

30 corn taco hard shells

TOPPINGS (OPTIONAL)

Sour cream

Guacamole (see recipe)

Chopped onions or sliced green onions

Diced and seeded tomatoes

Shredded lettuce

Shredded cheddar cheese

Pico de gallo (see recipe)

To make filling, heat oil in a large frying pan over medium heat and sauté onions until translucent.

Heat a second large frying pan over medium heat and add half the cooked onions from the other pan. Add half the ground beef to each pan, breaking up the meat with a spoon, cooking until no longer pink.

To each pan add half the garlic, chili powder, cumin, and salt. Stir and cook for a minute. Drain off any extra fat and combine in one pan. Lower heat and add tomato sauce; mix thoroughly. Cook for another 10 minutes. If making in advance, store in refrigerator; then reheat 30 minutes before guests arrive. During the party, keep warm in a slow cooker or chafing dish.

To serve, place the filling, taco shells, and toppings in serving dishes for guests to make their own tacos.

Nacho Cheese Sauce and Chips

MAKES 5 CUPS

In Spanish, this sauce is called chile con queso (CHEE-lay kon KAY-soh). It can be partially made up to a couple days in advance and reheated gently. It must be kept warm when served. Do so in a slow cooker or in a chafing dish. Don't let the list of ingredients throw you off. The extra seasonings add a depth of flavor that far surpasses the Velveeta version of this sauce.

4 tablespoons (½ stick) butter
2 medium onions, chopped (about 1½ cups)
4 to 6 jalapeños, seeded and minced
½ cup chopped red pepper
4 medium tomatoes, finely chopped
4 cups shredded Monterey Jack cheese
4 cups shredded cheddar cheese
1 teaspoon cayenne pepper
1 teaspoon black pepper
1 teaspoon paprika
½ teaspoon salt
3 tablespoons flour
1½ cups half-and-half
Tortilla chips

In a large pan, melt the butter over medium heat. Add the onions and sauté until translucent, about 3 to 5 minutes, stirring often. Add the jalapeños, red pepper, and tomatoes. Continue to cook over medium heat until the vegetables are tender and there is juice from the tomatoes, about 10 minutes. (Can be prepared up to 2 days in advance to this point, then cooled and refrigerated for later use.)

In the same pan, over low heat, melt cheddar and Monterey Jack with vegetable mixture; add cayenne pepper, black pepper, paprika, and salt.

Meanwhile, in a bowl, whisk flour into the half-and-half; then slowly stir into the cheese mixture. Continue to heat, stirring occasionally, until the cheese is fully melted. Add more cream if the mixture thickens too much. Keep warm in a slow cooker or chafing dish. Let guests drizzle the sauce over tortilla chips.

Guacamole for a Crowd

MAKES ABOUT 5 CUPS

You'll need to plan ahead to have the avocados ripe when you need them. Look for ones that aren't rock-hard at the store. Keep them in a paper or plastic bag to help ripen them. When preparing the guacamole, save the avocado pits to place in the finished dish, which will keep it from getting brown too quickly. Usually sour cream isn't added to guacamole, but when prepared for a crowd, it will help extend this avocado mash further.

6 avocados, peeled and pitted
¼ cup fresh lime juice (2 limes)
1 cup sour cream (optional)
½ cup finely chopped white onion
2 small tomatoes, finely chopped
2 fresh jalapeños, seeded and minced (optional)
1 teaspoon salt

Dice the avocadoes and place them in a bowl; toss with lime juice and mash with a fork, leaving some in small chunks. If using sour cream, add now and mix thoroughly. Add the onion, tomatoes, jalapeños, and salt.

Place plastic wrap directly on the surface to keep from browning. (Prepare no more than a few hours before serving.) Refrigerate until ready to use.

Variation: Add ½ cup or more diced roasted red peppers. They add a slightly sweet, smoky flavor to the dip.

Pico de Gallo

MAKES ABOUT 4 TO 5 CUPS

If you don't have fragrant ripe tomatoes, don't bother making this. No bottled salsa can compare with homemade, including this traditional one, pico de gallo (PEE-koh day GI-yoh), which is based on fresh tomatoes and chile peppers. This recipe calls for jalapeños, a pepper that ranges in flavor from fairly mild to very hot, but you won't know how hot simply by the appearance; you'll have to taste it. Use care when handling jalapeños and other spicy chiles because the oil on the chile can be painful if it gets into your eyes or nose. Either use rubber gloves when seeding the peppers, or wash hands thoroughly afterwards. Much of the chile's "heat" sizzles in the seeds and inside veins of the pepper; these parts generally are discarded.

4 to 6 ripe tomatoes, seeded and chopped
    (see Note)
1 small onion, chopped (about ½ cup)
¼ cup to ½ cup chopped fresh cilantro
1 jalapeño or more, seeded and diced (optional)
Salt

Combine tomatoes, onion, cilantro, and jalapeño. Season with salt. Let stand for at least 30 minutes to allow the flavors to mingle. Serve at room temperature or slightly chilled.

> **Note:** *To seed a tomato, slice it in half, then gently squeeze it to remove some seeds and juice. With your fingers, remove any remaining seeds. This will keep the salsa from being too juicy.*

Cinnamon-Fudge Bars

MAKES 24 OR 30, DEPENDING ON SIZE

1 cup (2 sticks) butter, plus extra for greasing the pan
8 ounces unsweetened chocolate (see Note)
5 eggs
2 teaspoons vanilla extract
½ teaspoon almond extract
3¾ cups sugar
1⅔ cups flour
1 tablespoon cinnamon
1 teaspoon salt
Powdered sugar, for garnish (optional)

Preheat oven to 400° F. Grease a 9 x 13-inch pan with butter.

Melt butter and chocolate over low heat, stirring until smooth; set aside.

In the large bowl of an electric mixer on low speed, beat eggs and extracts together. Add sugar, flour, cinnamon, and salt; beat until thoroughly mixed. Add melted chocolate and mix. Pour batter into prepared pan and bake 30 minutes, or until top has a firm crust. Edges will be dark, if not slightly burned. Cool completely before cutting. Trim edges off, if necessary. Dust with powdered sugar, if desired. Cut into small bars and store in an airtight container.

Note: *Try using high-end chocolate, such as Ghirardelli or Scharffen Berger.*

SUMMER

MENUS

Dinner at the Lake   88
Peach Lemonade
Fresh Tomato Soup
Walleye with Pecan-Dill Butter
Broccoli Slaw with Blue Cheese
Wild Rice Pilaf
Banana-Chocolate Ice Cream Pie

Fourth of July Picnic   98
Orange-Mint Iced Tea
Chicken Drumsticks with Ginger and Garlic
Asian Noodles with Pea Pods and Peanut Dressing
Grilled Summer Vegetables with Curried Onion Chutney
Sesame or Rice Crackers
Almond Shortbread

Upscale Dinner on the Grill   106
Sangria
Grilled Tuna Steaks with Two Olive Sauces
Tomato and Mozzarella Salad
Grilled Focaccia
Grilled Summer Squash
Frozen Tiramisu Parfait

Mediterranean Picnic   114
Pesto-Stuffed Eggs
Mediterranean Torte
Summer Greens with Feta Vinaigrette
Kalamata Olives
Chocolate Meringues

Lazy Summer Dinner   120
Hibiscus-Pineapple Iced Tea
   or White Wine Spritzer
Bruschetta
Grilled Shrimp and Scallops
Rotini with Summer Vegetables
Tropical Sorbet Terrine

Pizza on the Grill   126
Cherry Lemonade Fizz or Blonde Bloody Mary
Grilled Individual Pizzas
Caramelized Onion Dip
Chicken-Feta Salad
Crispy Ice Cream Sandwiches

Sweet Corn Bliss   136
Watermelon Daiquiri
   or Watermelon-Ade and Iced Coffee
Roasted Corn on the Cob with Flavored Butter
Pork Burgers with Cayenne Mayonnaise
Cabbage Salad with Spicy Lime Vinaigrette
Plums with Raspberry-Mascarpone Frozen Yogurt

A Crossroads Dinner   146
Mint Tea
Tabbouleh Salad
Lamb Kebabs with Harissa
Basmati Rice
Raita
Pita Bread
Lemon Granita

Summer

RECImPES BY COURSE

Make soup and freeze.

UP TO 1 WEEK IN ADVANCE

Toast nuts and prepare Pecan-Dill Butter.

UP TO TWO WEEKS IN ADVANCE

Make ice cream pie.

UP TO 2 DAYS IN ADVANCE

Make soup, if not made earlier.

UP TO A DAY IN ADVANCE

Make wild rice.

UP TO EIGHT HOURS IN ADVANCE

Prepare slaw.

Make lemonade.

Dredge walleye in seasonal flour.

LAST-MINUTE PREP

Add peaches to lemonade.

Cook walleye.

Shortcut Savvy

Buy preshredded broccoli slaw, preshredded red cabbage, and bottled Italian vinaigrette.

Buy prepared wild rice (available canned or frozen); then add vegetables to it.

Use prepared pie crust or buy ice cream pie.

DINNER AT THE LAKE

For 8

Peach Lemonade
Fresh Tomato Soup
Walleye with Pecan-Dill Butter
Broccoli Slaw with Blue Cheese
Wild Rice Pilaf
Banana-Chocolate Ice Cream Pie

LATE MORNING AT THE LAKE, with cloudless sky and shimmering water. As you dip your toes into the cool water, the screen door slams and there's a shout: "We're here!"

Welcome to summer and all the company it brings, especially if you have a lakeside cabin.

The head cook also should be able to enjoy the lake, and not just the view from behind the stove, so here's a menu for company that can be pulled together quickly.

Using common ingredients available at the small markets that dot the countryside and lakeside, this menu adds an interesting flavor twist to the summertime standards: peaches with lemonade, tomato soup with carrots and leeks, blue cheese with slaw, walleye with dill and pecans, ice cream pie dripping with flavor. The *Mmm* the cook hears won't be from the mosquitoes.

All of these dishes but the walleye are portable enough for picnics and those inevitable Fourth of July gatherings (keeping in mind the pie is frozen). Better yet, houseguests can bring these items to the cabin, and let the cook get back to dipping toes in the lake.

Peach Lemonade
MAKES ABOUT 4 QUARTS; 8 (8-OUNCE) SERVINGS

8 ripe peaches, peeled and pitted
2 (12-ounce) cans frozen lemonade concentrate, thawed
Water or sparkling water
Additional peach slices or fresh mint leaves, for garnish (optional)
Wooden skewers, for garnish (optional)

Cut up peaches slightly and place in blender or food processor to purée. If using a blender, add a little of the lemonade concentrate (which makes it easier to blend).

Purée the fruit, add more lemonade concentrate, and mix together. For a large pitcher, add fruit mixture to remaining lemonade concentrate, and add as much water (or sparkling water) as lemonade package directs. For the garnish, if desired, place alternating peach slices and mint leaves on a skewer for each glass of lemonade.

Variation: Use nectarines instead of peaches (and leave their skins on).

Beverage

Add fresh peaches or nectarines to lemonade for a refreshing drink with the fragrance of summer. The fruit should be very ripe to provide good flavor. The drink needs to be made the same day it is served or the fruit will begin to discolor and lose its pretty orange hue. If made in advance, the lemonade will need to be stirred before serving because the fruit gathers at the top. For more novelty, make the drink immediately before serving and use sparkling water. Peach lemonade can be served with or without alcohol. For adults, add some vodka, substitute sparkling water for tap water, and call it a Peach Fizz.

Fresh Tomato Soup
MAKES ABOUT 3 QUARTS; 12 (1-CUP) SERVINGS

Although it's the same salmon color as soup-from-a-can, that's about the only resemblance this recipe bears to its not-fresh-at-all distant cousin. It's adapted from a twenty-five-year-old recipe from Marian Morash in *The Victory Garden Cookbook*.

4 pounds ripe tomatoes
3 tablespoons oil
2 medium onions, chopped (about 1½ cups)
2 leeks, chopped (about 1 cup) (see Notes)
2 medium carrots, sliced (about 1 cup)
1 garlic clove, chopped
½ teaspoon sugar
2 tablespoons flour
6 sprigs parsley
1 celery rib with leaves
8 cups chicken broth, divided
Salt and freshly ground pepper
½ cup milk or cream (optional)
¼ cup loosely packed fresh basil leaves, sliced in julienne strips (optional)

Peel, seed, and coarsely chop the tomatoes (see Notes). You should have about 6 cups.

In a 6-quart saucepot, heat oil over medium heat and sauté onions and leeks until wilted and golden. Add carrots, garlic, sugar, and 2 cups of the tomatoes; cook uncovered over medium heat, stirring together, until the mixture thickens and the moisture evaporates, from 10 to 25 minutes. Whisk in the flour and cook for 2 to 3 minutes, stirring.

Add parsley and celery to the saucepan, along with the remaining tomatoes and 3 cups of the broth. Cook for 10 to 15 minutes until mixture thickens slightly. Add the remaining 5 cups broth and simmer for 20 minutes. Remove parsley and celery and discard. Using a food processor or blender, lightly purée the soup, leaving some bits of vegetables intact to keep texture in the soup. Season to taste with salt and pepper. (Can be made ahead up to 2 days in advance and refrigerated, or frozen.)

Return soup to the saucepan to reheat. If desired, add milk or cream for a creamy soup, and basil. Heat through and serve.

Notes:

- *To peel tomatoes, make a small X in the smooth end of tomato and drop several into boiling water for about 30 seconds, until the peel starts to loosen. Remove tomatoes from boiling water and plunge into ice water. Repeat with remaining tomatoes. When cool, the skin will slip off easily.*
- *To seed tomatoes, slice them in half, then gently squeeze to remove some seeds and juice. With your fingers, remove any remaining seeds.*
- *Leeks look like giant green onions. To clean them, trim root end and cut off white end to use. Slit the white portion from top to bottom and wash thoroughly.*

COOK'S NOTES

Don't let the simple name—Fresh Tomato Soup—put you off; there's nothing plain about this soup, other than it being just plain good. This is one that even serious soup lovers will slurp. That includes my family. We eat soup almost every day, even at restaurants, even for snacks. When I find a recipe that we all like, we're in soup heaven. This is such a recipe. The flavor comes from plenty of ripe tomatoes, with extra oomph from carrots, onions, and leeks. After the vegetables simmer together, the soup is puréed lightly so that small bits of vegetables remain to add texture (so be careful if you really do slurp).

Save this recipe for when you have a surplus of ripe tomatoes. If they're not available, skip the soup. In seasons past, I've made and frozen gallons to savor in the depths of winter when the only thing rosy in my kitchen are wind-burned faces.

This recipe is easily adapted to whatever produce you have available. If you don't have leeks, just add more onions. If you have more tomatoes, use more. (If you have fewer, you know what you can do.) The fresh basil adds wonderful fragrance and flavor. It's an easy recipe to double if you have a big enough stockpot.

Walleye with Pecan-Dill Butter
SERVES 8

In Minnesota, walleye is considered the best of the lake fish, as its supermarket price attests. Fillet sizes vary at the market from very small—2 or 3 ounces—to half-pound fillets. Those large sizes may put a gleam in the fisherperson's eye, but for the cook, the smaller fish are (or should be) preferred. Like almost everything that grows, the smaller version is more tender and flavorful than its larger counterpart. As for walleye, the small fillets seem to melt in the mouth.

For this walleye preparation, toasted pecans are added to a traditional herbed butter flavored with dill and green onions. Some people like nuts; others don't. These can be omitted and the dill butter is still wonderful with fish, as it would be for other meat (such as steaks or chicken breasts) or vegetables.

In chef terminology, any butter whipped together with herbs or other flavorings is called a compound butter. That whipping incorporates air into the butter and makes it softer and more spreadable when served cold. The flavorings, of course, add interest.

PECAN-DILL BUTTER
1 (1¾-ounce) package chopped pecans (about ½ cup)
8 tablespoons (1 stick) butter, softened
1 tablespoon fresh lemon juice
⅛ cup minced fresh dill or 2 teaspoons dried dill weed
1 tablespoon finely chopped green onions or shallot

WALLEYE
4 pounds walleye fillets in whatever size you catch or buy
1 cup flour
Paprika (Hungarian hot paprika is especially good)
Salt and white pepper
Cooking oil

FOR PECAN-DILL BUTTER

Toast pecans in a dry small saucepan over low heat until they have become fragrant, stirring occasionally so they don't burn (see Notes). Set aside to cool.

Whip softened butter with electric mixer or by hand. Gradually add lemon juice and mix in thoroughly. Stir in dill, green onions, and toasted nuts.

This can be made up to a week in advance. The butter can be molded into a log shape before refrigerating. First, cut a 6- to 8-inch sheet of plastic wrap or wax paper and plop the butter mixture onto the wrap. With a spatula or knife, shape the butter into a log much like a stick of butter. Wrap the plastic or wax paper around the butter, twist the ends securely, and refrigerate or freeze.

Just before cooking the walleye, pull the butter out of the refrigerator and slice into 8 to 16 individual pieces. Use a knife dipped in lukewarm water to make slicing easier. The butter pats will be added to the fish at the end of cooking (see "For Walleye" directions).

FOR WALLEYE

Rinse fillets and pat dry with paper towels. Add flour to a pie pan and season to taste with paprika, salt, and pepper. Lightly coat, or dredge, fillets with flour on both sides.

Add just enough oil to coat the bottom of a large frying pan. Heat oil over medium heat; then add fish. (If you have two large frying pans, use them; otherwise you will need to fry the fish in two batches.)

Cook over medium heat for 5 to 10 minutes, depending on thickness of fillets, turning once when first side is nicely browned. Once fillets are flipped, dot them with slices of Pecan-Dill Butter; the butter should begin to melt while the fish is still cooking. The fish will be white and opaque when done, and can be easily be pulled apart with a fork. Serve immediately on top of a bed of Wild Rice Pilaf (see recipe on page 95).

Variation: Instead of dredging the fish in seasoned flour, brush it lightly with vegetable oil and then dredge it in a combination of 1 cup panko breadcrumbs (a light, large breadcrumb, originally from Japan, that makes a wonderful coating) tossed with ¼ cup finely grated Parmesan cheese and 1 tablespoon dry Italian seasoning. Bake in a 425° F oven for 15 minutes until done. For this variation, skip the Pecan-Dill Butter.

Notes:

- *In the classic version of this recipe, shallots are used instead of green onions. But shallots are unlikely to be found at small country markets. If they are available, by all means use them.*

- *Toasting the pecans adds a little extra flavor, but it is not necessary. It also can be done over a campfire if you're at the lake, or in an oven at home.*

- *The paprika gives the fish a nice color when done. Hungarian hot paprika is especially nice; it adds just a hint of spice.*

Cole slaw makes its
annual appearance this
time of year at most
gatherings around a pic-
nic table. Those shreds
of cabbage leaves, mari-
nated in one of a hand-
ful of dressings, haven't
changed much over the
years. But some picnick-
ers prefer a change of
taste. For them, let's
turn to a much-ignored
part of another popular
vegetable, the broccoli
stem. Part of the same,
healthful cruciferous
family as the cabbage—
the name broccoli comes
from the Italian word
for "cabbage sprout"—
slaw made from broc-
coli stems isn't as great
a stretch of imagination
as one might initially
think. And it certainly
is a functional use, since
many cooks use only
broccoli florets and dis-
card the stems. A precut
version is available in
some supermarkets.

Broccoli Slaw with Blue Cheese

MAKES ABOUT 7 CUPS; 14 (½-CUP) SERVINGS

The most time-consuming task for making any slaw is cutting up the veg-etables into julienne, or matchstick-size pieces. Chefs use a simple, hand-operated machine called a mandoline. Inexpensive plastic versions are available in kitchen specialty shops. Or use a grater and shred the broccoli.

There's no need to cook the broccoli in this recipe because the dress-ing will soften it. If you like crunchy slaw, make it shortly before serving. For less crunchy slaw, make it earlier in the day.

Any favorite slaw dressing can be used. A simple vinaigrette with crumbled blue cheese makes for spectacular taste. For a really fast version of this salad, use bottled Italian vinaigrette with packaged broccoli slaw and packaged red cabbage. Crumble a little blue cheese on top for made-at-home taste. The blue cheese is the most unusual of the ingredients this menu uses. If you're not certain your countryside market carries it, bring a supply from home.

6 broccoli stalks (see Note)
2 carrots, peeled
1 cup sliced red cabbage (about ⅛ medium head)
½ medium red onion or 1 large white onion
½ cup white wine vinegar or apple cider vinegar
¼ cup olive oil
Salt and white pepper
1 (4-ounce) package blue cheese, crumbled, divided

Cut broccoli stalks, carrots, cabbage, and onion into julienne (matchstick) pieces; place all in a large bowl.

Mix together vinegar, olive oil, salt, and pepper in small bowl. Add to vegetables and toss; add most of crumbled blue cheese and toss again. Re-frigerate until serving. Top with remaining blue cheese just before serving.

Note: *Six stalks of broccoli should yield about 5 cups of pieces cut into matchsticks, or juliennes. If buying whole broccoli, you will need to purchase about 2½ to 3 pounds; save the florets for another use. If buying precut broccoli slaw, you will need about 12 ounces.*

Wild Rice Pilaf

MAKES ABOUT 9 CUPS

Walleye and wild rice are a natural pairing, particularly when served at the lake cabin. For an extra flavor boost, I use a little chicken broth to replace some water when preparing wild rice—a single can of broth is sufficient. To keep the kitchen cooler during dinner preparations, make the wild rice early in the day or the night before and store it in the refrigerator. To reheat the pilaf, add ½ cup water or broth to the rice, cover the pan, and gently warm over low heat. The reheating takes much less time than the initial cooking.

2 cups uncooked wild rice
6 cups water (or part chicken broth)
1 teaspoon salt (if salted chicken broth is used, additional salt is
    unnecessary)
2 medium onions, chopped (about 1½ cups)
3 ribs celery, chopped (about 1½ cups)
2 tablespoons butter

Rinse wild rice in cold water and remove any debris (a strainer works well for rinsing). Add wild rice, water, and salt to large pot.

Bring to a boil; then lower heat to a simmer and cover. Simmer until tender, 30 to 55 minutes (cooking time depends on type of wild rice—see package directions).

If you like your wild rice pure, stop here. Otherwise, while the rice cooks, sauté onions and celery in butter in a frying pan. Add the mixture to the rice when it is cooked.

Banana-Chocolate Ice Cream Pie
SERVES 8 (see Note)

You can count on guests in the summer—and you can count on them wanting a treat. This frozen dessert should please both the summer crowds and the cook. Think of it as an upscale ice cream pie, a cross between a Dairy Queen Blizzard and a banana malt in a pairing made in dessert heaven: bananas, chocolate, and vanilla wafers.

Easy to make, the pie can be made ahead in anticipation of the next batch of visitors. To make it really fast, turn to a commercially prepared vanilla-wafer crust or a graham-cracker crust. With the premade crust, you probably will have a little extra ice cream mixture left over. If so, plop it in paper muffin cups to freeze for individual treats.

The pie won't last for months in the freezer because the bananas will darken and look unappealing. But ice cream doesn't last that long anyway—especially not in a pie this good (there will be no leftovers). It will be fine in the freezer for at least a couple of weeks.

VANILLA WAFER CRUST
36 vanilla wafers
6 tablespoons butter or margarine, melted

PIE FILLING
1 quart vanilla ice cream
4 ounces semi-sweet chocolate, divided
3 very ripe bananas

FOR VANILLA WAFER CRUST
Place wafers between 2 sheets of plastic wrap and crush with a rolling pin. (You should have about 1½ cups crushed wafers.) Thoroughly mix with melted butter and press into the bottom and sides of a 9-inch pie pan. Chill for 10 to 15 minutes until firm.

FOR PIE FILLING

Soften ice cream until it can be stirred easily. Break up 3 ounces of chocolate into shavings with a grater or with a knife.

In a large bowl, mash bananas by hand or with an electric mixer. Add softened ice cream and mix thoroughly. Stir in chocolate shavings and mix thoroughly. Pour ice cream mixture into pie shell and freeze. Before serving, melt remaining ounce of chocolate and drizzle on top of pie.

> **Note:** *This recipe makes a single 9-inch pie, which for eight servings will yield small pieces. If you want to be prepared for raves, make two pies and offer seconds.*

COOK'S NOTES

For the Banana-Chocolate Ice Cream Pie, use very ripe bananas, which are the most flavorful. Or use up your frozen bananas. You know about frozen bananas, don't you? Bananas too ripe to eat, with blackened skins, don't have to be tossed out. They can be frozen for another use —such as banana bread, banana malts, or this ice-cream pie. Once thawed, they're really mushy and unsuitable for anything but a purée used in something else. (They also can be dangerous if they fall out of the freezer when frozen—like very cold rocks that definitely don't bounce. So stuff them in the freezer carefully.)

For the pie, use good-quality ice cream. As cooks are fond of saying, this dessert is only as good as its ingredients. (Actually, it's good no matter what you do to it; but quality ingredients make it really good.) Place the filled pie pan in the freezer on a cookie sheet so that, if the shelf isn't perfectly level, ice cream won't drip onto the freezer floor. (No need to ask how I figured this out.)

Make Ahead

UP TO A DAY IN ADVANCE

Make iced tea.

Make orange juice ice cubes.

Cook chicken drumsticks.

Make peanut dressing for salad.

Blanch pea pods for salad.

Prepare chutney.

Make shortbread.

UP TO 8 HOURS IN ADVANCE

Cook noodles for salad.

Grill vegetables.

LAST-MINUTE PREP

Reheat chicken drumsticks or bring them to room temperature.

Assemble salad.

Add fruit to tea.

Shortcut Savvy

Use premade flavored iced tea.

Buy a dip for the grilled vegetables instead of making chutney.

Use commercial peanut dressing.

Buy fortune cookies or almond cookies.

FOURTH OF JULY PICNIC

For 6

Orange-Mint Iced Tea
Chicken Drumsticks with Ginger and Garlic
Asian Noodles with Pea Pods and Peanut Dressing
Grilled Summer Vegetables with Curried Onion Chutney
Sesame or Rice Crackers
Almond Shortbread

FOR MANY PICNICKERS, the Fourth of July celebration marks the middle of summer. How you look at the occasion may be more a reflection of personality than the reality of the calendar: Is the summer half over? Or are the best weeks to come?

However you measure the season, burgers and hot dogs do just fine for the first few picnics of summer. By mid-season, however—about the time the ash from the charcoal piles up, the picnic blankets are stained and sticky, and the coolers are grungy—the dull-menu doldrums set in.

Tired of takeout fried chicken at your picnic? Here's a meal for you, the roving picnicker, whether you're gliding along the waters or lounging on the shore. The meal also suits the backyard picnicker with grill and refrigerator handy. This menu offers the flavors of Asia for hungry midwesterners: drumsticks cooked in a ginger-garlic sauce.

What's a picnic without salad? This one looks as good as it tastes: cellophane noodles, pea pods, cucumbers, and carrots drizzled with a peanut dressing.

Grilled or broiled vegetables—made ahead or prepared at mealtime—beat the usual celery and carrot sticks. A curried onion chutney replaces the standard dip of sour cream and onion soup mix. Crisp sesame or rice crackers from the store add an interesting twist and provide a good substitute for potato chips.

Top off the meal with a simply wonderful shortbread cookie (bet you can't eat just one) and fruit-flavored iced tea that's snappier than anything from a bottle, and you've got a picnic worth remembering.

Also worth remembering are these familiar words for summer meals: keep cold foods cold, and hot foods hot.

Let's picnic.

Beverage

Flavored iced tea is perfect for a picnic. This one is very refreshing with a hint of fruit that complements the Asian menu nicely. For more orange flavor, use an orange-flavored tea, such as Earl Grey. Double or triple the quantities of tea if you expect a thirsty crowd.

Orange-Mint Iced Tea

MAKES 8 CUPS

Orange juice for ice cubes
8 cups water
8 bags of black tea
12 or more fresh mint leaves, divided
Sugar (optional)
1 orange, cut in slices
1 lemon, cut in slices

Pour orange juice into an ice-cube tray and freeze to make ice cubes.

To prepare tea, bring 8 cups water to a boil. Pour over tea bags and 6 mint leaves in a pitcher or other container. (For sweetened tea, add sugar to taste at this point and stir to dissolve.)

Let tea steep for about 10 minutes; then remove tea bags. Cool tea completely and remove mint. Refrigerate, covered. Cut fruit slices in half.

To serve tea, pour it into a pitcher or insulated jug and add orange-juice ice cubes, 6 mint leaves, and fruit slices. Or serve individually in tall glasses, with a mint leaf, orange-juice cubes, and slices of both lemon and orange.

If the tea becomes cloudy when it is refrigerated, add a small amount of boiling water to clear it up. Cloudiness can occur if the tea is not completely cool when refrigerated.

Variation: To make sun tea, combine tea and water in a clear jar or pitcher and let sit in the refrigerator for several hours.

Chicken Drumsticks with Ginger and Garlic

SERVES 6

About 3 pounds chicken drumsticks

¼ cup sesame oil

8 to 10 garlic cloves, chopped

4 nickel-sized slices of fresh ginger root, cut in half (or 1 teaspoon ground ginger)

½ teaspoon black pepper

½ cup sugar

½ cup teriyaki sauce

½ cup soy sauce

1 cup water

1 tablespoon commercial Chinese hoisin sauce (optional; see Notes)

In large pot, brown drumsticks over medium heat, working in batches (all the drumsticks won't fit in the pan for browning at one time). Drain any grease from the pan.

In a medium bowl, mix together the sesame oil, garlic, ginger, pepper, sugar, teriyaki sauce, soy sauce, and water; add to pot. Return all the drumsticks to the pot and toss to coat in the liquid.

Cook, uncovered, over medium-high heat for 20 to 25 minutes, or until chicken is cooked through, stirring often. Remove chicken and set aside. (If you are not using hoisin sauce, chicken is done at this point; also remove and discard ginger slices.)

Add hoisin sauce to sauce in the pot and cook on high heat for 10 minutes, until sauce starts to thicken. Stir often to prevent burning. Add chicken and cook an additional 5 minutes, coating chicken with sauce. Remove slices of ginger and discard. To serve right away, pour sauce on chicken. To serve at room temperature later or to transport elsewhere in a covered container, discard sauce (it gets gloppy). Keep refrigerated until shortly before serving. The chicken also can be reheated.

Continued on page 102.

Variation: If you prefer to grill or broil the chicken, first marinate it overnight with the same ingredients, but do not add the water. Include the hoisin sauce, if available. The chicken gets much less of a garlic-ginger flavor when it's marinated this way, but it is extremely moist and tender.

Notes:
- *Figure 2 to 3 drumsticks per person—and bring a damp cloth or wet wipes for cleanup. These are finger-lickin' good, but messy.*
- *Hoisin sauce (HOY-sihn) is a thick, sweet, and spicy sauce widely used in Chinese cooking. It makes a nice glaze on the chicken, but it is not necessary. Most supermarkets carry the bottled sauce in the Asian food section.*

Asian Noodles with Pea Pods and Peanut Dressing
SERVES 6 TO 8

Not your every-picnic pasta salad. For the prettiest presentation, transport these elements in separate containers and make up the salad on a platter or in individual portions once you get to the picnic. The cellophane noodles, also called bean threads, are translucent threads made from the starch of green mung beans. Trust me, they taste better than their description sounds. The noodles come packaged in dry form. Many supermarkets carry them in the Asian food section, and they also are available in Asian markets. Other thin noodles could be substituted, including curly Japanese ramen noodles, vermicelli, or soba noodles.

PEANUT DRESSING (MAKES ABOUT 1 CUP)
¼ cup chunky peanut butter
½ cup orange juice
2 tablespoons soy sauce
2 tablespoons sesame oil
1 tablespoon rice wine vinegar

NOODLES AND PEA PODS

2 cups (about ½ pound) pea pods (snow pea or sugar snap)

1 (about 5-ounce) package cellophane noodles, or ramen, vermicelli,
    or soba noodles

Vegetable oil

½ head of lettuce (such as butter or Boston), loosely torn

1 cucumber, unpeeled, sliced

1 carrot, grated

Several sprigs of fresh cilantro, chopped or torn

FOR PEANUT DRESSING

Whisk together peanut butter, orange juice, soy sauce, sesame oil, and vinegar.

FOR NOODLES AND PEA PODS

Snap off the ends of the pea pods and remove the attached string (unless these are stringless): Snap each stem end off, breaking toward the inside curve of the pea; then continue pulling down the inside curve to remove the long string attached to the stem. (Snap peas taste better without the string.) Blanch the pea pods by dropping into boiling water for 1 minute, then cool immediately with cold water.

Prepare noodles according to package directions. Toss with a little vegetable oil to prevent noodles from sticking together. Set aside.

To present salad family syle, line bowl or platter with lettuce. Top with noodles, pea pods, cucumbers, and carrot. Drizzle with ½ to ¾ cup Peanut Dressing. Garnish with cilantro.

Grilled Summer Vegetables with Curried Onion Chutney

SERVES 6 TO 8

Any summer vegetables can be grilled, but the following work well with the rest of the summer menu. The curried dip is particularly good with sweet onions. To serve six people, one of each vegetable below (in the case of the green onions, one bunch) will yield more than enough.

Continued on page 104.

CURRIED ONION CHUTNEY (MAKES ABOUT 1½ CUPS)
3 large sweet onions, chopped (about 3 cups)
2 to 3 garlic cloves, minced
1 to 2 teaspoons curry powder
1 tablespoon vegetable oil
2 tablespoons sesame oil or water or rice wine vinegar
Sesame or rice crackers

VEGETABLES
1 eggplant (small Japanese variety is particularly nice)
1 zucchini
1 yellow squash
1 red bell pepper
1 yellow bell pepper
1 bunch green onions
1 head radicchio (red-leafed, slightly bitter variety of lettuce)
Canola, corn, or olive oil
Salt and freshly ground pepper

FOR CURRIED ONION CHUTNEY
In a large frying pan over medium heat, sauté onions and garlic with the curry powder in oil for about 10 minutes or until lightly brown. Remove from heat and let cool slightly.

In a blender, combine onion mixture and sesame oil. Purée mixture coarsely, leaving some chunks. Refrigerate until use. Serve at room temperature with grilled vegetables and sesame or rice crackers (available in the Asian foods section of supermarkets or at Asian markets).

FOR VEGETABLES
Preheat grill, or use broiler. Prepare vegetables as follows:

Eggplant: Peel or not, depending on your preference and its variety. Cut into ¼-inch slices.

Zucchini and squash: Do not peel; cut into ¼-inch slices.

Bell peppers: Cut into lengthwise slices, about ½-inch thick, so they can be easily handled on the grill.

Green onions: Cut off root end. Remove outer white skin of onion.

Radicchio: Quarter the small head.

After cutting vegetables, brush lightly with oil; season to taste with salt and pepper.

To grill outdoors, put vegetables in a single layer on a mesh tray over the hot coals and turn occasionally. Heat until lightly browned and grill marks appear on vegetables. (You may have to do this in separate batches.) To prepare inside, put the vegetables under the broiler for a few minutes, turning often. Refrigerate, if preparing in advance.

Bring vegetables to room temperature and serve with Curried Onion Chutney.

Almond Shortbread

MAKES 40 TO 45 BARS

⅔ cup sliced blanched almonds, chopped
1 cup (2 sticks) butter, at room temperature
½ cup sugar
2½ cups flour
1 teaspoon almond extract
Zest from 1 lemon (about 1 tablespoon)

Preheat oven to 350° F. In a saucepan over low heat, toast almonds until they are lightly browned, stirring often to prevent burning. Remove from heat.

In a mixing bowl, cream butter and sugar until smooth and creamy. Add flour, almond extract, and lemon zest; mix thoroughly. Stir in toasted almonds by hand.

Grease a 9 x 13-inch pan. With fingers, pat dough firmly into pan. Bake for 30 minutes, or until lightly brown. Immediately cut into bars. (If you wait until the bars are completely cool to cut them, they will crumble.) For a little different shape, try cutting them into diamonds. (To do so, make 5 cuts lengthwise down the long edge. Make 8 or 9 other cuts on the diagonal.) Cool bars completely in pan; then remove. Store in airtight container.

Prepare both olive sauces.

Assemble parfaits.

UP TO EIGHT HOURS IN
ADVANCE

Make sangria.

UP TO 1 HOUR IN ADVANCE

Assemble tomato salad.

Prepare grill.

LAST-MINUTE PREP

Add juice to sangria.

Preheat grill.

Grill tuna steaks.

Grill squash.

Grill focaccia.

Take parfaits out of freezer
10 to 15 minutes before
serving.

Shortcut Savvy

Use store-bought focaccia.

Use prepared tapenade and
thin with a little olive oil
into a saucelike consistency
to replace the olive sauces.

Buy a prepared ice cream
dessert.

UPSCALE DINNER ON THE GRILL

For 6

Sangria
Grilled Tuna Steaks with Two Olive Sauces
Tomato and Mozzarella Salad
Grilled Focaccia
Grilled Summer Squash
Frozen Tiramisu Parfait

I ADMIT IT. I don't like to cook in the summer. There are those who do—cooks who gush about summer meals as though hours spent in a warm kitchen during sun-drenched days were one of life's greatest pleasures.

I am not one of those cooks. I'd rather be the one outdoors, puttering in the garden, tossing a softball, or lounging on a beach blanket, book in hand. Cook? Who me?

Which is not to say I don't like to eat in the summer. Just that I'd rather be outdoors than eat, a trait that doesn't go well with those who share my name and dinner table.

So we compromise. We eat outdoors. We entertain outdoors. And we, like millions of others, cook outdoors. (Not so incidentally, there in the open, cooking duties tend to be more equitably shared—perhaps because there are fewer places to hide.) Judging by the aroma wafting about my neighborhood between 6 and 7 PM, we are not alone.

In praise of summer, here is a menu for entertaining that keeps the cook where the cook ought to be in summer: outdoors.

This meal makes the most of fresh fruits, vegetables, and herbs from the garden or the farmers' market. With dinner cooking quickly on the grill, there is plenty of time for doing what should be done in summer: nothing in particular.

Ah, to summer. Let us raise our lemonade glasses high.

Out-of-doors, of course.

Beverage

Sangria blends the refreshing flavors of red wine and fruit, which pair well with this grilled meal. Use an inexpensive table wine; a fruity pinot noir would be a good choice.

Sangria
SERVES 6

5 cups light red wine, such as pinot noir
5 oranges (cut 2 of them into ¼-inch-thick slices and reserve 3 whole)
2 lemons, cut in ¼-inch-thick slices
1 lime, cut in ¼-inch-thick slices
3 cups ice cubes

In a pitcher or juice container, combine wine and fruit slices and refrigerate, covered, for a few hours in the refrigerator. Juice the remaining oranges. Just before serving, add the orange juice and the ice cubes. Serve immediately.

Grilled Tuna Steaks with Two Olive Sauces
SERVES 6

For dinner, let's throw a few steaks onto the grill—tuna steaks, in this case, which look surprisingly like small slabs of meat. For those who say they don't like fish, take note: tuna doesn't taste like fish. Nor does tuna taste like chicken. The mild flavor is definitely tuna, which goes particularly well with olive sauces. Additional seasonings are not necessary before grilling because of the saltiness of the olives in the two sauces.

Some stores carry very large sizes of these steaks. I've even seen a three-quarter-pounder—almost two inches thick—which is a huge hunk for one person to eat. If you're one who plans ahead, call in advance and request a particular size tuna steak from your supplier. A 6-ounce portion is plenty; a half-pound is getting pretty big and a little pricey.

If you can find only the thick steaks, make them thinner by slicing them in half horizontally through the middle to make them thinner, which also makes them easier to grill. (Or once grilled, divide the steak into two portions for eating.)

6 tuna steaks
Two Olive Sauces (see recipes)

Preheat grill. Cook the fish on the grill over hot coals, turning once, for 5 to 10 minutes (longer if steaks are thicker than 1 inch). When done, the flesh becomes whitish and the meat flakes easily when poked with a fork. Do not overcook the fish, or it will be tough and dry (see Note).

Note: *Restaurants tend to cook tuna in the rare to medium range of doneness, which is how this particular fish tastes best. Food safety recommendations suggest that fish be cooked to an internal temperature of 140° F. From a practical standpoint, that means to cook over hot coals for 5 minutes per ½-inch thickness of fish. Unlike freshwater fish, which can harbor parasites, saltwater fish, such as this tuna, does not present the same health hazard with being slightly undercooked. Some cooks prefer tuna to be not much more than seared on both sides. For medium rare, the temperature would be 125° F.*

BLACK OLIVE SAUCE

Makes about 1 cup

¾ cup pitted, oil-cured Greek olives, such as kalamata

Grated zest of ¼ lemon

1 tablespoon fresh lemon juice

¼ cup extra-virgin olive oil

Pinch of freshly ground black pepper

2 tablespoons fresh thyme leaves, or 2 teaspoons dried and crushed

¼ cup water

In a blender or the bowl of a food processor fitted with a steel blade, place olives, lemon zest, lemon juice, olive oil, black pepper, and thyme. Purée to a smooth paste. Add water and purée again.

GREEN OLIVE SAUCE

Makes about 1 cup

¾ cup pitted green olives (preferably those sold individually instead of in a jar)

½ sprig fresh rosemary, leaves only, finely chopped, 1 teaspoon dried and crushed

¾ teaspoon finely chopped fresh sage, or ¼ teaspoon dried sage

1 teaspoon finely chopped fresh flat-leaf parsley

1 garlic clove, peeled and minced

⅛ cup extra-virgin olive oil

1 tablespoon rice wine vinegar

Salt and freshly ground black pepper

¼ cup water

In a blender or the bowl of a food processor fitted with a steel blade, place olives, rosemary, sage, parsley, garlic, olive oil, and vinegar. Purée to a smooth paste. Season to taste with salt and pepper. Add water and purée again.

COOK'S NOTES

The Sicilian combination of tuna and olives goes together like cinnamon and apples or ham and cheese. For this meal, two olive sauces complement the grilled tuna, served either on top of or beside the fish. To create a design, place the sauces, individually, in a plastic squeeze-style bottle and make your squiggles on the food or plate. Or simply spoon the sauces onto the fish.

Each sauce takes only a few moments at the blender to prepare. The two add contrasting color to the fish. One is made from oil-cured Greek olives, which are a purplish-black. The other is from the familiar green variety (without the pimiento). If possible, stick with the cured olives that are sold individually in delis and at supermarket olive bars. They have more flavor than do those in a jar. If short of time, stick with one sauce. Either can be made a day or two in advance; mix with a spoon before serving.

Tomato and Mozzarella Salad
SERVES 6

The Italians call this simple salad *caprese* (kah-PRAY-say). Slices of tomato are interspersed with fresh basil leaves and mozzarella, then drizzled with high-quality olive oil. Its elegance and flavor led me to serve it at my daughter's summer wedding. Because it is dependent on incredibly flavorful tomatoes, don't make this salad unless you have them. The salad calls for fresh mozzarella, which comes in a ball; it's not the version used to top pizza. Most groceries will carry it where they have their specialty cheeses. On rare occasions, most often at a cheese shop, you'll see buffalo mozzarella for sale. Until recently, I puzzled over that description. How do you milk a buffalo? Could it be that some poor milkmaid had to deal with this animal? Or did the name come from a city, as it does for Buffalo wings? Then I discovered, sheepishly, that buffalo mozzarella is made from the milk of a water buffalo. Whew. That actually makes it sound even more exotic.

3 to 4 ripe fragrant tomatoes, cut into ¼-inch slices
6 to 8 ounces fresh mozzarella, cut into ¼- to ½-inch slices
18 or more fresh basil leaves
Extra-virgin olive oil
Coarse salt and freshly cracked pepper

Assemble salad, either on individual salad plates or family-style on a single platter, by placing alternating slices of tomato and mozzarella to create a row of overlapping slices. Either add fresh whole basil leaves in between slices, or cut basil into thin slices (this is called a chiffonade, pronounced shihf-uh-NAHD) and sprinkle atop the tomatoes and cheese. Drizzle a little olive oil over the top; then sprinkle a little salt and pepper on top. Serve at room temperature.

Variation: Use both yellow and red tomatoes and alternate the slices. Ripe heirloom tomatoes are great for this.

Grilled Focaccia

To keep this meal preparation easy for the cook, turn to a local bakery to buy focaccia, which is readily available. This Italian flat bread takes on summer-like overtones when tossed onto the grill for a few moments to warm it; it will also pick up a smoky flavor. Once it is warm, brush a little olive oil on top, then sprinkle with some freshly grated Parmesan cheese and freshly ground black pepper. Two (10- to 12-inch) focaccias will feed six. They are widely available in supermarket bakeries. Or prepare homemade pizza crust (which is essentially what focaccia is). See recipe on page 189. Make a half-portion and divide dough in half; roll out to ½-inch thick round. Let rise, covered with oiled plastic wrap for about 1½ hours. Preheat oven to 400° F. Shortly before baking, make indentations with your finger or the handle of a wooden spoon in 2-inch intervals over the entire surface of the dough. (The indentations let the olive oil get absorbed by the dough.) Drizzle each crust with ¼ cup olive oil and sprinkle with ½ teaspoon coarse salt. Bake until golden, about 25 minutes. Cool and later grill briefly, if desired.

Grilled Summer Squash
SERVES 6

3 small summer squash, unpeeled
Olive oil
Salt and white pepper

Cut squash on the diagonal in about ¼-inch-thick slices. Brush olive oil on both sides; then sprinkle with salt and pepper. Place squash pieces on mesh grid over grate with hot coals. Watch carefully—the squash needs only a minute or two to cook on each side; turn once. Squash is ready when skins soften and juices begin to form.

Frozen Tiramisu Parfait

SERVES 6

One word says it all: unbelievable. Prepare up to a day in advance so it's ready when you are.

About 1½ pints (3 cups) coffee ice cream (see Notes)
2 to 3 tablespoons rum, or ¼ teaspoon rum extract mixed with 3 table-
    spoons water
About ¼ cup double-strength brewed coffee or regular espresso (you
    can also use instant espresso powder dissolved in ¼ cup water)
1 (3-ounce) package (24 ladyfingers) (see Notes)
1 (8-ounce) container mascarpone cheese (see Notes)
½ cup powdered sugar
2 tablespoons chocolate liqueur, divided
Unsweetened cocoa powder, for garnish

Soften ice cream for about 10 minutes.

Mix rum and coffee in a shallow dish. Soak ladyfingers in the liquid; then remove and cube the ladyfingers.

With an electric mixer, beat mascarpone cheese and powdered sugar.

In each of 6 serving dishes, put a layer of ladyfinger cubes. Top with a small scoop of ice cream and a small amount of mascarpone mixture. Drizzle a teaspoon of chocolate liqueur. Repeat with another layer of lady-finger cubes, ice cream, mascarpone, and liqueur. Cover and freeze for at least 2 hours.

To serve, keep at room temperature for 10 to 15 minutes. (Most guests will prefer this dessert more malleable than when it's frozen solid.) Top with a sprinkle of cocoa powder and serve immediately.

Notes:

- *For this parfait, use whatever freezer-proof glassware or dishes you have that can accommodate 6 to 8 ounces of dessert (that's ¾ to 1 cup). This includes parfait or wine glasses; mugs or margarita-style glasses; or small soup bowls, ramekins, or even custard cups. The amount of ingredients you need will vary according to the size of the dish or glassware that you use. Trust your own judgment on this. Keep the ingredients in proportion and remember this is dessert, not a main course. Less is more.*

- *If you can find only coffee ice cream with espresso beans rather than simply coffee-flavored ice cream, that's okay. If you're desperate because you can't find any kind of coffee ice cream, buy vanilla ice cream, soften it a bit, and add a little high-powered coffee as you beat it with an electric mixer. Or just use vanilla ice cream. This is a very flexible recipe, so the cook should be flexible, too.*

- *Ladyfingers are soft spongelike cookies rarely used other than in desserts such as tiramisu. Packages of them can be found in the freezer section of upscale supermarkets, near the phyllo products. Can't find them? Use frozen (and thawed) pound cake or sponge cake, instead.*

- *Mascarpone (mahs-kahr-POH-nay) is a barely sweet Italian soft cheese similar to cream cheese. It's sold in the cheese section of most supermarkets, near the ricotta.*

MEDITERRANEAN PICNIC

For 6

Pesto-Stuffed Eggs
Mediterranean Torte
Summer Greens with Feta Vinaigrette
Kalamata Olives
Chocolate Meringues

IT HAPPENS TO THE HARDIEST of picnickers: the moment of truth when you cannot swallow yet another forkful of potato salad, baked beans, or tube steak.

What seems so enticing at Memorial Day becomes a tad boring by the Fourth of July and unbearable by Labor Day. And yet, each year we eagerly await that first picnic with the anticipation more often reserved for a new experience.

Call it selective memory. The charm of dining alfresco—fresh air, blue sky, warm sun, and friendly companions—makes us overlook last summer's unmemorable meals. So let's have a menu for grownup tastes, in this case with Mediterranean flavors.

This summer menu offers a movable feast to be prepared ahead and transported in coolers and wrappings so that picnickers have only to dish up the meal. But pack that picnic basket carefully, and use insulated containers to keep hot food hot and cold food cold. An extra layer of plastic wrap or bags gives added protection to potentially leaking food in containers. And don't forget the cutting board, sharp knife, salt and pepper, corkscrew, and blankets. A waterproof ground cover, such as an old shower curtain or tarp, when placed under your picnic blanket, will protect you from last night's dampness.

Pesto-Stuffed Eggs
MAKES 24 STUFFED EGGS

A little innovation goes a long way when it comes to flavor. These stuffed eggs are made the traditional way, except for a small addition of pesto, the quintessential Italian sauce made by blending fresh basil, garlic, pine nuts, olive oil, and Parmesan cheese. That small addition of pesto packs a big flavor impact in these eggs.

Because such a small amount of pesto is added to the recipe, instead of preparing the sauce at home, buy a good-quality sauce at the store, where it's usually found in the refrigerated section—unless, of course, you've got your own homemade version stashed away. Add a little more or less pesto to the eggs to suit your tastes. The leftover pesto—and there will be plenty of it—can be tossed with cooked pasta for a simple dinner.

Be sure to keep the eggs cold when transporting them to the picnic— and don't let them sit out in the sun for long. Leftovers for nibbling should be kept in the cooler—not on the picnic table. Mini-muffin tins work well for transporting the eggs.

12 eggs
6 tablespoons mayonnaise
About 2 tablespoons pesto, commercial or homemade
Salt and white pepper

Continued on page 116.

COOK'S NOTES
The flavor of Greek kalamata olives is distinctly different from the Spanish green olives or ripe black olives that are so readily available. The small, purple-black kalamata olives are sometimes found on the supermarket shelf, but they are more likely found at a deli counter. They're easy to pack up for a change of pace at a picnic.

In a large saucepan, cover eggs with water and bring to a boil. Remove from heat, cover, and let sit for 15 minutes. Drain and plunge into ice-cold water until eggs are cool.

Peel eggs and slice in half lengthwise; empty yolks into a bowl. Mash yolks with fork. Add mayonnaise and pesto; mix thoroughly. Season to taste with salt and pepper.

Fill egg whites with yolk mixture. Cover with plastic wrap, and refrigerate until serving.

Mediterranean Torte
MAKES 6 SERVINGS

There are sandwiches . . . and then there are sandwiches. For lack of a better description, this falls loosely into the category, even though it requires a fork to eat. Stuffed within a shell of bread dough are layers and layers—and more layers and layers—of sweet Italian sausage, spinach, mushrooms, cheeses, and more. Suitable to eat at any temperature, it's best when served on the warmer side.

To speed up the preparation process, use prewashed spinach. It costs more, but it saves a substantial amount of time. Keep in mind that the bread dough is awkward to work with. The dish, however, is worth the effort. It's also wonderful as a brunch dish or as a light lunch.

1 (1-pound) loaf frozen bread dough
1 pound bulk sweet Italian sausage
3 tablespoons butter
1 garlic clove, minced
1 medium onion, sliced (about ¾ cup)
8 ounces mushrooms, sliced (about 2 cups)
2 cups loosely packed fresh spinach leaves, chopped
1 egg white
4 teaspoons water, divided
2 cups grated mozzarella, divided
2 tomatoes, diced and well drained
¼ cup sliced good-quality olives
1 cup grated cheddar cheese
1 egg yolk

COOK'S NOTES

To bring to a picnic, bake the torte first, then wrap in aluminum foil. Add several layers of newspapers around the torte and cover it all with a towel or two—just as your grandma used to do with her hot picnic dishes. The torte will make six servings, which should be enough to feed that many hungry picnickers when side dishes are served. But the torte is so good (and seconds are so tempting) that you may want to make two if you have any doubts. The ingredients in the torte—and their amounts—are easy to alter according to preferences, whether it's less cheese or more vegetables.

Defrost frozen bread dough overnight in refrigerator, or in microwave on defrost, turning every 20 seconds until done.

Preheat oven to 350° F.

Brown sausage in a pan over medium heat. Drain thoroughly and set aside.

Melt butter in pan over low heat; add garlic, onion, and mushrooms. Increase heat to medium and sauté until limp, and add spinach. Cook for only a few minutes until spinach is wilted slightly. Drain mixture thoroughly and set aside. (Can be done in advance to this point.)

Grease a 9-inch springform or deep-dish pie pan. Divide dough almost in half, with one part slightly larger. Roll out largest half of dough and place in bottom of springform pan. Dough should extend up sides and slightly over edge of pan for crimping later.

Make egg wash by mixing together egg white and 2 teaspoons water. Brush egg wash on bottom of torte. (This prevents ingredients from leaking through the dough.) Reserve remaining egg wash for later.

To layer torte, spread 1 cup of the mozzarella on the bottom, followed by the sausage, tomatoes, olives, cheddar cheese, mushroom-spinach mixture, and remaining 1 cup of mozzarella. Roll out remaining dough and cover top of torte.

Brush egg wash on edges of dough, then crimp together. (The egg white will work as a glue. The bread dough doesn't stay pressed together as easily as a pie crust does.) Decorate with any leftover bread dough, if desired, again using the egg white mixture to stick the decoration to the torte crust.

Mix together egg yolk and 2 teaspoons water. Brush the yolk wash on top of the torte to make the crust brown nicely, and cut several slits in top of crust. Bake for 1½ hours to be certain the center is thoroughly hot. Cover top of torte with aluminum foil when golden (after about 30 minutes), so that it won't get too brown. Remove from oven and let torte stand for at least 10 minutes before cutting into it. The internal temperature of the torte should be 165° F.

Summer Greens with Feta Vinaigrette
SERVES 6

¼ cup red- or white-wine vinegar
⅔ cup extra-virgin olive oil
3 tablespoons crumbled feta
Salt and freshly cracked pepper
3 to 6 cups mixed lettuces
2 tomatoes, chopped and well drained
Crumbled feta, for garnish

In a food processor or blender, mix vinegar, olive oil, and feta until smooth. Season to taste with salt and pepper. Toss lettuce and tomatoes in bowl. Toss with vinaigrette. Garnish with crumbled feta and sprinkle additional pepper.

Chocolate Meringues

MAKES 20

These tighter-than-air treats come from pastry chef Michelle Gayer of Minneapolis. For cocoa powder she prefers to use Valrhona. For chocolate chips she uses any leftover chocolate pieces, in any combination: bitter-sweet, semi-sweet, unsweetened, and white chocolate. Only make this on a day that is not humid.

½ cup egg whites (from about 4 eggs)
1 cup sugar
2½ tablespoons sifted unsweetened cocoa powder
½ cup chopped chocolate chips

Preheat oven to 350° F (see Note). Line 2 baking sheets with parchment paper.

In a double boiler over medium heat, whisk egg whites and sugar and simmer, stirring occasionally, until sugar is dissolved. Pour mixture into the bowl of an electric mixer fitted with a whip attachment. Whip egg-white mixture on medium speed for 5 minutes; then increase to medium-high speed for 5 to 10 minutes, until mixture is stiff but not dry.

Using a rubber spatula, fold cocoa powder into egg-white mixture until well incorporated; then fold in chocolate chips. Place heaping tablespoons of batter onto the parchment-paper-lined baking sheets. Bake 18 minutes, rotating the baking sheets halfway through baking time. Remove from oven and cool on baking sheets until ready to serve. Store in a single layer in an airtight container for up to 1 day.

Variation: If you're at home, serve sorbet or ice cream on top of the meringues.

Note: *If using a convection oven, preheat to 300° F and reduce baking time to 15 minutes.*

Make Ahead

A DAY OR MORE IN ADVANCE

Make sorbet dessert.

UP TO 8 HOURS IN ADVANCE

Prepare pasta salad.

Blanch onions, if desired.

Make hibiscus tea.

UP TO 1 HOUR IN ADVANCE

Combine the tomatoes and basil.

LAST-MINUTE PREP

Finish iced tea with pineapple juice.

Preheat grill.

Grill the bread for the bruschetta.

Add Parmesan to pasta salad.

Grill seafood.

Shortcut Savvy

Buy prepared pasta salad.

Buy rainbow-flavored sherbet and serve with fresh fruit.

Beverage

Is the weather tropical yet? Whether or not, sip Hibiscus-Pineapple Iced Tea. Or make a white wine spritzer.

LAZY SUMMER DINNER

For 6

Hibiscus-Pineapple Iced Tea or White Wine Spritzer
Bruschetta
Grilled Shrimp and Scallops
Rotini with Summer Vegetables
Tropical Sorbet Terrine

SUMMER AT ITS ESSENCE means simplicity. Nowhere is this more true than in the kitchen, where the enterprising cook favors simple flavors, simple methods, and simple meals. This menu takes advantage of that carefree approach to dining, as well as the bounty of the home garden. The cook who also wields a hoe has only to ramble over to the garden for the tomatoes, basil, zucchini, and red and yellow peppers that make this menu distinctive. This is a meal that calls out for the out-of-doors: blue sky, warm sun, a gentle breeze, and a simple grilled meal.

Let's get comfortable with a drink as effortless as the menu itself: hibiscus iced tea combined with pineapple juice. Need something even easier? Combine white wine and sparkling water for a season-pleasing spritzer. Move on to a starter of grilled bread with tomatoes and basil. Grilled seafood takes center stage with a pasta salad of garden vegetables. Layers of colorful sorbet finish off the meal with just the right note of contentment.

Hibiscus-Pineapple Iced Tea
SERVES 6

3 bags hibiscus tea (see Notes)
Ice cubes
6 cups pineapple juice, fresh if possible, divided (see Notes)
Fresh pineapple wedges, strawberries, or mint for garnish

To prepare tea, bring 3 cups water to a boil. Pour over tea bags and brew until very red in color. Cool to room temperature. Just before serving, place ice cubes in 6 tall glasses. Pour 1 cup pineapple juice into each glass. Very slowly add ½ cup tea to each glass, tilting the glass to minimize blending tea with pineapple juice so that there are layers of color. Garnish with fresh pineapple, strawberries, or mint. Serve immediately.

Notes:
- *Hibiscus tea is available in food co-ops, or use Red Zinger tea from Celestial Seasonings (hibiscus is the primary ingredient in the blend).*
- *Any fruit juice could be substituted with this tea and it would taste both good and summery.*

White Wine Spritzer

This is simply a blend of white wine and either club soda or sparkling water, usually prepared in proportions of half and half. Serve the drink with a slice of lemon or lime. A dry white wine will mean a dry tasting spritzer, and a sweet white wine, a sweet one. As a starting point, try either sauvignon blanc or pinot gris. Because the wine will be diluted, there's no reason to buy an expensive one. Keep both ingredients very cold; then mix together immediately before serving.

Bruschetta

MAKES 16 OR MORE

Whet the appetite of your guests with a delightful Italian antipasto, or appetizer, of bruschetta (broo-SHEH-tah or broo-SKEH-tah). It's simply a version of garlic toast—chewy bread preferably grilled over the coals, then rubbed with a garlic clove and topped with olive oil and a tomato-basil mixture. Roma tomatoes work particularly well because they aren't as juicy, which makes the bread soggy. Other tomatoes work fine when seeded, which helps eliminate too much juice.

3 or 4 ripe, medium-size tomatoes, seeded, chopped,
    and drained
¼ cup extra-virgin olive oil, plus more for brushing bread
½ teaspoon coarse salt
¼ teaspoon freshly ground black pepper
15 to 20 fresh basil leaves
1 large loaf (about 1 pound) chewy Italian or French bread,
    cut into ½-inch-thick slices
2 large garlic cloves, peeled

In a medium glass bowl, mix tomatoes with olive oil, salt, and pepper. Tear the basil leaves into small pieces and add to tomato mixture. Let stand at room temperature for 30 minutes or more.

Preheat the broiler or grill. Toast the bread until lightly browned on both sides. Rub one side of each slice with the garlic. Brush with olive oil. If the bread slices are too large to handle easily, cut them into smaller serving pieces. Spoon tomato mixture onto toast and serve immediately.

Notes: *To seed a tomato, slice it in half and then gently squeeze to remove some seeds and juice. With your fingers, remove the remaining seeds.*

Grilled Shrimp and Scallops

SERVES 6

The key to cooking scallops and shrimp together on a skewer is to have them the same size so they will be done at the same time. Scallops are fragile and should be placed on the skewer through their sides, not through the round face of the scallop. Unless the scallop is completely done, it may be difficult to remove from the grill. If it is sticking slightly to the grill, let it cook for a moment longer and it should come off easily.

12 to 18 small pearl onions, about 1 inch or less in diameter (purple, if available)
1 pound (at least 12) sea scallops
1 pound (at least 18) medium-size shrimp, peeled except for tail (see Note)
Melted butter or olive oil
Seasoned salt (optional)
Fresh herbs, such as oregano, rosemary, or chives, minced (optional)
6 (12-inch) skewers

If you prefer to minimize the strong taste of raw onions, blanch them in boiling water for 1 minute; then plunge immediately into cold water. This will also improve their color; however, blanching is not necessary if you prefer a strong onion flavor.

On each of 6 skewers place 3 shrimp and 2 scallops interspersed with 2 or 3 whole onions. Immediately before grilling, brush seafood with melted butter or olive oil, sprinkle lightly with seasoned salt and minced fresh herbs, and place on grill for 5 minutes or less, turning once, or until done, watching constantly. (Shrimp will be orangish-pink when done; scallops will be opaque white and very firm.) Serve immediately.

Variation: Toss the shrimp in pesto sauce before grilling.

Notes:
- *Figure three shrimp and two scallops per person for an ample entree.*
- *Skewers should be at least 12 inches long. If wooden skewers are used, they should be soaked in water for at least 20 minutes before use.*

COOK'S NOTES

Two grilling accessories will make cooking seafood easier:

1. Double-pronged skewers, which give more support to delicate foods such as scallops.
2. A screen-like accessory that's placed directly on the grill. The seafood is then cooked on the screen, which prevents small items from falling through the larger grate and also helps keep them from sticking.

Another method to keep the seafood from sticking is to oil the grate—before it is heated—with vegetable oil or a nonstick cooking spray.

Rotini with Summer Vegetables
SERVES 6 TO 8

Zucchini and yellow and red bell peppers give this pasta salad both summer flavor and color. Here the vegetables are tossed with corkscrew-shaped pasta called rotini (ro-TEEN-ee), though any pasta can be used. Salad proportions are generous; count on plenty of pasta for leftovers.

16 ounces rotini (corkscrew) pasta
⅔ cup olive oil
¼ cup lemon juice
2 teaspoons Dijon mustard
Salt and white pepper
3 small zucchini, unpeeled
1 yellow bell pepper
1 red bell pepper
5 or 6 green onions, sliced, including green part
½ cup freshly grated Parmesan cheese

Prepare pasta according to package directions.

Mix together olive oil, lemon juice, and mustard; season to taste with salt and pepper. Toss with pasta, using only as much dressing as needed; reserve remaining dressing to toss with pasta immediately before serving.

Chop zucchini and peppers. Add to pasta along with the green onions and toss together. Immediately before serving, toss with Parmesan cheese.

Tropical Sorbet Terrine

SERVES 12

This dessert is so incredibly beautiful, I served it over and over one summer, to the delight of my guests. It continues as a summer standby. These layers of sorbet serve as a refreshing finish, with pineapple, lime, and lemon offering both a lovely rainbow palette and subtle flavors. It is the simplest of desserts to prepare, nothing more than flavors of sorbet or sherbet that are layered. It should be made ahead so it freezes firm. Keep it on hand in the freezer in anticipation of unexpected summer guests. If time is really short, serve up some rainbow sherbet from the grocery store with a sprinkling of whatever fresh fruit is in season.

1 pint pineapple sorbet or sherbet
1 pint lime sorbet or sherbet
1 pint lemon sorbet or sherbet
Fresh fruit (such as raspberries) or mint leaves for garnish

Line a 9 x 5-inch loaf pan with wax paper or plastic wrap (aluminum foil will not work). Let pineapple sorbet sit at room temperature for about 20 minutes to soften. Empty into loaf pan and smooth out. Return pan to freezer while lime sorbet sits at room temperature to soften.

Repeat with lime layer and return pan to freezer while lemon sorbet softens at room temperature. Add lemon sorbet to frozen layers; freeze until hard. Cover top of sorbet lightly with a layer of plastic wrap or wax paper.

To serve, remove sorbet from pan by lifting out wax paper or plastic wrap. Slice into individual servings. Garnish with fresh fruit or mint leaves. Serve immediately.

UP TO A WEEK OR MORE IN
ADVANCE

Make pizza shells.

Caramelize the onions
(freeze them if it's more than
a day or two in advance).

Make ice ring, if using, or
freeze cherry tomatoes or
yellow pear tomatoes for
ice cubes.

Make ice cream sandwiches.

UP TO A DAY IN ADVANCE

Make the dip.

UP TO 8 HOURS IN ADVANCE

Prep pizza toppings (chop,
dice, or shred, as needed).

Purée the mixture for Blonde
Bloody Mary.

LAST-MINUTE PREP

Make lemonade fizz.

Preheat the grill.

Cook pizzas individually as
needed.

Leave the ice cream sand-
wiches at room temperature
for about 10 minutes before
serving.

PIZZA ON THE GRILL

For any size crowd

Cherry Lemonade Fizz or Blonde Bloody Mary
Grilled Individual Pizzas
Caramelized Onion Dip
Chicken-Feta Salad
Crispy Ice Cream Sandwiches

WITH PICNICS AND REUNIONS popping up like dandelions in June, it's worth remembering that food defines a family as surely as the shape of a face or breadth of a smile. Culturally, we are what we eat. That may mean Grandma's cinnamon buns, Aunt Helen's potato salad, or cousin Cedric's black-eyed peas. It all depends on your family. Those favorites need to be at the table—indoors or outdoors—of any large gathering where there is a sea of similar faces. But don't forget something new. That's what keeps the meal interesting.

Regardless of the size of your group, this menu will work well. Grilled individual pizzas will keep the crew busy. Guests can custom-make their own with toppings from peppers to pepperoni and cheeses galore (mozzarella, provolone, Parmesan, and feta). There should be enough choice to please the pickiest of hungry eaters. Then add your family's favorite salads to the menu, or any one of the side dishes included here.

Does your crowd like a dip? (Silly question. All crowds do.) A caramelized onion dip offers a delicious twist. Does pasta salad seem old hat? Try one with tomato, chicken, and feta.

What to drink will depend on your crowd. If you've got children along, consider a variation on the kiddie cocktail, which is nothing more than soda dressed up with a dash of grenadine and a skewer of fresh fruit. In this case we'll add some fizz to lemonade with sparkling water, then splash in some grenadine and serve it with some maraschino cherries and other fruit. It's like sangria for the under twenty-one set, though guests of any age find it refreshing.

If you want something spicier for the adults, try a Blonde Bloody Mary.

Shortcut Savvy

Buy premade individual pizza crusts.

Buy preshredded cheeses, available in economy-size packages at discount grocery stores.

Skip the caramelized onions used in the dip and replace with dried onion soup mix for a chip dip (see directions on soup mix package).

Use commercially made cookies for the outside layers of the ice cream sandwiches.

Beverage

Be sure to have a non-alcoholic choice available, such as Cherry Lemonade Fizz. For others, offer some summer spice with a Blonde Bloody Mary.

COOK'S NOTES

With the exception of the pizza dough, the amounts of ingredients for this menu's recipes aren't written in stone; add more or less according to your tastes. Much of this menu can be done in advance.

Plan for plenty to drink, especially if it's a hot day. To be sure you have enough to quench the thirst of partygoers, count on 2 (8-ounce) cups per person Each 12-ounce can of lemonade will make 2 quarts, or enough for 8 drinks. Leftover punch? Make frozen pops by placing the lemonade mixture in small paper cups or in plastic molds. If you're feeling particularly festive and have leftover maraschino cherries, drop one or two in the bottom of the mixture. Partially freeze; then push a wooden stick or plastic spoon into each container to be used as a handle. Freeze.

Cherry Lemonade Fizz
MAKES 8 (8-OUNCE) SERVINGS

This punch makes use of grenadine, a syrup that gives drinks a red, cherry-like color and flavor. This flavoring is what turns soda into kiddie cocktails in such drinks as the Shirley Temple (7-Up and grenadine) and the Roy Rogers (cola and grenadine, or basically a cherry cola). Use the grenadine sparingly; too much turns a drink cloyingly sweet. Grenadine is available in supermarkets in the beverage-mix aisle, as well as at liquor stores.

1 (12-ounce) can frozen lemonade, thawed (or other lemonade mix to make 2 quarts)
6½ cups sparkling water
2 tablespoons grenadine
Ice ring (optional; see Note)
Skewers of fruit: maraschino cherries, pineapple chunks, berries

Right before serving, make lemonade according to directions on can, substituting sparkling water for water. (The lemonade will foam up at first but will quickly settle down.) Add grenadine and stir to mix. Add ice ring, if desired.

If the beverage is served from a punch bowl, place fruit on skewers and have ready on a plate nearby. Or serve the fruit in individual bowls near the punch with a fork or tongs for guests to help themselves.

Note: *For this ice ring, prepare it with lemonade using plain rather than sparkling water. Add maraschino cherries or slices of orange, lemon, or lime.*

Blonde Bloody Mary

SERVES 1

What to do with your bumper crop of yellow tomatoes, besides adding color to salsa? These very pretty, very spicy drinks are based on a recipe from Scala's Bistro in San Francisco. If you don't have yellow tomatoes, you certainly could use the traditional red version. Any ripe tomato will do, as long as it's flavorful. And you don't have to add alcohol. I always have a jar of sliced jalapeños handy in the refrigerator for other cooking; they work well for this drink. Freeze small cherry tomatoes and use them as ice cubes.

6 to 8 ounces juice from small yellow or cherry tomatoes
Dash Worcestershire sauce
Dash green hot sauce
⅛ cup sweet and sour mix (optional; available at liquor stores)
Dash white pepper
Jalapeño slices
¼ cup vodka (optional)
Fresh dill sprig, for garnish
Pickled green bean, if available, for garnish
Frozen cherry tomatoes, for ice cubes

To make juice, purée tomatoes in blender or food processor. Thin with water to taste, if desired, unless you prefer a thick drink. Add Worcestershire sauce, green hot sauce, sweet and sour mix, and white pepper. Add jalapeño slices, 1 or 2 at a time, and purée with juice. Taste, adding additional jalapeño slices, if desired. (Be careful; it gets very hot, very fast.) Add vodka and blend. If desired, run the drink through a sieve to get rid of the jalapeño seeds and bits of tomato skin. Serve in a tall glass with a dill sprig and pickled green bean, with frozen tomatoes for ice cubes.

Grilled Individual Pizzas

MAKES 9 (5- TO 6-INCH) PIZZAS

If you have a lot to make, try doing separate batches on different days, which is how I made pizza shells for a hundred people. (By the last day, I was really fast.) Schedule the pizza-crust making to accommodate your other prep (that is, don't leave it to the last minute). If you're making this for a big crowd, it's best to partially bake the crusts so they are easier to handle at grilling time. The homemade version has a distinct rustic look, which is another way of saying it has irregular sides; that is, it does not have a perfectly round shape. If you need to make a lot of pizza crusts, double the recipe. Continue with double batches rather than multiplying the recipe too many times. This is a great recipe to have ready in the freezer for unexpected guests or informal extemporaneous gatherings.

CRUST
2 envelopes dry yeast
½ teaspoon sugar
1½ cups warm water (105° to 115° F)
3½ cups flour
1 teaspoon salt
Olive oil

PIZZA ASSEMBLY TOPPINGS
Commercial pizza sauce (squeeze bottles are useful for a crowd)
Olive oil (for white pizzas)
Variety of pizza toppings (shredded cheese, diced vegetables, cooked or
    cured meats, etc.)

FOR CRUST
In a bowl, stir yeast and sugar into 1½ cups warm water. Set aside for 10 minutes, or until foamy; stir again. Measure flour and salt into a large bowl; add yeast mixture and mix thoroughly by hand. The dough will be sticky.

Turn dough out onto a lightly floured surface. Knead, adding a little flour if necessary, for 5 to 10 minutes, until dough is no longer sticky. (Or knead with an electric mixer with attachment for 5 to 7 minutes.)

Lightly oil dough and place in a bowl large enough to allow it to double in volume. Cover bowl tightly with plastic wrap that has been oiled on the side that touches the dough. Let stand at room temperature for at least 1 hour, or until doubled in volume. At this point, dough can be refrigerated for several hours or overnight. Do not punch dough down.

To form pizza crusts: With floured hands, pull off enough dough to make a ball 2 to 3 inches in diameter. Roll out dough into a 5- or 6-inch circle. Place on lightly greased cookie sheet. Repeat, using remaining dough to make 8 more pizza crusts. Cover and set aside in refrigerator.

To parbake crusts for future use: Preheat oven to 400° F. Bake the crusts on a lightly greased cookie sheet for 3 to 4 minutes or until crusts are just firm (do not brown). Remove them from the oven and pierce in several spots with a fork to release steam (they will have puffed up in the oven). Cool the crusts and, in an airtight container, either freeze for up to several weeks or store in the refrigerator for up to 4 days.

FOR PIZZA ASSEMBLY

Raise the grate on the grill as far from the coals as possible. Bring coals to medium heat (you should be able to hold your hand over the coals for 3 to 5 seconds). You don't want a blast furnace effect or the pizzas will burn. You may want multiple grills going if you have many pizzas to make.

Have pizza sauce and toppings ready for guests to assemble. Let them know they shouldn't pile the ingredients high. Stick to about ½ inch. With too much atop, the pizza crust will burn before the ingredients become warm or the cheese melts.

Place the pizzas on the grill and lower the grill cover. If pizzas are being added frequently to the grill (which is likely with a crowd), place a pie pan over individual pizzas to maintain steady heat. Watch the pizzas carefully, because grilling will take only a few minutes. They are ready when the cheese has melted.

If pizza crusts are not parbaked: Lightly grease the grill before starting the coals. Place crusts on heated grill and turn over after a few minutes when the crusts have become firm. Repeat on second side (do not let either side get brown). Remove crusts from grill and pierce any puffed areas. Add toppings and finish pizzas on grill as directed.

CARAMELIZING ONIONS

For onions to be caramelized, they must be cooked slowly over low heat. This takes time—up to 1½ hours, depending on the pan used and how many onions are cooking—but it's no effort at all. Just put the onions on the stove to cook and then do something else, checking on the onions every once in a while—clean house, garden, or wash the car and cook all at the same time.

The onions cook faster in a shallow pan than in one with tall sides, such as a Dutch oven. But the latter may be necessary because of the sheer amount of onion, which eventually cooks down to a much smaller amount (4 big onions caramelize into 1 cup).

You can prepare the onions in advance and freeze them for later use. Better yet, make a bunch to freeze so you can pull them out anytime for summer guests.

Caramelized Onion Dip
MAKES 3 CUPS; ENOUGH FOR ABOUT 9 GUESTS

Call this the "Better than Lipton" onion dip. It's simply terrific. Once you taste this, you'll never go back to dehydrated onion again. The caramelization process brings out the onion's inherent sweetness and gives the dip a rich, dense flavor. Vidalia, OsoSweet, or other sweet onions, which are in season in the spring and summer, are particularly flavorful in this dip, though any onion will do.

The recipe calls for big onions, but that's strictly to cut the peeling time for the cook. The dip will taste best when the flavors have a chance to mingle, so make this a day in advance and you'll be set. Serve with store-bought vegetable-flavored chips or with fresh vegetables.

1 tablespoon olive oil
4 large onions, preferably sweet such as Vidalia or OsoSweet
    (about 4 cups coarsely chopped)
2 cups sour cream
2 tablespoons lemon juice
Salt and white pepper
Chopped chives, for garnish (optional)

Add olive oil to large frying (or braising) pan or Dutch oven and heat. (The frying pan is preferable because the caramelizing process will go faster.)

Over low to medium heat, cook onions uncovered and slowly, until the moisture leaves the onions and they turn lightly brown and become nearly a purée as they caramelize. This takes a long time, at least 1 hour and maybe more depending on the type of pan you're using and the amount of onions. Don't give up and turn up the heat or the onions will burn. Remove the onions from the pan and cool. If working in advance, either refrigerate or freeze the onions in a tightly covered dish or in a plastic freezer bag. To thaw, place the onions in the refrigerator for several hours.

To finish the dip, mash the onions with a fork. Stir in the sour cream. Add the lemon juice and season to taste with salt and white pepper. To serve, garnish with chives, if desired. Serve with chips or vegetables.

Chicken-Feta Salad
MAKES 16 (½ CUP) SERVINGS

This recipe is adapted from D'Amico & Sons, a longtime restaurant in Minneapolis. After years of ordering the salad off the menu, I finally asked for the recipe on behalf of the *Star Tribune* readers. Those readers, I should note, included my mother, sister, kids, and me, who all love the dish.

8 boneless, skinless chicken breast halves (about 2½ pounds)
Salt and pepper
Olive oil
16 ounces pasta (penne, bowties, rotini, or other)
3 medium-size tomatoes, chopped (about 1½ cups)
1 cup pitted kalamata olives
1 cup crumbled feta cheese
½ cup chopped flat-leafed parsley
½ cup bottled Italian vinaigrette (Parmesan Italian is especially good)

Preheat oven to 350° F.

Season chicken breasts to taste with salt and pepper; lightly drizzle olive oil over top. Roast, uncovered, for 10 minutes in oven. Then cover and continue baking for additional 15 minutes or until cooked through. Remove from oven, cool chicken, dice, and reserve or refrigerate for later use.

To prepare salad: Boil pasta in salted water, cooking according to package directions. Drain pasta, cool, and set aside.

In a large bowl combine chicken, pasta, tomatoes, olives, feta cheese, and parsley; toss with vinaigrette and serve.

Variation: Toss the tomatoes in olive oil and roast in a 350° F oven for about 30 minutes, or until tender, before using them for the salad. This method brings out their inherent sweetness.

Crispy Ice Cream Sandwiches
MAKES 18 (2 X 3-INCH) SANDWICHES

4 tablespoons (½ stick) butter
1 (10-ounce) bag regular-size marshmallows (about 40)
2 teaspoons vanilla
6 cups crispy rice cereal
1 quart ice cream, any flavor

Melt butter in a large pot. Add marshmallows and melt over low heat. Remove from heat and add vanilla. Add cereal and mix thoroughly.

With butter or a nonstick spray, grease two 9 x 13-inch pans (see
Note). Press the cereal mixture firmly into the pans, making the bars about
¼ inch thick.

Soften ice cream slightly. Meanwhile cut bars into desired size, making
sure there is a mate for each bar. Spread the ice cream over half the bars,
and top ice cream with another bar to make a sandwich. Wrap individually and return to freezer. Before serving, if frozen firm, let stand at room
temperature for about 10 minutes.

Variation: Add a layer of melted chocolate on top of the ice cream before
the second bar is placed on it.

> **Note:** *You can use other size pans; just keep in mind that in the end the
> bars need to be about ¼ inch thick. You can make the bars thicker in one
> pan and later cut them in half to get ¼-inch-thick bars.*

All food is the gift of the gods and has something of the miraculous, the egg no less than the truffle.

....

SYBILLE BEDFORD

SWEET CORN BLISS

For 6

Watermelon Daiquiri or Watermelon-Ade or
    Iced Coffee
Roasted Corn on the Cob with Flavored Butter
Pork Burgers with Cayenne Mayonnaise
Cabbage Salad with Spicy Lime Vinaigrette
Plums with Raspberry-Mascarpone Frozen Yogurt

IT WAS THE SEASON'S FIRST CORN. He chomped on an ear of yellow-white hybrid, nibbling from left to right until he finished the row without missing so much as a kernel. Then he was on to the next, moving his way along the ear as though it were a typewriter carriage: left to right and down a row. Then another row and another until the ear had gone 'round and the kernels were gone. Only then did he look up. Melted butter dripped from his wrist; a few corn kernels stuck to his chin. His face glistened from a smudge of grease. He smiled, and the remainder of the corn imbedded in his teeth smiled with him.

This is summer bliss—and the reason we eat corn on the cob only with those close to us. They are the ones who don't mind us wearing our corn because they are wearing theirs, too.

What else to eat when corn is center stage? Let's keep it simple.

WATERMELON

If summer could be symbolized by a single food, it would be a slice of watermelon, sweet with the scent of sunshine and warm earth, dripping with flavor. And, by the way, offering one of life's true pleasures: seeds for long-distance spitting.

Limited to a simple juicy slice or occasional pickle, or shaped into a decorative holder of more versatile fruit, watermelon is underused in this country. We may dabble with watermelon-flavored candy, gum, and even gelatin, but the rest of the world is wiser with this subtle flavoring. From Latin America to the Far East, the juice of watermelon is sipped and savored in a variety of thirst-quenching drinks.

Thick and refreshing, watermelon juice has the texture of just-squeezed orange juice. Because of the seeds, it takes a little more time to extract the juice from a watermelon than from, say, an orange. But even that can be quickly done with a knife. Only the black seeds need to be discarded, and they're often bunched together in the fruit.

It does get a little messy while cutting up the watermelon because of the juice that seeps off the cutting board and onto the counter and, sure enough, drips onto the floor before you can yell, "Where's the sponge?" But, hey, it's summer, so seed the watermelon outside where sticky floors don't matter.

Obviously, watermelons are not squeezed like an orange to retrieve the juice. Its pretty pink flesh needs to be chopped into large chunks that will fit into a blender or food processor where, in a matter of moments, it becomes purée, or juice. Roughly 2 cups of watermelon chunks puréed equal 1 cup of juice. If you don't like the pulp, strain the juice through a sieve before serving.

As you experiment with watermelons, you will find some that are intensely flavorful and others that taste more like water than melons. You can't tell the difference before the melon is cut, and even then you occasionally can be fooled. Generally, the lusher pink ones seem to carry more flavor than the pale ones.

Beverage

Use watermelon as a base for drinks. With a really sweet watermelon, the juice won't need any embellishments. But for juice that needs a little more flavor, add an equal portion of prepared lemonade to make a simple watermelon-ade. Or experiment with the addition of other juices. If you combine the watermelon juice with lime juice and rum, you've got the makings of a daiquiri, frozen or otherwise. Or serve iced coffee with either the meal or with dessert.

Watermelon Daiquiri
MAKES 1 LARGE DRINK

2 cups watermelon (1-inch) chunks
¼ cup light rum
2 tablespoons fresh lime juice
2 tablespoons orange-flavored liqueur, such as Triple Sec

In a blender or food processor, purée the watermelon with the rum, lime juice, and orange flavoring. Pour into a glass and serve, or, if you want an icy drink, freeze in a separate container for several hours or overnight.

Another way to prepare the daiquiri is to first freeze small chunks of watermelon in a single layer, and then purée them with the other ingredients. Serve immediately.

Watermelon-Ade
MAKES 8 CUPS

8 cups watermelon, seeded and cut into chunks
4 cups prepared lemonade

In a blender or food processor, purée watermelon in batches, about 2 cups at a time. In a large pitcher, combine watermelon purée and lemonade. Mix thoroughly and pour into glasses with ice cubes. If watermelon-ade is left undisturbed for awhile, the watermelon juice and the lemonade will separate, with the watermelon floating to the top. Stir to remix.

Iced Coffee

Brew up extra-strong coffee (espresso is especially good). Pour hot coffee into a glass with ice and a metal spoon. (The spoon will keep glass from cracking.) Or make coffee in advance and chill; serve with ice. If desired, add a splash of half-and-half or Grand Marnier to the iced coffee.

Roasted Corn on the Cob with Flavored Butter

SERVES 6

There are as many ways to cook corn as there are kernels on an ear. But don't fret, whichever way you like is best. It's hard to be wrong when the ear is fresh and the butter is plentiful. Yet when the State Fair comes around and the fragrance of roasted ears of corn wafts through the air, I wonder as I stand in line for not one but two cobs of corn if my steamed version at home really is best, even when dripping in butter. Could anything beat nature's own food-on-a-stick roasted in the husk over coals?

Let's just say that roasting has its advantages, not the least of which is that for those of us who eat fresh corn almost daily through the season, this method adds a nice variety to mealtime. And here's the secret: there's nothing to it.

Don't let cookbooks or food "experts" throw you off with elaborate methods of soaking or other preparation. Not only is soaking unnecessary, but also it makes the corn take forever to roast. Some say to pull back the husks before roasting and pull out the silks; then to pull the husks back over the corn before putting it over the coals. Such a fuss for something as simple as corn on the cob. Don't bother. It would seem that the corn would be too hot to remove the silks after it is cooked. But contrary to logic, that's not the case. The silks pull away easily when the husks are cooked. Those of us with hardy fingers don't even need potholders.

THREE WAYS TO ROAST CORN

1. Unhusked: All you have to do to roast corn is leave it in the husk and toss it on the grill for about 10 minutes, turning occasionally. If you have a covered grill, you can cover it. If not, roast the corn a little longer. If you're cooking over a campfire, cook the corn in the embers. It's that simple.

2. Husked: Here's another approach, and almost as easy. You can roast the corn on the grill without the husks. This method lightly browns the corn. Just plop the husked cob right on the grill, basting it with butter, if you like. It needs very little time on the grill—less than 10 minutes—but how long is up to the cook and the intensity of the coals. Cook it until it looks lightly browned and your mouth begins to water.

Continued on page 140.

3. Partially husked: For a real treat if you feel like tinkering around with the grilling, cook the corn in the husk for 5 minutes, then pull back the husk and baste it with melted butter. Then return to the heat with the kernels directly on the grill. *Mmmm.* Makes me hungry just to think about it.

ALTERNATIVES TO ROASTING CORN

Some people don't even bother cooking sweet corn. They eat it raw, cut from the cob and used in a corn salsa or salad. Others boil or steam the cob. A few general cautions with these methods: Don't add salt to the water; it toughens the corn. And if you boil it, add the corn to boiling water instead of heating the water with corn already in the pot. Either way, corn doesn't need much cooking or it becomes tough. In my kitchen, I steam this summer treasure for only a few minutes—and it's perfect.

For others, the microwave is the method of choice, especially for just one or two cobs. These cobs can be cooked in or out of the husk. If cooking unhusked, wrap in a damp paper towel or place in a dish with a little water. Either way, microwave for 2 minutes for one ear, 5 minutes for two ears (perhaps that should be called a head of corn?). More than two ears and it's faster to steam the corn.

In theory, corn can be roasted in the oven, too. But it's not reasonable to cook corn under the broiler in the summer. Why would anyone want to heat up the kitchen like that? Then you may as well choose another method of cooking.

SEASONING

How to season the corn is another matter that cooks debate. Butter is the traditional topping in the Upper Midwest. But on a visit to the Pacific Northwest, where a food festival was in full swing, I enjoyed roasted corn served with an array of seasonings buffet-style, to the delight of the diners. Choices included a variety of flavored salt and pepper—including seasoned salt and cayenne pepper—as well as bottles of hot sauce and jalapeño peppers.

Some cooks use olive oil or flavored oils instead of butter for their seasoning. Garlic oil is one such option. In the South, some cooks prefer basting their roasted corn with barbecue sauce or wrapping the cobs in bacon. Whatever your choice, if you start with fresh corn, you can't go wrong.

6 to 12 ears of corn
Flavored Butter

Grill corn using one of the mentioned methods. Serve with Flavored Butter.

FLAVORED BUTTER
Makes 1 cup
1 cup (2 sticks) butter
Choice of seasonings:
    Juice of 1 lime and 1 teaspoon hot or sweet paprika
    1 teaspoon cayenne pepper
    1 teaspoon minced garlic
    1 teaspoon minced chives
    Sea salt to taste

Either melt the butter and add seasonings, or mix softened butter together with the seasonings to form a paste. If working with melted butter, pour the mixture into a mold or dish for the butter to solidify. (Your guests would be impressed with individual molds for each person.) If working with a paste, either smooth it into a container or roll it into a log and wrap in plastic wrap or wax paper until dinner when guests can take slices off the butter at the table. Refrigerate the butter until ready to serve. (Can be made a day ahead and stored in the refrigerator.)

Pork Burgers with Cayenne Mayonnaise
MAKES 6

This gives the old burger a new taste.

1½ pounds ground pork
2 teaspoons minced garlic
½ cup diced onion
2 tablespoons chopped fresh parsley
¼ cup chopped fresh sage, or 2 teaspoons dried

Continued on page 142.

Salt and pepper

6 buns

Cayenne Mayonnaise (see recipe)

Lettuce, for garnish

Onion slices, for garnish

Tomato slices, for garnish

Combine ground pork, garlic, onion, parsley, and sage; season to taste with salt and pepper. Form into 6 patties. (If making in advance, pack in an airtight container and refrigerate until ready to use.)

Grill or broil until desired doneness. (Pork can be cooked to an internal temperature of 160° F.) Toast buns on grill, if desired. Serve burgers on buns with flavored mayo and lettuce, onion, and tomato.

CAYENNE MAYONNAISE

½ cup mayonnaise

¼ teaspoon or more ground cayenne pepper (red pepper)

Mix together mayonnaise and cayenne in a small bowl. Refrigerate for at least 30 minutes before serving. (Can be made a day ahead.)

Cabbage Salad with Spicy Lime Vinaigrette
SERVES 6

This is a simple name for a simply perfect salad from chef Alex Roberts of Brasa Rotisserie in Minneapolis, Minnesota, who was the James Beard Foundation nominee for best chef in the Midwest. Roberts serves the salad very finely shredded; he uses a deli slicer at the restaurant, but at home a mandoline or grater works well. Prepackaged, finely shredded cabbage is sometimes available in the produce department.

SPICY LIME VINAIGRETTE
1 tablespoon coarsely chopped shallots or onion
¼ cup fresh lime juice (about 2 limes; see Notes)
1 teaspoon sugar
½ teaspoon salt
1 serrano chile, seeded and coarsely chopped, if desired
⅓ cup grapeseed oil (or other neutral oil)
⅓ cup sour cream at room temperature

CABBAGE SALAD
½ head green cabbage (or a 10-ounce bag of finely shredded cabbage)
¼ cup chopped fresh flat-leaf parsley
¼ cup chopped fresh cilantro leaves
¼ cup chopped fresh mint leaves
Salt and pepper
Sesame seeds, toasted (see Notes)

FOR VINAIGRETTE
Mix shallots with lime juice, sugar, and salt. Let stand for 10 to 15 minutes. In a blender, purée shallot mixture with chile, oil, and sour cream until smooth; set aside.

FOR CABBAGE SALAD ASSEMBLY
Using a mandoline or grater, shred cabbage as finely as possible. In a bowl, toss cabbage with parsley, cilantro, and mint. Add about ½ cup vinaigrette to taste and toss. Season to taste with salt and pepper. Add more vinaigrette, if desired. Garnish with sesame seeds. There will be extra vinaigrette left over that can be used to toss with any other salad.

Notes:
- *To get the most juice out of the limes, roll them in your hands or on the counter to soften them up first.*
- *To toast sesame seeds, heat them in a dry saucepan over low heat for a few minutes, stirring occasionally as they lightly brown and become fragrant.*

Plums with Raspberry-Mascarpone Frozen Yogurt

SERVES 6

From Kirk Bratrud, chef of the Boat House on Barker's Island in Superior, Wisconsin. He suggests steeping the plums in an inexpensive merlot, which will have a fruity flavor.

3 plums
½ cup honey
2 cups red wine (such as merlot)
1 cinnamon stick, broken
5 whole cloves
3 whole allspice berries
1 pint (2 cups) mascarpone cheese at room temperature
1 quart frozen raspberry yogurt, slightly softened

Wash plums, cut them halfway through and pit them. Arrange tightly in a noncorroding saucepan. Pour honey over plums, add merlot, and scatter spices, being sure plums are submerged. Over medium heat, bring plums and liquid to a simmer. Lower heat and cook until plums are barely soft, about 5 to 10 minutes. (If they cook too long, they will lose their shape.) Using a strainer spoon, remove plums to a bowl and cool to room temperature.

Continue to cook sauce until reduced by more than half to a thin syrup. (You will end up with about ¾ cup sauce.) Strain through a fine-meshed sieve. (If making in advance, refrigerate sauce.)

In a large bowl, mash mascarpone into the frozen yogurt. (If making in advance, refreeze in a covered container.)

To serve: Bring plums to room temperature. Slightly warm sauce over low heat. Place a small scoop of slightly softened yogurt into each parfait glass or small plate or bowl, such as a ramekin. Using the back of a wet spoon, make an indentation in the yogurt to support a plum half and place one on top. Ladle 2 tablespoons sauce over plum and yogurt.

Note: *If raspberry frozen yogurt is unavailable, vanilla frozen yogurt could be used, with puréed raspberries added (or not). Or substitute strawberry frozen yogurt.*

A dinner invitation, once accepted,
is a sacred obligation. If you die before
the dinner party takes place,
your executor must attend.

....

WILLIAM MCALLISTER

A CROSSROADS DINNER

For 6

Mint Tea
Tabbouleh Salad
Lamb Kebabs with Harissa
Basmati Rice
Raita
Pita Bread
Lemon Granita

WE WERE WANDERING through the Grand Bazaar in Istanbul, Turkey, hungry and hot as vendors vied for our attention with promises of good deals on the carpets, silver, and spices they had for sale. In the corner a little café promised relief in the form of lamb kebabs and pita bread. We took the bait and, once refreshed, returned to the crowded shops. For centuries, Turkey was the crossroads of the world as traders made their way through the region, bringing culinary traditions, as well as spices and other goods, from one country to the next. The result was an amalgam of memorable flavors. Like those early traders, I've incorporated traditional recipes from the expansive region, in this case for a menu that pays homage to those crossroads. Influenced by a hot climate, Middle Eastern, Mediterranean, and North African flavors are made for summer. Turn them into a refreshing meal with grilled lamb kebabs, seasoned with a spice blend popular in North Africa. Add the traditional cooling agents—raita (the Greek variation of the traditional yogurt sauce), a salad of bulgur wheat and parsley from the Middle East, rice from India, Moroccan mint tea, and icy granita from Italy—and you've got a made-in-the-shade summer meal wherever your dinner plate may be.

Mint Tea
SERVES 6

6½ cups almost boiling water
3 bags of green tea, or about 1 tablespoon green tea leaves
20 spearmint leaves
2 teaspoons sugar

Bring the water almost to a boil (green tea leaves need water a little less hot than black tea leaves so the tea doesn't become bitter). Pour a little of the boiling water into the teapot to warm it; then discard the water. Add the tea and the rest of the hot water. Let steep for 2 to 3 minutes. Add the mint and sugar. Serve immediately, or cool and serve cold.

Tabbouleh Salad

SERVES 6

In parts of the Middle East, where this is a traditional salad often served among the appetizer plates called "meze," tabbouleh (tuh-BOO-luh) is scooped up into lettuce. The base of the salad is bulgur wheat and parsley. Bulgur is wheat kernels that have been steamed, dried, and crushed; it has a chewy consistency. It can be found in the health-food section of supermarkets, in the aisles with rice and Middle Eastern foods, and in the bulk-food section. Sometimes it's in a box that simply says Tabbouleh Salad.

1 cup bulgur wheat
2 cups water
⅓ cup olive oil
⅓ cup fresh lemon juice (about 3 lemons)
1 bunch fresh parsley (either Italian flat-leaf or curly-leaf), chopped
1 medium onion, finely chopped (about ¾ cup)
1 large cucumber, peeled, seeded, and diced (about 1 cup)
2 to 3 tomatoes, seeded and chopped (about 1½ cups)
Salt and pepper

Measure bulgur into a medium-size bowl. Bring 2 cups water to a boil; pour over bulgur, cover, and let sit for about 30 minutes, until bulgur has absorbed the water. Drain any excess.

Combine the olive oil and lemon juice, and toss with the bulgur. Add the parsley, onion, cucumber, and tomatoes. Season to taste with salt and pepper. Refrigerate until 30 minutes before serving; it tastes best when it's not too cold.

Variation: Add ¼ cup or more chopped mint to the salad.

Lamb Kebabs with Harissa

SERVES 6

Harissa (hah-REE-suh) is a North African spice mixture.

HARISSA (MAKES 1 CUP)
2 tablespoons chile powder, such as ancho or
    chipotle (see Notes)
¾ teaspoon minced garlic (about 2 garlic cloves)
1 tablespoon fresh lemon juice
½ cup extra-virgin olive oil
1 teaspoon salt
1½ teaspoons ground cumin

LAMB KEBABS
3 pounds boneless lamb shoulder or leg
Vegetable oil
12 to 18 skewers (see Notes)

FOR HARISSA
Combine chile powder, garlic, lemon juice, olive oil, salt, and cumin. Adjust seasonings as preferred. If desired, make additional harissa to serve on the side with the kebabs. (Don't reuse the harissa that was mixed with the raw lamb because of food safety reasons.)

FOR LAMB KEBABS
Trim exterior fat from lamb and discard. Cut lamb into 1½-inch cubes and toss in harissa shortly before cooking.

Preheat the grill or the broiler. Oil grate or broiler pan for easier turning of the meat. Place meat on skewers, leaving a small space between pieces of meat. Cook over high heat until meat is at preferred doneness, turning once after about 5 minutes, and cooking an additional 2 or 3 minutes for medium rare. Serve kebabs atop a bed of rice.

Notes:

- *The cook controls the intensity of the heat in harissa. If you use dried ancho chiles (which are large and mild), you'll have a milder flavor than if you use small dried red peppers such as cayenne. (Often, the packaging indicates the level of heat for a particular chile. Chipotles, for example, are rated 5.5 on a 10-point scale; ancho chiles are at 3.5.)*

  You can find the chiles already ground in some supermarkets that carry a variety of Mexican chile seasonings. Or you can buy the dried peppers whole and grind them yourself. To grind whole dried chiles, first remove the stems and, if possible, scrape out the seeds if the peppers are hot (wear gloves to protect your hands from the oils). Process to a powder using a blender or food processor. A 1-ounce package of dried chiles makes more than enough ground chile for this recipe.

- *If you're using wood skewers, soak them for about 20 minutes before using.*

Basmati Rice

SERVES 6

Basmati rice has a nutty, perfumed aroma. The cooking method in this recipe comes from Raghavan Iyer, a Minneapolis author of several Indian cookbooks, including *660 Curries* and *The Turmeric Trail*. Before the rice is cooked, he rinses it several times to remove the starch. Then he soaks the rice for 30 minutes. This method makes for perfect fluffy—and fragrant— rice. It can be made in advance and reheated by covering the rice with boiling water, and then draining it.

1½ cups uncooked basmati or other long-grain rice
2¼ cups cold water

To rinse rice, place it in a medium saucepan and add enough water to cover. Rub the grains of rice with your fingers to remove the starch and any dust; drain. Repeat several times, draining each time, until the water is clear.

Once clean, add 2¼ cups cold water to the rice and soak for 30 minutes. Bring to a boil, stirring once; reduce heat to medium-high. Cook uncovered 5 to 6 minutes, stirring occasionally until most of the water has evaporated.

Reduce heat to low. Cover and cook 5 minutes; remove from heat and let stand covered 5 to 10 minutes. Fluff with a fork before serving.

Raita

MAKES ABOUT 2 CUPS

Some variation of this cucumber yogurt dip (called RI-tah in India) is served all over the Middle East and along the Mediterranean to cool the palate when spicy foods are served. For smaller pieces of cucumber, grate it.

½ cucumber, peeled and seeded
1 cup plain nonfat yogurt
½ small onion, diced (about ½ cup)
Salt and white pepper

Pat the cucumber with paper towels to get it as dry as possible. Dice to make about ½ cup.

In a medium bowl, combine the cucumber, yogurt, and onion; stir to mix. Season to taste with salt and pepper. Marinate for at least 1 hour in the refrigerator to blend flavors.

Lemon Granita
SERVES 6

This is best served the day it is prepared, when the ice crystals are large and flaky. They almost look like tiny snowflakes. Meyer lemons are particularly good with this.

3 cups water
1 cup sugar
Zest of 2 lemons
Juice of 6 large lemons (about 3 cups)

In a saucepan, boil the water, sugar, and lemon zest together until the sugar dissolves. Remove from heat and mix in the lemon juice. Cool.

Pour into a shallow container, such as a 9 x 13-inch pan, and cover. Freeze until the edges are frozen, about 1 to 2 hours. Remove the pan from the freezer and, using a fork, scrape the ice, moving from the edge to the center. Return to the freezer.

Repeat at least 3 times, every 30 minutes or so, until the mixture has become large ice flakes. Serve the same day as made.

Note: *Do not let the granita freeze solid, or you will lose the flaky texture.*

FALL

MENUS

Kick Off the Season Dinner   154

Garlic-Thyme Soup with Homemade Croutons

Stuffed Chicken Breasts with Roasted Red Pepper Sauce

Rice Pilaf with Sage

Squash Sauté

Devil's Food Cake with Milk Chocolate–Sour Cream
    Frosting

Oktoberfest Dinner   162

Hungarian Goulash

Spaetzle

Red Cabbage with Bacon and Caraway

Rye or Pumpernickel Bread

Easy Apple Strudel

Autumn Flavors   170

Gingered Squash Soup

Caramelized Leek, Goat Cheese, and Sun-Dried
    Tomato Triangles

Braised Short Ribs

Creamy Polenta

Cranberry-Pear Crisp

Southwestern Dinner   178

Pineapple Salsa and Pico de Gallo

Quesadillas with Brie and Roasted Red Peppers

Southwestern Black Beans

Pork Tenderloin with Chorizo and Salsa Verde

Chocolate Mini-Tortes with Cinnamon Cream Sauce

Game Night Pizza   186

Caesar Salad

Smoked Duck and Caramelized Onion Pizza

Shrimp, Avocado, and Tomato Pizza

Feta, Sun-Dried Tomato, and Artichoke Pizza

Hazelnut Biscotti

Slow-Cooked Pork Dinner   196

Butterhead Lettuce with Parmesan
    and Fresh Mushrooms

Sesame Pork Roast

Sour Cream Mashed Potatoes

Roasted Green Beans

Gingerbread with Lemon Sauce

A New Bird   204

Spinach with Apple, Blue Cheese, and Walnuts
    with Shallot Vinaigrette

Roast Capon with Wild Mushroom Sauce

Riced Potatoes

Roasted Carrots with Thyme

Orange–Chocolate Chunk Cheesecake

Thanksgiving Feast   212

Fall Fruit Salad

Orange-Marinated Brined Smoked Turkey

Focaccia Dressing with Chanterelles and Sage

Easy Cranberry Relish

Balsamic-Glazed Pearl Onions

Pumpkin Ice Cream Pie or Maple Pumpkin Pie

FALL

RECESPE BY COURSE

Make Ahead

UP TO 2 DAYS IN ADVANCE

Make soup and croutons.

Make red pepper sauce (use chicken broth or water instead of drippings; the latter can be used if the sauce is made after the chicken is cooked).

UP TO 8 HOURS IN ADVANCE

Make cake and frosting.

Stuff chicken.

Make pilaf.

Clean and slice squash.

LAST-MINUTE PREP

Reheat soup.

Bake chicken.

Reheat pilaf.

Sauté squash.

Shortcut Savvy

Buy prepared croutons.

Skip the Roasted Red Pepper Sauce; the stuffed chicken breasts are flavorful enough to serve without the sauce.

Buy a dessert from the bakery.

KICK OFF THE SEASON DINNER

For 8

Garlic-Thyme Soup with Homemade Croutons
Stuffed Chicken Breasts with Roasted Red Pepper Sauce
Rice Pilaf with Sage
Squash Sauté
Devil's Food Cake with Milk Chocolate–Sour Cream Frosting

THIS IS THE SEASON for dining formally, as entertaining makes a quick retreat to the indoors, packing away its casual alfresco style along with the picnic tables and potato salad as surely as we do the flip-flops and tank tops of warm weather. Whether we dress up or dress down, we're together at the table without a hint of sunburn in sight, as we reach for the sustenance of the new season: the heavier flavors so welcome to savor as we stave off the chill of the evening.

The courses are simple but elegant presentations. A bowl of steamy garlic soup and slices of chicken breast stuffed with spinach and a garlic-herb cheese lend an air of formality. Rice pilaf, sage, and squash offer comfort and a reminder that the growing season—and farmers' markets—are coming to a close. Dessert shifts from casual to formal, too, as we return to the oven with a luscious chocolate cake. As the sun gets lower in the horizon, we find ourselves back at the hearth.

Garlic-Thyme Soup with Homemade Croutons

SERVES 8

24 garlic cloves or more (about 3 heads)

2 tablespoons olive oil

4 medium onions, chopped (about 3 cups)

3 ribs celery, chopped

1¼ cups white wine

10 cups chicken broth

1½ tablespoons chopped fresh thyme, or 1½ teaspoon dried thyme

Homemade croutons, for garnish (see recipe)

Fresh thyme leaves, for garnish

To easily peel garlic cloves: Separate the cloves and scald them in boiling water for 1 minute. Slip off and discard the skins and the water.

In a large stockpot, heat olive oil. Add garlic cloves and onions; sauté until onions are soft. Add celery and sauté for a few minutes more. Add wine and simmer for 10 minutes.

Add broth and thyme; bring to a boil. Reduce heat, cover, and simmer for about 45 minutes. Purée soup in a blender or food processor, and return it to the pan. Reheat soup before serving. Garnish with homemade croutons and fresh thyme leaves, if desired.

HOMEMADE CROUTONS

Makes 2 cups

2 cups of ½-inch cubed hearty bread, such as dark rye or multigrain

2 tablespoons olive oil

1 teaspoon dried Italian seasoning (available in the spice department) or
   1 tablespoon grated Parmesan

Preheat oven to 325° F. Toss bread with olive oil until lightly coated. Sprinkle Italian seasoning or grated Parmesan on the bread and toss again. Spread out bread cubes on a baking sheet and bake 10 minutes. Shake pan to turn cubes over and bake 5 to 10 minutes longer, or until golden brown. Cool and store in airtight container.

Beverage

Start out with an Italian prosecco sparkling wine and follow up with a Spanish Rioja or Oregon pinot noir. For dessert, offer coffee.

Stuffed Chicken Breasts with Roasted Red Pepper Sauce

SERVES 8

STUFFING
½ (10-ounce) package frozen chopped spinach, thawed and squeezed to
   remove excess moisture (see Note)
2 (4- to 5-ounce) packages soft garlic and herb cheese spread, such as
   Rondelé or Alouette

CHICKEN
8 large boneless and skinless chicken breast halves (6 to 8 ounces each)
Salt and pepper
4 tablespoons (½ stick) butter, melted

ROASTED RED PEPPER SAUCE
1 (12- to 13-ounce) jar roasted red peppers
¼ to ½ cup pan drippings from chicken, chicken broth, or water
2 tablespoons red wine vinegar

FOR STUFFING
In a bowl, mix spinach and cheese together; set aside.

FOR CHICKEN
Preheat oven to 400° F.

Pound chicken breasts until uniformly thin, about ¼ inch thick. Season
with salt and pepper. Smooth about 2 tablespoons spinach-cheese stuffing
over each breast. Fold in the long sides of the chicken and roll the breast up;
close with a skewer.

Place chicken breasts in a shallow roasting pan without crowding.
Brush tops with melted butter. Bake uncovered for 25 to 30 minutes, basting a few times. Remove from heat and let rest for at least 10 minutes. To
serve, remove skewers and slice each breast into four portions. If preparing individual plates, fan out portions on rice pilaf or atop a pool of the red
pepper sauce.

FOR RED PEPPER SAUCE

Drain peppers and rinse off any black particles. Purée roasted peppers in a blender or food processor; then transfer to a saucepan. Add enough pan drippings, chicken broth, or water to make a sauce of desired consistency, starting with ¼ cup. Add vinegar and heat thoroughly. Serve under, alongside, or drizzled on top of the chicken, or pour into a serving dish to pass at the table.

Note: *Reserve the extra ½ package of frozen spinach for another use, such as stuffing a pork tenderloin. If you prefer, you can substitute fresh spinach for frozen. In that case, coarsely chop about 5 ounces to make ⅓ to ½ cup, and mix it, uncooked, into the cheese.*

Rice Pilaf with Sage

SERVES 8

4 tablespoons (½ stick) butter or olive oil
1 medium onion, chopped (about ¾ cup)
2 cups uncooked long-grain rice
1 teaspoon salt
4 cups chicken broth or water
1 tablespoon chopped fresh sage
¼ cup chopped fresh parsley

Melt butter in a large saucepan over low heat, increase heat to medium and sauté onion until translucent. Add rice and salt; cook for about 3 minutes until the rice starts to brown, stirring to coat all the rice grains with butter. Add chicken broth and sage; bring to a boil. Stir once, then cover and cook over low heat for about 15 minutes, until the liquid is almost absorbed and the rice is tender. Do not stir again. Remove from heat and let sit for 5 minutes before serving. Stir in the parsley and serve. (If making this in advance, reheat in the oven with the chicken, adding about ¼ cup water to the mixture to keep it from drying out.)

Squash Sauté
SERVES 8

¼ cup olive oil
2 or 3 medium zucchini (about 2 pounds), cut into ¼- to ½-inch slices
    (see Note)
2 or 3 small yellow summer squash (about 2 pounds), cut into ¼- to
    ½-inch slices
Salt
½ cup freshly grated Parmesan cheese, for garnish

Heat oil in saucepan. Add zucchini, summer squash, and salt to taste; cover and cook about 8 minutes, until squash is tender. Garnish with Parmesan cheese.

> **Note:** *If the zucchini skin seems tough, then peel it. (This shouldn't be necessary with smaller zucchini.)*

Devil's Food Cake with
Milk Chocolate–Sour Cream Frosting
SERVES 8 TO 12

From Lucia Watson, chef-owner of Lucia's Restaurant in Minneapolis, Minnesota, and James Beard Foundation nominee for best chef in the Midwest.

CAKE
½ cup sifted unsweetened cocoa powder
1 cup boiling water
2¼ cups flour
½ teaspoon baking soda
1 teaspoon baking powder
½ teaspoon salt
8 tablespoons (1 stick) butter
1½ cups light brown sugar
3 eggs
1 teaspoon vanilla
½ cup buttermilk (see Note)

FROSTING:
6 ounces milk chocolate, cut into pieces
4 tablespoons (½ stick) butter
1 tablespoon light brown sugar
1 teaspoon vanilla
½ cup sour cream

FOR CAKE
Preheat oven to 350° F. Grease and flour 2 (8-inch) round cake pans.

In a small bowl, whisk together cocoa powder and boiling water; set aside to cool.

In a large bowl, sift together flour, baking soda, baking powder, and salt; set aside.

In another large bowl, cream 8 tablespoons butter and 1½ cups brown sugar until light and fluffy. Add eggs and 1 teaspoon vanilla; continue beating until smooth. Add about ⅓ of the flour mixture to the butter mixture and beat until smooth; add ½ the cocoa mixture and beat until smooth; add ½ the buttermilk and beat until smooth. Repeat process until all ingredients have been incorporated into the batter.

Pour batter into the prepared pans and bake about 25 to 35 minutes, or until the cakes spring back when gently touched with your fingers. Take cakes out of the oven and cool on a wire rack for 10 minutes before removing from the pans.

FOR FROSTING

In a small saucepan, melt the chocolate over low heat, stirring constantly. Set aside to cool.

In a medium bowl, beat together 4 tablespoons butter, 1 tablespoon brown sugar, 1 teaspoon vanilla, and sour cream until light and fluffy. Gradually add the chocolate and continue to beat until fluffy. Place one layer of cake on a serving plate and spread the top with one-third of the frosting for a layer of filling; place the second cake layer on top of the first layer and spread the rest of the frosting over the top and sides of the cake.

Note: *Powdered buttermilk is a good product to have on hand for baking such as this. It's available in the baking section of supermarkets.*

OKTOBERFEST DINNER

For 6

Hungarian Goulash
Spaetzle
Red Cabbage with Bacon and Caraway
Rye or Pumpernickel Bread
Easy Apple Strudel

UNDER THE OPEN-AIR AWNING of the Cafe Glockenspiel in Salzburg, Austria, we were torn between scenery and hunger. In front of us, the wide-open plaza—Mozartplatz—beckoned with street vendors and history. At our table, an impatient youngster implored us for food.

Hunger won, and we shifted our gaze to the menu in German before us.

We searched the listings for familiar phrases. *Hahn* means chicken. *Schwein*, pork. *Spargel*, asparagus. Still early in our trip, we read the menu slowly, painstakingly, as we paged through a traveler's dictionary to look up uncertain terms. With relief, and some surprise, our eyes stopped at the mention of *gulasch* on the menu. As we sounded out the letters, pulling its syllables apart like a lesson in phonetics, the word rang familiar. *Gu-lasch.* Goulash. Ah, yes. A familiar dish in unfamiliar territory.

As it turned out, the meal bore no resemblance to the macaroni hot dish by the same name that we made at home. Which was all for the better, the hot dish being fast but not terribly memorable. Gulasch, however, was another dish. Our first bite of the hearty paprika-flavored stew was not to be our last.

During family travels throughout Germany and Austria, when in doubt about a meal, at least one of us—usually that same impatient youngster—ordered the simple, now comfortingly familiar stew of beef and onions. From Frankfurt, Germany, to Vienna, Austria, the dish was on each menu, sometimes served with veal, other times as a soup (gulaschsuppe).

No matter what version of the stew we ate, on the platter alongside was a pile of spaetzle, squiggles of dough about the size of a child's little finger. More often than not, a mound of red cabbage accompanied the dish.

We were hooked on the whole meal and, once home, determined to re-create it. And we did. (Actually, I did. The only joint effort was in eating. But we were all in agreement; it was—and is—really good.)

It's the season for Oktoberfest, so let's celebrate with a menu of flavors from Germany and Austria, with a little Hungary thrown in (and with plenty of German beer for the occasion). All three countries were once part of the same empire, and the foods, consequently, cross present-day borders with ease.

Beverage

For this German-influenced meal, German beer is an excellent choice. For those who prefer wine, go with a lighter red Burgundy or pinto noir with the goulash. Or go the Hungarian route with Egri Bikavér (EH-grih BIH-kah-vahr), Hungary's most famous red wine (quality varies a lot so avoid the cheapest bottle). For the strudel, sip on a Tokay, Hungary's famous sweet wine from the region of the same name.

Hungarian goulash (we'll use the American spelling), known as *gulyas* in Hungary, isn't much more than beef and onions braised in a paprika-flavored sauce. Although described as a stew, the goulash, with its thin sauce, seems more like a variation on beef stroganoff.

Guten appetit!

Hungarian Goulash
SERVES 6

3 pounds boneless beef chuck steak (or boneless stew meat or sirloin), trimmed of fat and cut into 1-inch cubes
4 tablespoons oil, divided
3 large onions, cut into slices (about 3 cups)
2 tablespoons red wine vinegar
3 tablespoons Hungarian sweet paprika
1 (10½-ounce) can beef broth, divided
1 tablespoon tomato paste
Salt and pepper
Sour cream, for garnish
Finely chopped parsley, for garnish
Additional Hungarian sweet paprika, for garnish

In a Dutch oven or large pot, brown cubes of meat in 2 tablespoons oil; remove from pan. Add 2 tablespoons oil to the pan and over medium heat sauté onion slices until limp. Return browned meat to the pan with onions, along with vinegar, paprika, and 1 cup beef broth.

Cover mixture, bring to a simmer, and braise for about 45 minutes, or until meat is tender, adding additional beef broth if liquid cooks away. During the last 5 minutes, stir in tomato paste; season to taste with salt and pepper (see Note).

Serve goulash on top or alongside spaetzle or egg noodles. To garnish, top with a dollop of sour cream and sprinkle with finely chopped parsley and paprika.

COOK'S NOTES

This dish makes use of paprika, which is made of ground up sweet red peppers,. This gives the stew its rich red color and, not so incidentally, puts vitamin C into the mixture. (A Hungarian scientist won a Nobel Prize for research into the vitamin content of paprika. It has more vitamin C than citrus fruits.) Hungarian paprika has a more pungent flavor than does the spice sold without the country designation. It comes in both a hot and sweet version; the sweet works well with the goulash recipe.

Variation: Instead of braising the meat, the mixture can be cooked in a pressure cooker for 10 to 15 minutes (with all the ingredients but the garnishes in the pot), depending on the cut of meat used. Or prepare the meat in a slow cooker for 3 hours on high or 6 to 9 hours on low.

Serve goulash with a hearty bread, such as rye or pumpernickel, in the German fashion with plenty of butter. This bread, traditional for the meal, is readily available at supermarkets and bakeries.

Note: *The sauce will be very thin if served the European way, as described here. However, if you or your guests prefer a thicker, gravylike sauce, remove the meat and vegetables at the end of cooking, and thicken the sauce with a little flour. Then return the meat and vegetables to the sauce before serving.*

Spaetzle
MAKES 6 CUPS (6 TO 8 SERVINGS)

This version of spaetzle is lightly flavored with nutmeg, which gives it an unexpected flavor to savor. If you don't like nutmeg, don't use the flavoring. Spaetzle can be made 24 hours in advance and refrigerated, then reheated.

3 cups flour
½ teaspoon salt
¼ teaspoon nutmeg
3 eggs
1 cup milk
1 tablespoon (or more) water

In a medium bowl, thoroughly mix flour, salt, and nutmeg. In a large bowl, beat eggs until foamy; mix in milk.

Add flour mixture to egg mixture a little at a time, beating by hand, until the flour is thoroughly incorporated. Add 1 tablespoon water and mix the batter thoroughly. If batter is too stiff to go through the holes of a colander or spaetzle maker, add additional water, 1 tablespoon at a time. (See Note.)

Bring water to a boil in a large, wide kettle (wider pots will cook more spaetzle at one time). Place either a colander with large holes or a spaetzle
Continued on page 166.

maker over the boiling water. Add the batter to either utensil, pressing the batter through the holes and dropping the spaetzle into the water. Prepare only as many as will fit in the width of the kettle.

Cook the spaetzle, uncovered, for 2 to 3 minutes. Spaetzle will rise to the surface when done. Remove with a slotted spoon and place in a bowl. Repeat with remaining batter.

If using immediately, cover the bowl to keep spaetzle warm while you cook the remaining batter. If preparing for later use, place spaetzle in a large bowl of ice water to cool; then drain thoroughly, cover, and refrigerate. When ready to serve, reheat spaetzle in one of three ways: in a saucepan with a little butter, in a microwave if you want to avoid the use of butter, or in boiling water, briefly; then drain.

Variation: Omit the nutmeg and flavor with a little mustard, either dry powder or from a mustard jar.

Note: *Spaetzle (SCHPEHT-suhl) are a cross between pasta and dumplings. Originating in southwestern Germany, in the region of Swabia, spaetzle are popular throughout Germany and Austria, where they often are served in place of potatoes. Most American cookbooks suggest that, to form the spaetzle, the batter be pushed through a colander with large holes. But that's a lot of work, and an inexpensive spaetzle maker cuts the time considerably. For those Scandinavians with a potato ricer in the cupboard, that device could be substituted (they also squeeze food through small holes).*

The spaetzle maker, which is available in kitchen specialty shops, looks like a flat grater with a little box on top to hold the batter. Like the potato ricer, the spaetzle maker does a single task and does it really well. If you like your first taste of spaetzle, you may want to buy the inexpensive gadget. If you use a colander as a substitute, you'll need to thin out the spaetzle with water until it can easily go through the large holes. The first time I tried the spaetzle maker, the recipe took about 30 minutes to complete; later it became much faster.

Red Cabbage with Bacon and Caraway

SERVES 6 TO 8

1 small head red cabbage (see Note)

5 slices bacon

2 tablespoons bacon drippings or salad oil

5 tablespoons vinegar

1½ teaspoons sugar

¾ teaspoon dry mustard

1 teaspoon caraway seeds

Shred cabbage, either by hand or with a mandoline or grater. Set aside.

To make dressing, fry bacon in a large pan until crisp. Remove bacon from pan and place on paper toweling to absorb excess fat. When cool, crumble bacon into small pieces and set aside.

Drain all but 2 tablespoons bacon drippings from the pan (or use salad oil). Add vinegar, sugar, and dry mustard to the pan. Bring to a boil and remove from heat. Add cabbage and toss in dressing for about 60 seconds, until cabbage is slightly cooked from the heat of the dressing.

Put cabbage in serving bowl and toss with crumbled bacon and caraway seeds. Serve immediately.

Note: *The big pieces you get from shredding cabbage by hand work well for this recipe. Coarsely shredded red cabbage is available in some supermarkets (a 10-ounce bag contains about 10 cups).*

COOK'S NOTES

Though red cabbage is the traditional side dish for goulash, for this meal it's given a slightly different presentation, tossed with caraway seeds and a warm bacon dressing like the one used with the more familiar wilted-spinach salad. If you don't like red cabbage, use the dressing with fresh spinach. The caraway seeds, which give rye bread its distinctive flavor, come from a plant in the parsley family that is native to Europe. With its strong flavor, caraway should only be used sparingly.

Easy Apple Strudel
SERVES 6

A German cook might raise an eyebrow at this recipe, but no one else will. This old family recipe is *wunderbar*.

CRUST
2½ cups flour
1 tablespoon sugar
1 teaspoon salt
1 cup shortening
1 egg, separated
½ cup milk

FILLING
1 cup sugar
1 tablespoon cinnamon
5 tart apples (such as Granny Smith), peeled and cored
2 to 3 tablespoons butter, cut in small pieces

TO MAKE CRUST
In a large bowl, thoroughly mix flour, 1 tablespoon sugar, and salt. With a fork or pastry blender, cut in shortening. In a small bowl, whisk egg yolk and milk together and add to dough, mixing in thoroughly.

Divide dough into 2 pieces, with one slightly larger than the other. Take the larger half and roll into rectangle about 8 x 14 inches. Place on an ungreased jelly roll pan (see Notes).

TO MAKE FILLING AND FINISH STRUDEL
Preheat oven to 350° F.

In large bowl, mix together 1 cup sugar and the cinnamon. Slice apples about ¼-inch thick and add to cinnamon sugar. Spread apple filling over crust, leaving ¾ inch bare around the edges. Dot with butter.

Roll out remaining dough and place on top of apple filling. Fold edge of bottom crust over top edge and crimp as for pie. Cut a few slits in the top of the strudel. Brush top crust with egg white.

COOK'S NOTES
Apple strudel is another traditional German dish. Although cookbooks often suggest that it be made with phyllo leaves, the paper-thin pastry used with many Mediterranean dishes, our samplings across Germany and Austria didn't turn up a single strudel made like this. What we found was heavy-duty strudel that was much like pie crust in texture. So is the one in this recipe.

Bake for 25 minutes or until crust is lightly browned and firm. Remove pan from oven and let strudel cool slightly on pan. To serve warm, cut into individual pieces. Or keep intact and cut later, served at room temperature.

Variation: A dab of cinnamon-flavored whipped cream on top makes a wonderful finish to this dessert. But for this menu, with the sour-cream-topped goulash, whipped cream for dessert is a bit much. Save the suggestion for another meal.

Notes:
- *To save time, replace the fresh apple filling with 1 (21-ounce) can apple pie filling.*
- *Be sure to use a sheet with rims to prevent the filling from running off the sides while baking.*

Make Ahead

UP TO A DAY IN ADVANCE

Cook squash; make soup.

Prep the meat.

Thaw the phyllo.

Make leek appetizer.

Make pear crisp.

UP TO 3 HOURS IN ADVANCE

Cook meat.

LAST-MINUTE PREP

Make polenta.

Reheat crisp.

Shortcut Savvy

Use prepared puréed squash, available either frozen or as baby food.

Buy prepared fruit crisp.

Beverage

For the soup, serve either an unoaked chardonnay or chablis. For the short ribs, move on to a petite sirah or Rioja. For the cranberry pear crisp, go with a pear liqueur, such as pear eu de vie.

AUTUMN FLAVORS

For 6

Gingered Squash Soup
Caramelized Leek, Goat Cheese, and Sun-Dried Tomato Triangles
Braised Short Ribs
Creamy Polenta
Cranberry-Pear Crisp

AS SURELY AS I REACH for my wool coat and warm mittens when the leaves turn to crimson and gold, so do I pull out the soup pot and casserole dishes that were set aside for months. Once again the windows steam up from the bubbling pots on the stove and make a cozy nest of the warm kitchen. The heady perfume of dinner fills every corner and seeps out-of-doors, teasing passersby with hints of an upcoming meal. We nestle in for the coming cold months, wrapping ourselves in the hearty flavors of the season that keep us warm and content.

For this menu we start out with a lightly gingered squash soup with a color alone that shouts fall. Small phyllo bites of warm, savory caramelized flavors serve as an accompaniment for this starter. Or offer them earlier as an appetizer with wine. For the main course long-cooking braised short ribs show how a great meal doesn't require a lot of time in the kitchen for the cook. An age-old starch—polenta—dresses up the menu. For the finish a cranberry-pear version of the traditional apple crisp offers just the right change of taste.

Gingered Squash Soup
SERVES 6

About 3 pounds winter squash, such as delicata or butternut (about
    4 cups cooked) (see Note)
1 tablespoon (or more) grated fresh ginger root
3 cups vegetable stock (or water or chicken stock)
Salt and white pepper
1 teaspoon ground nutmeg
1 cup heavy cream
Sour cream, for garnish

Preheat oven to 350° F. Cut squash in half and scoop out seeds. (If the squash is too hard to cut in half, poke holes in it with a knife and microwave for several minutes to soften.)

Place squash halves face down in a lightly oiled baking dish or on a baking sheet; cover with aluminum foil. Bake until the pulp is soft, about 1 hour. Scoop pulp from the skin; discard skin.

In a large, heavy saucepan over medium-high heat, stir together cooked squash, ginger, and stock. Bring to a boil; then reduce heat. Simmer for about 20 minutes, breaking up squash with a spoon. Remove soup from heat and purée with a food processor or blender until smooth. If desired, strain for a smoother texture. Season to taste with salt and pepper and add nutmeg.

Stir in cream and heat throughout. Serve hot, garnished with a small dab of sour cream.

Note: *You can use any hard-skinned winter squash for this soup, including cooking pumpkin (but not the oversized type used for jack-o'-lanterns).*

Caramelized Leek, Goat Cheese, and Sun-Dried Tomato Triangles
MAKES 32 APPETIZERS

Goat cheese too tangy for you? Use cream cheese. This goes nicely with the squash soup. Or serve it separately as an appetizer. Adapted from a recipe by chef Jonathan Gelman, who served this to a conference of food editors in Napa Valley.

½ cup dry-packed sun-dried tomatoes, cut into ¼-inch dice
1 tablespoon minced red onion
2 tablespoons minced shallots
1½ teaspoons olive oil
1 tablespoon red wine vinegar
1½ teaspoons brown sugar
¾ cup finely diced leeks (about two leeks)
1½ tablespoons butter
12 ounces (1½ cups) goat cheese (chèvre), at room temperature
1½ tablespoons chopped fresh thyme
Salt and freshly ground pepper
8 sheets of phyllo dough (see Note)
¼ cup melted butter

In a small pan over medium heat, sauté the tomatoes, onions, and shallots in olive oil, stirring frequently, until the onions are softened, about 5 minutes. Add the vinegar and sugar and sauté, stirring constantly, until the vinegar evaporates. Remove from heat, and reserve.

In a large pan over medium heat, sauté leeks in 1½ tablespoons butter, stirring frequently, until they are golden, about 10 minutes. Remove from heat, fold in the goat cheese and thyme, and season to taste with salt and pepper. Stir in the onion-tomato mixture.

Unfold the phyllo dough; keep unused sheets covered with damp paper toweling. Lightly brush 1 sheet of phyllo with melted butter. Top with another sheet of phyllo; brush lightly with butter. Using a sharp knife, cut the phyllo dough in half, widthwise. Cut each half into 4 even strips across the short side, giving you 8 strips.

Place a generous ½ tablespoon of the goat cheese mixture at the base of 1 strip. Fold a corner of the strip over the filling to enclose it. Continue to flag-fold the strip into a neat triangle. Lightly brush the edges with a little butter. Continue with remaining strips. Chill triangles for 20 minutes. (Can be made in advance to this point and refrigerated or frozen.)

Preheat oven to 350° F. Bake the triangles until they are golden brown, 15 to 20 minutes. Cool briefly on a baking rack. Serve warm.

Note: *Remember that phyllo dough, found in the freezer section of the supermarket, comes frozen and must defrost overnight in the refrigerator, so plan accordingly.*

Braised Short Ribs

SERVES 6

½ cup flour
Salt and freshly ground black pepper
About 12 beef short ribs (about 3 pounds), excess fat trimmed (see Notes)
2 tablespoons vegetable oil
3 medium carrots, chopped into ½-inch pieces (about 1 ½ cups)
2 medium onions, quartered
2 tablespoons chopped garlic
3 cups beef or chicken broth, or water
3 bay leaves
4 fresh sage leaves, or 1 teaspoon dried (optional)
4 sprigs fresh thyme, or 1 teaspoon dried (optional)

Preheat oven to 350° F.

In a pie plate or shallow bowl, season flour generously with salt and pepper. Dredge ribs in the flour. Heat oil in a large heavy skillet or Dutch oven. Brown the ribs in batches; set meat aside. Pour off all but 2 tablespoons fat from the pan, and cook carrots and onions over medium heat, about 5 minutes. Add the garlic and sauté for an additional minute.

Combine the ribs and vegetables in a Dutch oven or a casserole dish with a cover. Add broth, bay leaves, sage, and thyme. Cover and roast for 2½ to 3 hours, or until the meat falls away from the bone.

Remove the meat from the pan and place on a plate, covered, to keep warm. Strain the liquid, discarding vegetables. Return liquid to Dutch oven or heavy pan and skim off all but 1 tablespoon of fat. On the stovetop over high heat, heat sauce until it thickens and reduces slightly. Serve with polenta.

Variation: For additional flavor, add a 12-ounce bottle of dark beer to the liquid and reduce the broth to 2 cups. Or add a can of crushed tomatoes.

Variation: Serve the beef with mashed potatoes or sauerkraut instead of polenta.

Notes:

- *How many ribs you need will depend on the size of those available and on your guests. Generally plan on two per person.*
- *Other cooking methods: With a Dutch oven, you can cook this on top of the stove at a simmer. You also can make this recipe in a slow cooker. For either one begin by browning the ribs and sautéing the vegetables on the stovetop.*

  For a crusty exterior to the ribs, whichever cooking method is used, the ribs can be browned after they are cooked. To do so, increase the oven temperature to 450° F and place the ribs on a roasting rack in a pan. Sprinkle with salt and pepper and bake for about 10 to 12 minutes while the sauce is thickening.

COOK'S NOTES

Beef short ribs are not to be confused with the more familiar back ribs, which are mostly bones. Short ribs are the meaty version cut from the end of the rib. They tend to be fatty (which is why you cut off any exterior fat and remove the drippings after browning them) and tough (which is why they cook a long time). That combination of fatty and tough means a flavorful meal that needs little attention from the cook. If you plan ahead, salt the meat a day or two before it is braised to enhance the flavor of the meat. Just sprinkle the meat lightly with salt, cover, and refrigerate. No need to rinse off the salt before browning, but don't add more salt to the dredging flour. Really planning ahead? You could prepare the ribs a couple days in advance; then reheat them in a 350° F oven, covered, for about 30 minutes.

COOK'S NOTES

Popular in northern Italy, polenta is a cornmeal mush that is particularly good with roasted meats. Don't let the word "mush" throw you. Think of it as a creamy alternative to mashed potatoes.

Creamy Polenta

SERVES 6 TO 8

5½ cups water, divided (see Note)
1 teaspoon salt
1 cup yellow cornmeal (see Note)
8 tablespoons (1 stick) butter, cut into small pieces
¼ cup freshly grated Parmesan

In a large saucepan, bring 4 cups water to a boil with salt. Meanwhile, in a medium bowl, stir together another 1½ cups water and cornmeal. Gradually add the cornmeal to the boiling water, over medium heat, stirring constantly. Reduce the heat to low and cook until the cornmeal is thick, about 10 minutes, stirring occasionally. Stir in butter and Parmesan. Serve immediately.

Variation: Substitute a blue cheese, such as Gorgonzola, instead of the Parmesan.

> **Note:** *A fast-cooking version of cornmeal is sometimes available at the supermarket. If using that, follow the cooking instructions on the package. You can substitute chicken broth for water, or use half water and "half chicken broth.*

Cranberry-Pear Crisp
SERVES 6 TO 8

FILLING

8 ripe pears, peeled, cored, and cut in ¼-inch slices

1 tablespoon lemon juice

2 cups fresh cranberries

¼ cup granulated sugar

1 teaspoon cinnamon

TOPPING

1 cup rolled oats

¾ cup flour

½ cup firmly packed brown sugar

8 tablespoons (1 stick) butter, softened and cut into pieces

Whipped cream, for garnish

Preheat oven to 350° F.

Toss the pear slices in lemon juice and combine with cranberries in an ungreased 9 x 13-inch baking pan (see Notes); toss with granulated sugar and cinnamon.

In a bowl, mix oats, flour, brown sugar, and butter with a fork until crumbly. Sprinkle over fruit mixture. Bake for 30 minutes, or until the fruit is tender and the topping is lightly browned. Serve warm, at room temperature, or chilled. Top with a dab of whipped cream.

Notes:

- *Prefer apples to pears or cranberries? The fruit in this recipe can be mixed and matched however you prefer, even substituting apples for one of the fruits. Keep in mind that the ¼ cup granulated sugar is for the cranberries, because of their tartness; if you eliminate or decrease the cranberries, the granulated sugar should also be cut.*
- *Want some style for serving? Bake these in individual ramekins instead of a 9 x 13-inch pan.*

UP TO 2 WEEKS IN ADVANCE

Make Chocolate Mini-Tortes
and freeze them.

Grind ancho chiles, if
necessary.

UP TO A DAY IN ADVANCE

Make Pineapple Salsa.

Make Pico de Gallo.

Make Salsa Verde.

If using dry black beans, begin
soaking them.

Make Cinnamon Cream
Sauce.

UP TO 8 HOURS IN ADVANCE

Stuff tenderloins.

UP TO 2 HOURS IN ADVANCE

Make quesadillas.

LAST-MINUTE PREP

Heat Southwestern Black
Beans.

Cook tenderloins.

Assemble mini-tortes for
dessert.

SOUTHWESTERN DINNER

For 6

Pineapple Salsa and Pico de Gallo
Quesadillas with Brie and Roasted Red Peppers
Southwestern Black Beans
Pork Tenderloin with Chorizo and Salsa Verde
Chocolate Mini-Tortes with Cinnamon Cream Sauce

MAYBE IT'S THE DINNERWARE, those colorful platters of cornflower blue, desert rose, and cactus green, that catches our interest. Then again, maybe it's the margaritas.

Whatever the incentive, we've adopted Southwestern fare as our own with an embrace as wide as the Rio Grande. Call it Tex-Mex, Santa Fe, Mexican, or Southwestern, the name itself means less than the flavors do: spicy and earthy. This regional cooking with a centuries-old heritage creatively balances the many foodstuffs grown in arid, warm climates— the very places many midwesterners head after the leaves fall and the air catches a chill.

And so, this menu turns to the Southwest, where the dinner table typically holds a bottle of hot sauce and mealtime make uses of Southwestern staples: roasted red peppers, jalapeño and ancho chiles, tomatillo, chorizo, black beans, cilantro, and a vanilla bean.

Southwestern cooks pride themselves on improvisation, borrowing flavors and techniques from neighboring Mexico. Their results take a little more effort in the kitchen because fewer commercially made alternatives are available as backup. That's true, too, with this menu. But with some moderate planning and cooking ahead, this menu is manageable for the busiest of cooks.

Pineapple Salsa
MAKES ABOUT 2 CUPS

1 medium-size fresh pineapple, in ¼-inch dice (about 2 cups)
6 green onions, in fine slices (about ⅓ cup)
1 teaspoon diced fresh sage

In a bowl, toss together pineapple, onion, and sage. Let stand at least 30 minutes to allow the flavors to mingle. Serve at room temperature or slightly chilled.

Quesadillas with Brie and Roasted Red Peppers
SERVES 6

About 1 pound Brie cheese
6 or more flour tortillas
About 3 cups (12 ounce jar) roasted red peppers, chopped coarsely
3 avocados, sliced (see Note)
Vegetable spray coating or olive oil
Pineapple Salsa (see recipe on page 179)
Pico de Gallo (see recipe on page 83)

Cut off the edible rind of the Brie and save for nibbling later. Spread Brie over half of each tortilla, about ¼ inch thick. (If Brie is hard to spread, let it warm for a few minutes to room temperature.) Top Brie with a layer of roasted red peppers, then avocados. Fold empty half of tortilla over the layers of vegetables, forming tortilla into a half circle.

In a frying pan or electric skillet, spray a thin layer of vegetable coating, or add a few drops of oil. Place as many tortillas in the pan as will fit and, over medium heat lightly brown on both sides for only a few minutes, until the cheese has melted and the vegetables are warmed throughout. Repeat until all the tortillas are heated.

Cut tortillas into triangles (as you would a pie) and serve immediately with a variety of salsas, such as pineapple and pico de gallo.

Variation: You also could add cooked shrimp and chopped fresh cilantro.

Note: *To be sure the avocado is ripe when needed, buy it several days in advance.*

Southwestern Black Beans

SERVES 6

3 (16-ounce) cans cooked black beans (about 4½ cups)
1 garlic clove, minced (about 1 teaspoon)
1 medium onion, diced (about ¾ cup)
2 teaspoons olive oil
¾ cup water or chicken broth
1 teaspoon dried thyme
1 teaspoon dried oregano
6 large sweet red chile peppers, for serving (optional)

Rinse and drain beans. Sauté garlic and onion in olive oil.

Combine beans and sautéed garlic and onion in a saucepan; add enough water or chicken broth to cover. Add the thyme and oregano. Bring to a simmer and heat through; drain any remaining liquid.

To serve, slit an opening in the side of the sweet red chile peppers and remove the seeds. Stuff beans into each pepper (which looks quite dramatic on the plate).

Note: *To prepare dried black beans, soak 2 cups of them in 6 to 8 cups water overnight, discarding any beans that float and draining liquid. Or for a quick soaking method, put them in a saucepan with 6 to 8 cups cold water. Bring to a boil and simmer for 2 minutes. Remove from heat, cover, and let sit for 1 hour. Drain before cooking. To cook soaked beans, place them in saucepan and cover generously with water. Bring to a boil, reduce heat to a simmer, cover, and cook until tender, about 45 minutes. Drain.*

COOK'S NOTES

Until recently, cooks had to plan ahead to prepare dried black beans, which are also known as turtle beans. First the beans had to be soaked overnight; then simmered for about an hour, until tender. The alternative is a good choice: canned precooked black beans. Keep in mind, though, that black beans aren't difficult to cook from scratch. Only needing an occasional peek to be sure the cooking liquid hasn't simmered away, black beans take little actual attention; they just require advance planning.

Pork Tenderloin with Chorizo and Salsa Verde

SERVES 6

2 dried ancho chiles, or 1 well-rounded tablespoon ancho chile powder
   (or substitute 1 tablespoon ground red chili powder and 1 teaspoon
   ground cumin)
3 pounds pork tenderloins, trimmed of all visible fat (see Note)
3 to 4 links mild or hot chorizo sausage (about 12 ounces)
Olive oil
Salt and freshly ground black pepper
1 tablespoon butter or vegetable cooking spray
Salsa Verde (see recipe)

Preheat oven to 400° F.

Using a food processor or blender, grind ancho chiles to a powder. (Or use preground ancho chile powder; or make a spice blend from ground red chili pepper and ground cumin.) Set aside.

Cut tenderloins into several pieces the length of the chorizo (these smaller pieces will be easier to stuff). With a sharp knife, poke a hole through the center of each chunk of tenderloin. Stuff the chorizo into the hole in the tenderloin chunks (the hole will expand as you do this). Rub outside of each chunk with olive oil; then pat salt, pepper, and ground ancho chile onto the exterior of the meat.

Add butter or vegetable cooking spray to a heavy skillet and preheat on high heat. Sear the meat on all sides until lightly browned. Transfer meat to baking dish and place in oven. Roast 25 to 40 minutes, or until meat is thoroughly cooked. The roasting time will depend on the thickness of the tenderloin and chorizo. Remove the meat from oven at 155° F and let it sit until it registers 160° F. A 1-pound tenderloin, stuffed with chorizo, will take 25 to 30 minutes to cook. The 2-pound size may take 40 to 45 minutes. To check doneness, make a slight cut in the meat. The chorizo will slightly bleed its orangish color onto the meat, but don't let that throw off your inspection.

To serve, slice the meat in ¼- to ½-inch thick pieces. Top with salsa verde or another salsa.

Note: *Pork tenderloins vary in size from 1 to 2 pounds, so to serve six for this meal at least two will be needed. Choose tenderloins that are roughly the same size so they will be done at the same time. Do not use a premarinated tenderloin.*

SALSA VERDE
Makes about 2 cups

8 tomatillos, husks removed

1 small onion, chopped (about ½ cup)

1 clove garlic

1 jalapeño, seeded and sliced (optional)

½ cup chopped fresh cilantro leaves

2 tablespoons fresh lime juice

Dash salt

Wash tomatillos and cut them in quarters. In a food processor or blender, purée tomatillos with onion, jalapeño, garlic, cilantro, and lime juice. Add salt and mix.

COOK'S NOTES

For this menu the pork tenderloin is stuffed with chorizo (chor-EE-zoh), a spicy Mexican sausage. The tenderloins then are dusted with ground ancho chiles, which can range from mild to intensely flavored. Chorizo comes in different degrees of spiciness, so choose yours accordingly. You'll need only a few links of the sausage; save the rest of the package for another meal. Dried ancho chiles are deep reddish-brown in color; when fresh they are green and are called poblano chiles. Dried ancho chiles are usually found in the produce section of grocery stores.

The tart green sauce called salsa verde is made from tomatillos (tohm-ah-TEE-oh), which look like small green tomatoes. They are readily available in the produce section of the supermarket; choose ones that are firm, with tight-fitting husks. The sauce also uses cilantro, a fresh herb widely used in Mexican cooking. Asian cooks call it fresh coriander or Chinese parsley. Though cilantro is widely distributed, should you be unable to find it, the sauce is still good without it. The jalapeño in this recipe also is optional. If you want to ease up on the chiles in this menu, you can cut the jalapeño from the tomatillo sauce and it will still be tasty. To save time, this sauce could also be served as a salsa with the quesadilla, instead of making different salsas for that recipe.

Chocolate Mini-Tortes with
Cinnamon Cream Sauce

MAKES 8 INDIVIDUAL TORTES

MINI-TORTES
8 tablespoons (1 stick) unsalted butter, plus additional for greasing tins
4 (1-ounce) squares bittersweet chocolate, coarsely chopped
3 eggs
½ cup unsweetened cocoa powder, sifted
¾ cup granulated sugar

CINNAMON CREAM SAUCE (MAKES ABOUT 2 CUPS)
2 cups milk
3 tablespoons sugar
¼ teaspoon cinnamon
1-inch piece of vanilla bean
4 egg yolks

FINAL ASSEMBLY
Powdered sugar, for garnish
Cinnamon, for garnish
2 mangoes, sliced, for garnish (see Note)

FOR MINI-TORTES
Preheat the oven to 300° F. Butter a standard-size muffin pan.

Melt butter and bittersweet chocolate in microwave or double boiler. Cool to room temperature.

Beat 3 eggs until thick and frothy, about 1 minute. Beat in cocoa powder and then ¾ cup sugar at low speed to partially blend. Add melted chocolate mixture. Beat at high speed until thickened, about 1½ minutes.

Fill each muffin tin with ⅓ cup batter. Place the pan inside a larger pan filled with enough hot water to reach ½ inch up the sides of the muffin pan (a cooking method the French call *bain-marie*, pronounced bahn mah-REE). Bake for 30 minutes, or until tortes have risen slightly and are firm to the touch. Remove pan from water and cool on a rack. Invert cakes onto parchment or waxed paper. Tortes can be frozen up to 2 weeks. Defrost tortes inside the refrigerator; then bring to room temperature for serving.

FOR CINNAMON CREAM SAUCE

In a heavy saucepan, combine milk, 3 tablespoons sugar, and cinnamon. Split the vanilla bean in half lengthwise and scrape out the seeds into the milk; then add the bean pod. Warm over low heat, stirring occasionally, until the sugar is dissolved.

In a small bowl, whisk the egg yolks slightly. Add a little of the hot milk to the 4 egg yolks to warm them up, and whisk together. Add the egg mixture to the pan with the hot milk, and stir constantly to cook the sauce until it reaches 170° to 175° F (it will still be very thin, only slightly thicker than before).

Pour the sauce through a strainer and place in a container. Add the vanilla bean back into the sauce to flavor it further until you are ready to use it. Cover tightly and refrigerate. Before serving, remove the vanilla bean and bring the sauce to room temperature.

FOR FINAL ASSEMBLY

On each dessert plate, ladle a small pool of Cinnamon Cream Sauce. Place a mini-torte in the pool of sauce. To garnish, sift powdered sugar and cinnamon on top of each serving; arrange a few mango slices on the side.

Notes:

- *Vanilla beans are sold in the spice section of the supermarket.*
- *To be sure the mangoes are ripe when needed, buy them several days in advance.*

COOK'S NOTES

Mexican cooking often taps into chocolate, vanilla, and cinnamon. This dessert makes use of all three with a flourless torte so dense it's almost like a chocolate candy bar, served with a luscious vanilla sauce flavored with a hint of cinnamon. The recipe calls for bittersweet chocolate, but if you can't find that, semisweet can be substituted. The small tortes are prepared in individual portions, but they could be cooked in a small loaf pan, with the baking time adjusted slightly.

The French call this rich vanilla-based sauce crème anglaise (ahn-GLEHZ), but in any language it's a treat. Watch the sauce carefully during preparation because the eggs will scramble if you don't keep stirring the pan. Chefs make designs with sauces like this by putting them into a squirt-style bottle first (such as the plastic picnic bottle used for ketchup or mustard). The designs are then easy to create on the plate.

GAME NIGHT PIZZA

For 6

Caesar Salad
Smoked Duck and Caramelized Onion Pizza
Shrimp, Avocado, and Tomato Pizza
Feta, Sun-Dried Tomato, and Artichoke Pizza
Hazelnut Biscotti

THERE'S A LITTLE-KNOWN ITALIAN saying that goes something like this: You can take the pizza out of the kid, but you can't take the kid out of the pizza.

There's something casual, something kidlike—dare we say adolescent—about eating food with your fingers, which most certainly is part of pizza's appeal. But kids' tastes change, and pepperoni eventually loses some of its cachet.

Were it not for some creative chefs—who are really just kids at heart having fun in the kitchen—pizza might have been relegated to the pizza parlor or sturdy delivery box. Today it's getting another life as a gourmet food of sorts, one suitable for more mature tastes and menus.

For this menu we turn to a meal so casual it's simply a pizza party for grownup tastes. With smoked duck, sun-dried tomatoes, feta cheese, and shrimp—and not a speck of tomato sauce in sight—these distinctive pizzas are designed for adventurous taste buds.

Fall dinner parties can quickly evolve into TV dinners where batting averages or multimillion-dollar free-agent salaries or pass-completion percentages—instead of wine vintages—make up the conversation. The drink of choice with pizza might well be beer. For a gathering where unpredictable flavors are the essence, a selection of very different beers from local microbreweries offers an opportunity for a beer tasting.

The game plan for this menu is simple: The pizza dough, salad croutons, and dessert can all be made quickly the night before or earlier. At dinnertime, have your guests help toss the salad and top the pizzas. For a gathering of six, you're set with three (12-inch) pizzas, which normally serve two each. With salad and dessert, there's plenty to enjoy.

You know you're an adult when you need more than pizza for a meal. This menu calls for a modified Caesar salad, which may soon replace the traditional version made with raw egg, which is considered a health risk. This no-egg Caesar is every bit as good as the original, still tangy and distinctively garlicky. Even those with an aversion to anchovies should be pleased with this taste—which isn't remotely fishy—since they won't see any evidence of the tiny fillets. (The dressing calls for a "Bass-O-Matic" approach to the anchovies, which are puréed in a blender.) If in doubt about your guests' predilections, don't tell them what's in the dressing until after they've had seconds.

As for dessert, let's stick with the informal nature of this gathering, as well as the finger-food nature of a meal of pizza, and serve biscotti.

Caesar Salad
SERVES 6

DRESSING
4 flat anchovy fillets (rinsed for milder flavor, if desired), or about
    2 to 4 teaspoons anchovy paste (see Notes)
4 garlic cloves, minced
⅓ cup olive oil
3 tablespoons red wine vinegar
½ teaspoon dry mustard
¼ teaspoon salt
½ teaspoon pepper

SALAD
1 to 1½ heads of romaine lettuce, torn into bite-size pieces (see Notes)
2 cups Homemade Croutons (for recipe, see page 155)
½ cup grated Parmesan cheese

FOR DRESSING
In a blender, purée anchovies and garlic. Add olive oil, vinegar, mustard, salt, and pepper, and blend again.

FOR SALAD ASSEMBLY
Immediately before serving, place torn lettuce in a salad bowl. Pour dressing over lettuce and toss to coat. Add croutons and most of the Parmesan cheese; toss. Sprinkle remaining Parmesan over salad.

Notes:

- *Use whichever form of anchovies—fillets or paste—is practical for you. Anchovy paste comes in a resealable tube, much like a toothpaste container.*
- *If you prefer another lettuce, by all means use it. Butter lettuce? Curly lettuce? Take your pick. You're the cook.*

Pizza Dough
MAKES 3 (12-INCH) PIZZA CRUSTS

2 envelopes dry yeast
½ teaspoon sugar
1½ cups warm water (105° to 115° F)
3½ cups flour
1 teaspoon salt
Olive oil
Cornmeal

In a bowl, stir yeast and sugar into 1½ cups warm water. Set aside for 10 minutes, or until foamy; stir again. In a large bowl, stir together flour and salt; add yeast mixture and mix thoroughly by hand. The dough will be sticky.

Turn dough out onto a lightly floured surface. Knead for 5 to 10 minutes, adding a little flour as needed, until dough is no longer sticky. (Or knead with an electric mixer with attachments for 5 to 7 minutes.)

Lightly oil dough and place in a bowl large enough to allow it to double in volume. Cover bowl tightly with plastic wrap. Let stand at room temperature for at least 1 hour, or until doubled in volume. At this point dough can be refrigerated for several hours or overnight. Do not punch dough down.

When ready to form crusts, preheat oven to 400° F for parbaking or 450° F for complete baking. (See directions below to determine which baking method is appropriate. If baking completely and using pizza stones, warm up the stones at this point for about 45 minutes and do not grease them.)

Lightly grease pizza pans or cookie sheets and sprinkle a little cornmeal on the surface. Pull dough down from sides of bowl to remove the dough;

Continued on page 190.

slice into three equal sections. Roll out each section into a 12-inch circle.

Place rolled-out crusts into pizza pans or onto cookie sheets or stones. If you will be using toppings that are at all juicy, the pizza crusts should be partially baked before adding the toppings so that the crust won't get soggy. To parbake the crust, bake it at 400° F for 3 to 4 minutes, or until crusts are just firm (do not brown). Remove from oven and pierce any bubbles in the crust. If not parbaking the crust, brush with olive oil to keep it from getting soggy when the toppings are added.

Add pizza toppings (see following recipes). Finish pizza by baking for 8 to 10 minutes at 450° F or until crust is lightly browned. If crust is not par-baked, then bake pizza with toppings at 450° F for about 10 to 15 minutes.

Note: *A half recipe makes 2 (10-inch) pizzas or 1 (14-inch) pizza. Limit your baking to two pizzas at one time.*

TIPS FOR HOMEMADE CRUST

This pizza dough is so easy to make from scratch—and so good to eat—there's really no reason to substitute commercial packaged mixes. The dough will keep in the refrigerator for several days and can be frozen for several months. For less dough, the recipe can easily be halved. Or leftover dough can be shaped into bread sticks and baked.

If you're trying homemade pizza for the first time and don't want to invest in a special pan, an inexpensive alternative is a disposable aluminum pizza pan. The biggest problem with these lightweight pans is that they're flimsy and hard to handle; they also won't heat up as much as heavier ones. For more strength and a crisper crust, place the lightweight pan on a cookie sheet.

Serious pizza makers may want to invest in a pizza stone or pizza tiles, which heat up and help brown the bottom of the pizza crust. The stones and tiles come in a variety of sizes and are available in kitchenware shops. But pizzas certainly don't require this equipment; they can be shaped by hand and baked on a cookie sheet.

Smoked Duck and Caramelized Onion Pizza

SERVES 2

You don't have to be a hunter to consider this smoked duck pizza a fall treat. Smoked duck is available at many supermarkets in the deli department. Some specialty meat stores regularly carry smoked duck; other meat markets will smoke a duck on request, usually at a nominal charge. Duck meat is moister than chicken, which well suits a pizza's high oven temperature. Smoked chicken or turkey can be substituted, but then the meat needs to be topped with cheese so that it doesn't dry out while baking.

4 tablespoons (½ stick) butter
4 medium onions, thinly sliced (about 3 cups)
1 (3- to 4-pound) smoked whole duck
1 (12-inch) unbaked pizza crust
Olive oil
2 garlic cloves, minced
2 tablespoons chopped fresh rosemary, or 2 teaspoons dried rosemary
Freshly cracked black pepper

In a skillet over low heat, melt butter and add onions. Slowly cook onions over low heat, stirring occasionally, until they turn caramel colored, about 25 to 30 minutes. Remove from heat and set aside. Drain, if necessary.

Preheat oven to 450° F. Remove skin from duck; take meat off bones and chop meat. Brush pizza crust lightly with olive oil. Add caramelized onions; then top with duck meat and minced garlic. Sprinkle rosemary leaves and pepper on top. Bake for 8 to 10 minutes, or until crust is brown. (If crust is not parbaked, then bake pizza with toppings for about 10 to 15 minutes.)

Shrimp, Avocado, and Tomato Pizza
SERVES 2

"Lovely" may not be the term most people use to describe pizzas, but this one definitely is. It looks every bit as good as it tastes with shrimp, avocado, and fresh tomatoes adding color and flavor.

1 (12-inch) unbaked pizza crust
Olive oil
⅓ pound cooked or uncooked small shrimp, thoroughly drained of excess
    moisture (see Note)
1 ripe medium tomato, thinly sliced
1 ripe avocado, peeled and sliced
2 shallots, thinly sliced
2 tablespoons chopped fresh tarragon (or 2 teaspoons dried tarragon)
Freshly cracked black pepper
2 ounces provolone cheese, shredded
2 ounces mozzarella cheese, shredded

Preheat oven to 400° F. This crust needs to be partially baked before the toppings are added to avoid a soggy crust. Bake this crust for 3 to 4 minutes or until crust is just firm (do not brown). Remove from oven; pierce any bubbles in the crust. Increase oven heat to 450° F.

Lightly brush pizza crust with olive oil. Pat shrimp thoroughly dry and add to pizza. Top with tomato, avocado, shallots, tarragon, and black pepper. Sprinkle cheese over pizza. Bake 4 to 5 minutes, or until cheese is melted.

Note: *Either cooked or uncooked shrimp can be used. Smaller shrimp— but not tiny shrimp—are preferred.*

Feta, Sun-Dried Tomato, and Artichoke Pizza
SERVES 2

This Mediterranean-style pizza won't appeal to everyone. The flavors are intense. But it's my favorite.

1 (12-inch) unbaked pizza crust
Olive oil
1 jar (about 7 ounces) sun-dried tomatoes marinated in olive oil, drained well
About 12 ounces marinated artichokes, drained well (see Note)
About 3 ounces feta cheese

Preheat oven to 450° F. Brush pizza crust lightly with olive oil. Thinly slice sun-dried tomatoes and spread on pizza crust. Remove any tough outer leaves on the artichokes; then cut into bite-size pieces and scatter over pizza crust. Crumble feta cheese and sprinkle on top of other ingredients. Bake for 8 to 10 minutes, or until crust is brown. (If crust is not parbaked, then bake pizza with topping for about 10 to 15 minutes.)

Note: *Marinated artichokes in a jar taste better than the canned counterparts, which can have a tinny flavor. The jars typically weigh about 6½ ounces, so you would need 2 jars; cans weigh about 14 ounces, so 1 can is sufficient.*

COOK'S NOTES

If you're not the kind who likes tangy pizzas, try an all-mushroom one: Briefly sauté in butter 8 ounces of chopped button mushrooms with 4 ounces of a wild mushroom such as shiitake. Season to taste with salt, pepper, thyme, and basil; sprinkle with mozzarella and bake. Sprinkle a little freshly grated Parmesan on top immediately before serving.

Hazelnut Biscotti
MAKES 3 DOZEN

These biscotti aren't as hard as many. Instead, they are pleasantly chewable.

1½ cups hazelnuts (also known as filberts; see Note)
1 cup sugar
2 eggs
2 tablespoons milk
2½ cups flour
1½ teaspoons baking powder
¼ teaspoon salt
¾ teaspoon vanilla extract
½ cup semisweet or bittersweet chocolate, chopped

Preheat oven to 350° F. Butter and flour a baking sheet (or use parchment paper on the baking sheet).

Place hazelnuts in an ungreased pie pan and toast in the oven 8 to 10 minutes, or until fragrant. Wrap in a clean kitchen towel and let cool to the touch.

Rub the hazelnuts together inside the cloth to remove the peels. Separate nuts from peels and discard the peels. Chop the hazelnuts coarsely; set aside.

In a large bowl, beat together sugar, eggs, and milk. In another bowl, stir together flour, baking powder, and salt. Stir flour mixture into sugar mixture. Add the hazelnuts and vanilla, mixing dough with your hands until all ingredients are evenly incorporated into the dough.

On a lightly floured board, knead dough for 1 or 2 minutes until smooth; then shape into a flat log about 3 inches wide and a ½ inch high. Place the log on the prepared baking sheet. Bake on the middle rack of the oven for 30 minutes, or until set and lightly browned.

Remove the baking sheet from the oven, place the log on a cutting board, and cut into ⅛-inch diagonal slices. Place the slices cut-side down on the baking sheet and return the sheet to the oven for 10 to 15 minutes, or until the biscotti are very lightly colored. Place biscotti on wire racks to cool.

When biscotti are at room temperature, melt the chocolate over low heat in a saucepan or double boiler. Dip the biscotti halfway into the chocolate. Let the chocolate air-dry by laying the cookies on wire racks (it helps to put a piece of aluminum foil or wax paper under the racks, because the chocolate may drip.) Store in an airtight container.

Variation: Substitute chocolate mint for the semisweet or bittersweet chocolate.

Note:
- *Slivered blanched almonds could be substituted for the hazelnuts, if you want to skip the step of taking the peel off the nut. They still should be toasted for extra flavor.*

Prepare meat marinade.

Make vinaigrette.

UP TO 9 HOURS IN ADVANCE

Cook meat in slow cooker.

Clean beans and trim the ends of the beans, if desired.

Grate Parmesan and slice mushrooms.

Peel and cut potatoes and keep in cold water.

Bake gingerbread and make lemon sauce.

UP TO 1 HOUR IN ADVANCE

Clean lettuce and assemble salad.

LAST-MINUTE PREP

Cook and mash the potatoes.

Make gravy for the meat.

Roast the green beans.

Reheat lemon sauce and gingerbread, if desired.

SLOW-COOKED PORK DINNER

For 6

Butterhead Lettuce with Parmesan and Fresh Mushrooms
Sesame Pork Roast
Sour Cream Mashed Potatoes
Roasted Green Beans
Gingerbread with Lemon Sauce

IT'S EARLY NOVEMBER. Do you know where your good dishes are? Or the leaves for the dining room table? The silverware is probably tarnished and the linen tablecloth, the big one, will need a serious pressing. Get the iron ready.

Yes, it's the season of gathering around the dinner table—and perhaps an extra little table or two for those really big groups, which may or may not include children. (Do you recall the children's table of yesteryear, where kids were banished—to their delight? As a child, I sat at a crowded table of six where, without doubt, we had more fun and ate less than anyone at the more sedate table for adults. We laughed, we roared, we teased and tormented. And we inevitably hid our vegetables and tried to escape the mound of dreaded rutabagas—"beggies," as we called them—that always found their way onto the winter menu.)

From now until the first of the new year, we will find ourselves enjoying more company than we do for the entire rest of the year. That means one thing for the cook expecting a busy kitchen: Recipes. Lots of them. Good ones, new ones, tried-and-true ones. This menu is a place to start.

For me, with the first hint of fall in the air, I reach for the slow cooker, the busy person's favorite kitchen tool. There's nothing better than to come home to a kitchen fragrant with dinner ready. And entertaining couldn't be easier than with dinner almost cooking itself.

Sesame pork is a recipe that has traveled throughout my family faster and with more persistence than a chain letter. My aunt heard the recipe over the radio more than thirty years ago. She told my mother, who told her daughters. It is so popular that we all have been handing out recipe cards ever since. The ingredients—especially the spices—seem far too abundant, but they are correct. Yes, all that ginger and all those sesame seeds and ketchup are necessary for the resulting flavor. For the Svitak-Dean family, these are the flavors of fall.

The meal starts with a simple salad of earthy flavors. The Parmesan and mushrooms contain the fifth taste of food—beyond sweet, salty, sour, and bitter—called *umami* (oo-MAH-mee). This taste contains the essence of savory flavor—which is why it tastes so good. The meat is paired with mashed potatoes that have an extra layer of flavor, and with green beans roasted to perfection, in what is sure to become a favorite recipe that makes the e-mail rounds. A hearty gingerbread ends the meal with a delicate lemon sauce.

Shortcut Savvy

Buy packaged lettuce.

The slow cooker simplifies food prep, since the cook's work is done once the ingredients are in the pot.

Buy a dessert from the bakery.

Beverage

Serve a California chardonnay or oaked Australian chardonnay with both the salad and pork roast. For dessert, serve hot tea with the gingerbread.

Butterhead Lettuce with Parmesan and Fresh Mushrooms

SERVES 6

6 cups butterhead lettuce, such as Boston or Bibb (see Note)
4 to 6 ounces fresh mushrooms, sliced
6 tablespoons Parmesan shavings (see Note)
2 tablespoons white wine vinegar
1 teaspoon Dijon mustard
¼ teaspoon salt
Freshly ground black pepper
6 tablespoons olive oil

Portion lettuce leaves on salad plates. Top with mushroom slices and Parmesan.

To make vinaigrette, whisk together vinegar, mustard, salt, and pepper. Slowly whisk in olive oil. Drizzle on salad.

Variation: For a warm salad, sauté the mushrooms in a little olive oil before serving. This salad is also good with baby spinach leaves.

Notes:
- *To shave Parmesan, use a grater with coarse holes to make larger pieces (shavings) of the cheese.*
- *Butterhead lettuce comes in loose heads with floppy leaves. They are the most tender of lettuces.*

Sesame Pork Roast

SERVES 6

Basically, a braised piece of meat, this roast is easy to cook whether in a slow cooker, in the oven, or on top of the stove in a Dutch oven. When prepared in the slow cooker, the roast doesn't need to be marinated in advance because the meat marinates during the lengthy cooking time. But for ease in the morning, prepare the marinade the night before.

2 tablespoons sesame seeds

3 or 4 green onions, sliced (about ¼ cup)

½ cup ketchup

¼ cup soy sauce

2 tablespoons ground ginger

2 tablespoons molasses (any type)

2 teaspoons salt

½ teaspoon curry powder

½ teaspoon black pepper

1 cup water

2 tablespoons wine vinegar

4 pounds pork shoulder roast

3 tablespoons flour for gravy, if desired

Toast sesame seeds in a dry frying pan over low heat until golden and fragrant. Place seeds in a bowl with the green onions, ketchup, soy sauce, ginger, molasses, salt, curry powder, pepper, water, and wine vinegar; stir to mix thoroughly. Place meat in a large bowl and pour the marinade over the meat. Marinate, covered, 2 to 3 hours or overnight in the refrigerator.

To prepare in a slow cooker, place meat and marinade in the slow cooker, cover, and cook on low for 9 hours or on high for about 3 hours.

To prepare in the oven or on the stovetop, remove meat from marinade and pat dry. Brown it in a Dutch oven or frying pan. To continue in the oven, place meat and marinade in a covered casserole dish and roast at 300° to 325° F for 3 hours. (The roast should be falling apart when it's done.) To continue on top of the stove, place the meat and marinade in the pot and heat until the marinade is boiling. Reduce to a simmer and cover. Cook, turning meat once or twice, for 3 hours.

Serve with pan juices or make gravy.

To make gravy: Pour pan juices into a 2-cup measure. Skim off fat, returning 2 tablespoons of the fat to the pan. If defatted pan juices do not equal 2 cups, add enough water or chicken broth to reach the 2-cup measure. Whisk 3 tablespoons flour into fat in the pan and cook over medium heat on the stovetop until bubbly, scraping the bottom of the pan to release all the flavor from juices cooked to the pan. Slowly stir in pan juices and cook until gravy thickens, stirring constantly.

Sour Cream Mashed Potatoes
SERVES 6

2½ pounds russet potatoes, peeled and cut into chunks
Salt
¼ cup milk or cream
2 to 4 tablespoons butter
½ cup sour cream
White pepper

Place potatoes in a large pot; add 1 tablespoon salt and water to cover potatoes. Bring to a boil, then lower to a simmer and cook, uncovered, until tender, about 20 minutes, or until a fork can easily pierce the potatoes. Drain.

If you have a potato ricer, run the potatoes through that first. In the pot or a large bowl, add milk and butter to the potatoes. Mash by hand or with a hand mixer. Mix in sour cream and season to taste with salt and pepper.

Variation: Add about 8 roasted garlic cloves (about ¼ cup roasted garlic purée) to the potatoes and sour cream. Or, for a tangier flavor, substitute 4 ounces goat cheese (chèvre) for the sour cream.

Note: *Russet potatoes, also called Idaho potatoes, are the best ones for mashing because of their high starch content.*

Roasted Green Beans

SERVES 6

Why is it that the concept of roasted beans sounds so foreign? These are wonderful, inspired by those served at 20.21, Wolfgang Puck's restaurant at the Walker Art Center in Minneapolis. They remind me of green french fries.

1¼ pounds fresh green beans, ends trimmed, if desired
Olive oil
Coarse salt
Freshly cracked pepper (tricolor peppercorns look particularly nice)

Preheat oven to 350° F (see Note).

Toss in olive oil and place in baking dish. Roast in oven for 15 to 20 minutes or so, until the beans are cooked through. They will have shriveled slightly.

Remove from oven and sprinkle with coarse salt and pepper. Serve immediately.

Variation: Add a sprinkling of black sesame seeds, which are available in the spice section of upscale supermarkets. (However, black sesame seeds are not recommended for this meal because white sesame seeds are used in the roasted pork.)

Variation: Roast the beans with ½ cup raw cashews.

Note: *The beans can be roasted at whatever temperature your oven is already set at, if you are cooking something else at the same time.*

Gingerbread with Lemon Sauce
MAKES 8 OR 9 SERVINGS

From Beatrice Ojakangas, Duluth, Minnesota, cookbook author and in-
ductee into the James Beard Foundation Cookbook Hall of Fame. She has
been called the baker laureate of the nation.

GINGERBREAD

½ cup sugar

4 tablespoons (½ stick) unsalted butter, softened

1 cup flour

1 teaspoon ground ginger

1 teaspoon ground cinnamon

½ teaspoon ground allspice

¼ teaspoon salt

½ teaspoon baking soda

½ cup nonfat plain yogurt or buttermilk

¼ cup light molasses

1 egg, slightly beaten

LEMON SAUCE

½ cup sugar

4 tablespoons (½ stick) unsalted butter

2 tablespoons lemon juice

1 teaspoon grated lemon zest

¼ cup water

TO MAKE GINGERBREAD

Preheat oven to 375° F. Lightly grease an 8-inch square or round cake pan.

In a large bowl, cream together ½ cup sugar and 4 tablespoons butter.

In another bowl, mix flour, ginger, cinnamon, allspice, and salt. Blend
into the creamed ingredients until the mixture resembles moist crumbs.
Transfer one-third of the mixture to another bowl and reserve.

To the remaining mixture, add baking soda, yogurt, molasses, and egg.
Stir until the batter is evenly blended. Pour into the prepared pan. Sprinkle
evenly with the reserved batter. Bake for 20 to 25 minutes or until a toothpick inserted in the center comes out clean.

TO MAKE LEMON SAUCE

In a small saucepan, combine ½ cup sugar, 4 tablespoons butter, lemon juice, lemon zest, and water. Place over medium heat and bring to a boil, stirring constantly. Reduce heat to low and simmer for 4 minutes, stirring until the mixture is clear and slightly thickened. Serve warm over squares of gingerbread.

Make Ahead

UP TO SEVERAL DAYS IN ADVANCE

Thaw frozen capon in refrigerator.

UP TO A DAY IN ADVANCE

Prep and cut up carrots.

Prepare capon stock for mushroom sauce base.

Make cheesecake.

Toast walnuts for salad.

Make vinaigrette.

Prepare capon.

UP TO 3 HOURS IN ADVANCE

Roast capon.

Finish mushroom sauce.

UP TO 1 HOUR IN ADVANCE

Roast carrots.

Assemble salad.

LAST-MINUTE PREP

Cook and rice the potatoes.

Reheat mushroom sauce.

Carve meat.

For 6

Spinach with Apple, Blue Cheese, and Walnuts with Shallot Vinaigrette
Roast Capon with Wild Mushroom Sauce
Riced Potatoes
Roasted Carrots with Thyme
Orange Chocolate Chunk Cheesecake

TIME IS THE INGREDIENT in short supply for dinner parties these days. The thought of a table full of hungry guests—even friendly ones—can be daunting to the most enthusiastic of busy cooks.

But there's no need to abandon dinner parties by the side of the road just because you're stuck in the fast lane. Here's an elegant dinner menu that can be prepared with a modest amount of time, talent, and dirty dishes.

Most of the menu can be prepared at least a day in advance, with last-minute work limited to an easy salad assembly, and to minimal sautéing and simmering. With a practical menu in hand, one other question looms as the busy cook considers issuing invitations. Whether novice or experienced, the refrain is the same from kitchen to kitchen and cook to cook: Is there time to clean house? But that's another matter.

Spinach with Apple, Blue Cheese, and Walnuts with Shallot Vinaigrette
SERVES 6

VINAIGRETTE
¼ cup olive oil
2 tablespoons finely chopped shallots
2 tablespoons balsamic vinegar
½ teaspoon minced garlic
Salt and fresh ground pepper

SALAD
½ cup coarsely chopped walnuts
5 to 6 cups (about 10 ounces) baby spinach leaves
2 tart unpeeled apples, cored, thinly sliced, and dipped in lemon juice to prevent browning
⅓ cup crumbled blue cheese

FOR VINAIGRETTE
Whisk to blend olive oil, shallots, vinegar, and garlic. Season to taste with salt and pepper. Cover and refrigerate for at least 1 hour or up to a day ahead.

FOR SALAD ASSEMBLY
Toast walnuts in a dry saucepan over medium heat until fragrant, stirring occasionally. Set aside to cool.

To assemble salads, place a bed of spinach on each salad plate and top with apple slices, blue cheese, and walnuts. Drizzle with vinaigrette.

Shortcut Savvy

Use prepared chicken broth instead of making a capon stock for the mushroom sauce.

Buy a prepared potato dish.

Buy prewashed spinach.

Use bottled vinaigrette.

Substitute a bakery-made dessert.

Beverage

With this almost-retro meal, turn to a classic aperitif, such as Lillet (a blend of wine, brandy, fruits, and herbs) or Dubonnet (herb-flavored). Serve a medium-bodied Burgundy with the roast capon, and espresso with the cheesecake.

COOK'S NOTES

The capon is a little-
known treasure that will
enhance any home chef's
repertoire. The bird, which
in appearance looks like a
cross between a very large
chicken and a small turkey,
is actually a rooster that
has been neutered and fed
a fattening diet. Those
factors make the bird juicy
and flavorful with an abundance of white meat. The
largest capons are about 9
pounds; an 8-pound bird,
which this menu uses, easily feeds six.

This bird is less fatty
than chicken, more juicy
and tender than turkey.
Cooks making plans for
holiday meals may want to
take note of this practical
and flavorful alternative.
Capon is also delicious
barbecued on a grill.

Capons are a midwest-
ern product, with the birds
raised in Minnesota, Iowa,
and Wisconsin. There
are only two large proces-
sors in the nation: Pietrus
Foods of Sleepy Eye,
Minnesota, and Wapsie
Produce of Decorah, Iowa.

Roast Capon with Wild Mushroom Sauce

SERVES 6

WILD MUSHROOM SAUCE (see Note)
3½ cups chicken broth, divided
Neck and giblets from capon
½ cup white wine
4 tablespoons (½ stick) butter
¼ cup diced yellow onion
5 dried porcini mushrooms
¼ cup shiitake mushrooms
¼ cup oyster mushrooms
½ cup button mushrooms
1 tablespoon fresh chopped thyme, or 1 teaspoon dried thyme
¼ cup flour
Salt and white pepper

CAPON
1 (7½- to 8-pound) capon
Salt
1 large onion, peeled and quartered
2 to 3 carrots, washed and cut into chunks
Olive oil

FOR WILD MUSHROOM SAUCE

Combine 3 cups chicken broth, capon neck and giblets, and wine in a
3-quart saucepan to make a capon stock. Bring to a simmer and cook 30
minutes. Strain and keep hot. (Capon stock can be made ahead to this
point a day in advance, cooled, and refrigerated. Reheat before adding to
mushroom mixture. If you don't have time to make the stock, substitute
chicken broth in the sauce.)

In a small bowl or saucepan, warm the remaining ½ cup chicken broth
in the microwave or on the stovetop; add dried porcini mushrooms and
soak 30 minutes. Remove and chop mushrooms. Pour broth through a
strainer to remove sand; add broth to capon stock.

In another 3-quart saucepan, melt butter over medium heat and sauté
onions until soft. Add mushrooms and thyme and cook until juices begin to

run. Cook over low heat for 5 minutes, stirring occasionally. Mix in flour and cook 2 minutes.

Gradually stir in hot capon stock and add salt and pepper to taste. Simmer for 10 minutes, until sauce is thickened and smooth, stirring frequently. (If making ahead, reheat on low.)

FOR CAPON

Preheat oven to 350° F.

Rinse capon and dry thoroughly, reserving neck and giblets for Wild Mushroom Sauce. Sprinkle a little salt inside the cavity of the capon. Add onion and carrot chunks to cavity. (These will be discarded after capon is cooked.)

Rub exterior of capon with a little olive oil; sprinkle with salt. Place capon breast-side down in a shallow roasting pan, preferably on a rack because there will be a lot of drippings which will not be used; save them for gravy on another occasion. (Roasting with the breast down will keep the juices flowing into the breast meat.) Roast, basting occasionally, until done and leg moves freely (interior temperature should be 180° F). Allow about 22 minutes per pound—about 3 hours for an 8-pound capon.

For the last 20 minutes of roasting, turn capon over breast-side up. Increase temperature to 425° F to brown the breast. Before carving, cover capon loosely and let stand for 10 to 15 minutes. Serve with Wild Mushroom Sauce.

Note: *The more familiar—and less expensive—button mushrooms can be substituted for all the wild mushrooms, if preferred.*

Riced Potatoes

SERVES 6

About 3 pounds russet potatoes, peeled
Salt
Butter
Paprika, for garnish

Cut potatoes in half or quarters to allow them to cook faster. Place potatoes in a large saucepan; add water to cover and sprinkle with salt. Bring to a boil; then drop heat to a simmer. Cook potatoes until tender, 20 to 30 minutes depending on size of potatoes (check by sticking a fork into the potato; it should go in easily if it's done).

Drain potatoes. Using a potato ricer (see Note), squeeze potatoes through the ricer and into serving dish. To serve, top with a dab of butter and sprinkle with paprika, if desired.

Note: *A potato ricer is an inexpensive kitchen tool that's available in most kitchen specialty stores. It presses potatoes through a container with holes; the result looks somewhat like rice. "Riced" potatoes are very light. If you don't have a ricer—and don't want to buy one—mash the potatoes instead: Add ½ cup milk and 3 tablespoons butter; then, either by hand or with a hand mixer, mash or beat potatoes until desired smoothness. (Add more milk or butter, if preferred.) Season to taste with salt and pepper.*

Roasted Carrots with Thyme

SERVES 6

2 pounds peeled carrots, cut into large chunks of equal size
Olive oil or vegetable oil
Several sprigs fresh thyme, or ¼ teaspoon dried thyme
Salt and freshly cracked black pepper

Toss carrots with oil and thyme. Place in a medium baking pan and sprinkle with salt and pepper. Roast the carrots in the oven during the last hour of capon roasting. (If you are roasting these carrots on another occasion, cook them at 400° F for about an hour, or until they are tender.)

Orange–Chocolate Chunk Cheesecake
MAKES 1 (10-INCH) CAKE; 12 TO 20 SERVINGS

This recipe hails from Cafe Latté in St. Paul, Minnesota.

SHORTBREAD CRUST
1⅓ cups flour
⅓ cup unsweetened cocoa powder
½ cup powdered sugar
6 tablespoons (¾ stick) cold butter, chopped
Vegetable spray

CHEESECAKE
5 (8-ounce) packages cream cheese (2½ pounds), softened
1¼ cups granulated sugar
3 eggs, at room temperature
⅓ cup sour cream, at room temperature
2 tablespoons orange zest
½ cup fresh orange juice, at room temperature (about 2 medium oranges)
8 ounces chocolate (bittersweet or semisweet), coarsely chopped

CHOCOLATE GLAZE
⅓ cup cream
8 ounces chocolate (bittersweet or semisweet), broken into pieces
2 tablespoons corn syrup
Whipped cream, if desired

FOR SHORTBREAD CRUST
In a bowl, stir together flour, cocoa powder, and powdered sugar. Cut in butter with a pastry blender or with fingers or a fork. Mix until it comes together like pie dough. With vegetable spray, coat only the sides of a 10-inch springform pan with removable bottom. Press dough into bottom of pan. Refrigerate for 30 minutes.

Preheat oven to 400° F. Bake until lightly brown, about 15 minutes. Cool.

FOR CHEESECAKE

Preheat oven to 350° F.

In a mixing bowl, beat cream cheese and granulated sugar until smooth and creamy. Scrape sides of bowl. Add eggs one at a time, beating thoroughly after each addition. Mix in sour cream and orange zest. Gradually stir in orange juice. Fold in 8 ounces chocolate chunks.

Pour mixture on top of shortbread crust and bake for 1 hour to 75 minutes, or until cheesecake is golden in color and slightly domed on top. Cool completely.

FOR CHOCOLATE GLAZE

In a medium saucepan over low heat, warm cream until tiny bubbles form around edges—do not boil. Remove from heat and add 8 ounces chocolate; whisk until smooth (return to low heat, if needed, to fully melt the chocolate). Add corn syrup and mix well. Let chocolate glaze cool before spreading on top of cooled cheesecake. If desired, pipe whipped cream on top of the outside edge.

THANKSGIVING FEAST

For 12

Fall Fruit Salad
Orange-Marinated Brined Smoked Turkey
Focaccia Stuffing with Chanterelles and Sage
Easy Cranberry Relish
Balsamic-Glazed Pearl Onions
Pumpkin Ice Cream Pie or Maple Pumpkin Pie

IT'S THAT TIME OF YEAR when tradition comes with a capital T, which stands for Thanksgiving, and which may or may not stand for Turkey. Like other holidays rich with memories, this day arrives with the trappings of meals past: green bean casserole, marshmallow sweet potatoes, sage stuffing, or pumpkin pie that Grandma used to make.

But tradition has a way of hazing over the already less-than-brilliant colors of memory. For some, the notion of sweet potatoes blanketed in melted marshmallows conjures up delight; for others it's an appalling reminder of meals better forgotten. "We do it this way because we've always done it this way" doesn't hold up to careful analysis, let alone taste.

Where you fall along the spectrum of opinion on the holiday menu may depend on where you are as a participant in the event. If you're the one at the stove, this may be the holiday of reckoning. Years ago, those around the

Thanksgiving table probably weren't concerned about fat or calories. More than likely, there wasn't a vegetarian in the bunch. Guests liked the same old thing because they were the same old guests who showed up year after year without fail—and were plenty happy to do so because it meant they weren't doing the cooking themselves.

Today, with family members scattered across the country, the Thanksgiving table may include a broader spectrum of diners: family, friends, business associates, classmates of children, new relatives, exchange students, recent immigrants who, when faced with melted marshmallows, may wonder to themselves, if not aloud, "What is this stuff, and why is it on the table?"

What we remember about those meals of the past may be the warm companionship of those gathered together, the sense of plenty to share, the delight of enjoying food seldom available. (When it comes to marshmallows, that delight may be because of the knowledge that they won't be seen again for a year.) If you listen carefully to the guests on your list, there usually is at least one voice speaking out for change. Not necessarily a big change—you don't have to dump the turkey—but perhaps a simple update of the side dishes.

This year start a new holiday tradition by heeding that voice. Start the process with a variation on a theme from the traditional meal: balsamic pearl onions instead of creamed white onions, for example. Never before—and this is not an exaggeration—have there been so many choices for the

Shortcut Savvy

Too busy to do the whole meal? Settle on what's most important for you to cook. Then delegate the other cooking responsibilities; or buy, already prepared, the remaining foods for the meal. To help set the mood for the party, though, prepare something fragrant that will make the whole house smell wonderful.

Beverage

Start the celebration with asti spumante with the salad. Move to a Rhine Riesling kabinett or Beaujolais-Village for the turkey, and coffee for dessert.

cook, both in recipes and ingredients. This is the time to experiment—and, for the cook, that's where the adventure is.

Most of the recipes that follow are the inspiration of chefs in Napa Valley, who prepared a Thanksgiving menu for a conference of food editors who roundly offered *oohs* and *aahs*. The chefs' recipes show how even small variations offer a dramatic change. Consider the sage dressing: keep the herb, but substitute focaccia for white bread and add chardonnay and chanterelle mushrooms for a flavorful recipe. Simple changes, but the outcome is simply delightful.

Although there's a full feast's worth of recipes here, they aren't intended to replace your entire traditional Thanksgiving meal. A little variation goes a long way. Guests expecting familiar favorites may be appalled to find only the unfamiliar at the table. These recipes are offered to broaden the palates of your guests and, yes, to let the cook have some fun. Choose one or two new recipes to add to your traditional meal, keeping in mind that some predictability is necessary for this holiday. But don't just save these recipes until next Thanksgiving. Any one of them can be used throughout the holiday season. None is difficult to prepare. True, some take a little more time, but most are fairly quick to set up. The exception is the Orange-Marinated Brined Smoked Turkey, which takes a bit of the cook's attention.

Fall Fruit Salad

SERVES 12

This salad is very adaptable. If you don't have one ingredient—or don't want to have it—substitute something else. For example, frisée is suggested for the recipe. This pale yellow-green, feathery leaf has a slightly bitter taste. It's often used in the salad mix called mesclun. But another lettuce could be used. Likewise for the arugula or radicchio, both of which also have a somewhat bitter flavor that contrasts well with the fruit in this salad. Any selection of fall fruit—pears, apples, even kiwi—could be part of this salad. The recipe is from the late chef-instructor Catherine Brandel of the Culinary Institute of America in St. Helena, California.

3 shallots, minced
6 tablespoons balsamic vinegar
2 tablespoons sherry vinegar
¾ teaspoon salt
1½ cups walnut oil
3 pomegranates
1½ pounds assorted grapes (about 4 cups)
6 Asian pears
3 small heads frisée
3 medium bunches arugula, stems removed
3 heads radicchio, torn into bite-size pieces

Place minced shallot, vinegars, and salt in the bottom of a 1-quart bowl. After 30 minutes, whisk in nut oil and adjust seasonings, if necessary. (If preparing in advance, the oil can be whisked in right away.) Seed pomegranates. Wash grapes, pears, and salad greens. Just before serving, core and slice the pears. Toss with other fruit and vinaigrette. Combine frisée, arugula, and radicchio. Toss fruit mixture with greens and serve in bowl.

Variation: To serve on individual plates, arrange pears and grapes on a bed of greens, sprinkle with pomegranate seeds, and drizzle with vinaigrette.

COOK'S NOTES

The seeds are the only edible part of a pomegranate. To keep the mess out of the seeding process (the seeds turn everything they touch red), make a cut in the fruit big enough to insert both your thumbs. Then submerge the fruit in a bowl of water, pulling the fruit apart in two pieces. Loosen the seeds and discard any white pith. Drain the seeds. Working under water prevents the juice from squirting and staining anything it touches.

Orange-Marinated Brined Smoked Turkey
SERVES 12 TO 15

Not your grandmother's turkey. This recipe from chef Jeffrey Starr of Stags' Leap Winery in Napa, California, requires three days of marinating in brine (in the refrigerator, of course). The most difficult part of this is finding a container that is big enough to hold the turkey and still fit in the refrigerator (a large plastic dishpan or 5-gallon bucket works well), where the turkey will soak in the brine for 3 days. This turkey is moist and tender with a subtle blend of citrus and spice that comes in part from the fruitwood chips used in the smoking; they're available at cookware stores.

1 gallon (16 cups) orange juice
2 cups rice wine vinegar
2 cups apple cider vinegar
1 cup dark brown sugar
6 garlic cloves, crushed
¼ cup sliced fresh ginger root (see Notes)
1 bunch green onions, sliced
2 bunches cilantro, chopped
12 whole star anise (see Notes)
2 cinnamon sticks, crushed
2 tablespoons red pepper flakes
1 tablespoon whole cloves
2 tablespoons whole black peppercorns
1 cup kosher salt
1 (12- to 15-pound) turkey, giblets removed and discarded or saved for
    another use, such as stock)
About 2 pounds orange wood chips for smoking (or grapevine cuttings
    or hickory chips; see Notes)
Olive oil, as needed
Salt and pepper

Combine the orange juice, rice wine vinegar, apple cider vinegar, brown sugar, garlic, ginger, green onions, cilantro, star anise, cinnamon, red pepper flakes, cloves, peppercorns, and salt in a stockpot. Bring to a boil, reduce heat to low, and simmer for 45 minutes. Let cool. (May be prepared the day before you will begin brining the turkey; refrigerate in a nonmetal container.)

Thoroughly rinse and dry the turkey inside and out. Place in a large plastic, glass, or earthenware container that is not much wider than the diameter of the turkey and deep enough so that the brine can cover the bird completely. Pour in the brine; if it doesn't completely cover the bird, then turn the bird every 12 hours. Cover and refrigerate for 3 days.

About 4 hours before serving, soak wood chips in water for at least 30 minutes. (When the wet chips are placed on the fire, they will create an aromatic smoke that flavors the bird.) Place a drip pan on the fire grate of a kettle grill. Place 20 or 30 briquettes on either side of the drip pan. Light the briquettes and let burn until coated with white ash, about 30 minutes.

Meanwhile, remove the turkey from the brine and pat it dry; place on a roasting rack (either one especially for grills or one for the oven). Rub with olive oil, salt, and pepper.

When the fire is ready, place small handfuls of wet wood chips on the briquettes; then place the turkey, still on the roasting rack, in the center of the grill over the drip pan. Add about an inch of water into the drip pan and maintain it throughout the cooking.

Cover kettle with the lid. Partially open the vents in the lid and the bottom of the kettle. Try not to remove the lid too often or the temperature will drop too low, but check approximately every 45 minutes and replenish briquettes as needed, adding about 10 each time and also additional smoking wood. If the briquettes begin to burn too hot or flare up and blacken the turkey skin, gently damp down the fire with a small plant mister, taking care not to blow briquette dust into the drip pan if you're planning to use the drippings for gravy. If turkey skin is getting too dark, cover it with aluminum foil.

Smoke turkey for 2½ to 3 hours, or until a meat thermometer inserted in thickest part of breast (not touching bone) reaches 165° to 170° F. Carefully transfer turkey to a carving platter and let rest for about 15 minutes before carving. (Temperature will increase to 180° F.)

Notes:
- *Ginger root, with its knobby shape, is found in the produce department of supermarkets.*
- *Star anise is a small star-shaped pod, usually available where Asian foods are sold or in the spice section of supermarkets.*
- *Specialty wood chips can be found at kitchen stores.*

Focaccia Stuffing with Chanterelles and Sage
MAKES 12 SERVINGS

This recipe, from chef Jeff Starr of Stags' Leap Winery, makes a dry dressing in which the bread cubes retain their shape. Should you prefer a moister dressing, toss the mixture with about ½ cup chicken broth before transferring it to a baking pan.

1 pound focaccia, cut into 1-inch cubes
8 tablespoons (1 stick) butter, plus additional as needed
1 large onion, finely diced (about 1 cup)
1 large carrot, finely diced (about 1 cup)
1 celery rib, finely diced (about ¼ cup)
6 garlic cloves, minced
8 ounces chanterelles or other fresh mushrooms (wild or cultivated),
    washed and cut into long thin strips
¾ cup chardonnay or other dry white wine
1 small bunch sage, leaves only, finely chopped
Salt and pepper

Preheat oven to 350° F.

Place cubed focaccia in a large roasting pan or jelly-roll pan and toast in the oven, stirring occasionally. (Can be done ahead; store cooled bread cubes in a plastic bag at room temperature.)

Melt butter in a large sauté pan over medium heat; add onion, carrot, celery, garlic, and mushrooms. Sauté, stirring frequently, until mushrooms are cooked through, about 10 minutes. Add wine and simmer 5 minutes. Transfer mushroom mixture to a large bowl and toss thoroughly with toasted focaccia cubes and sage; season to taste with salt and pepper.

Transfer stuffing to a lightly buttered 9 x 13-inch baking pan that will hold the dressing to a depth of about 2 inches. (Can be made ahead to this point; cover pan with aluminum foil and refrigerate. Remove the pan from the refrigerator about 1 hour before it is to be baked; or increase the cooking time by 30 minutes.)

Cover with aluminum foil and bake for 30 minutes. Remove aluminum foil; brush the top of the dressing lightly with melted butter. Continue to bake until the top of the dressing is golden brown, about 10 to 15 minutes.

Note: *If your guests are partial to stuffing, you may want to increase the recipe by half or double—it's that good.*

Easy Cranberry Relish
MAKES ABOUT 3 CUPS

If you're going to put the time into the turkey, then you need something fast for the relish. This couldn't be easier—or better tasting. This favorite in the Dean household is simply chopped cranberries with lemon zest and some sugar to sweeten it up. I like to serve it in a cut glass bowl because the chopped cranberries look like jewels.

1 (12-ounce) package fresh cranberries
1½ cups sugar, or to taste
Zest from 1 orange or 1 lemon (or from both for extra flavor)

In a food processor or blender, coarsely chop the cranberries. In a large bowl, toss berries and sugar together.

Add zest to cranberries; stir. Refrigerate overnight in an airtight container to let flavors blend. Stir again before serving.

Balsamic-Glazed Pearl Onions

SERVES 12

From chef Laurie Souza of Franciscan Oakville Estate in Rutherford, California.

4 (10-ounce) packages pearl onions
¼ cup olive oil
2 tablespoons balsamic vinegar, divided
Freshly ground pepper

Boil the onions in salted water until they are just crisp-tender, 3 to 7 minutes, depending on the size; drain. Rinse in cold water to cool onions. Then cut off ends and remove and discard the papery outer skins. Take care not to trim too much off the ends or the onions will fall apart.

Over medium-high heat, heat a large skillet that either holds all the onions in one layer or do this in two batches. When the pan is hot, add the oil. When the oil is hot, add the onions, shaking the pan until they are all well coated with the oil. Add 1 tablespoon plus 1 teaspoon of the vinegar. Continue to sauté, shaking the pan occasionally, until the onions are golden brown, 6 to 8 minutes.

When the onions are golden, sprinkle in the remaining 2 teaspoons balsamic vinegar; season to taste with freshly ground pepper. Shake the pan briefly to distribute the vinegar. Taste for seasoning; add a dash more vinegar if desired, but there should be just a hint of it.

Variation: Substitute cipollini onions for the pearl onions. These are small, somewhat flat onions, slightly bigger than pearl onions. Peel them, toss in olive oil, and drizzle with balsamic vinegar. Then bake at 350° F in a covered dish until soft, about 40 minutes.

Note: *Trimming and skinning the onions are time consuming tasks with this many onions; plan your time accordingly. This is a great job to spread among helping hands.*

Pumpkin Ice Cream Pie

MAKES 3 (9-INCH) PIES OR 36 (3-INCH) PIES

This recipe is a family favorite. It makes a lot of dessert very quickly, which is one reason I like it. The other is that the pumpkin ice cream offers a perfect finish for a heavy Thanksgiving meal; it has a lighter texture and color than the usual pumpkin pie. For individual portions, which look especially nice, either buy or make 3-inch graham-cracker crumb crusts. (The mini-pies are easily removed from their aluminum pans for more attractive serving.) One 9-inch pie pan of filling equals 12 (3-inch) individual servings.

½ gallon vanilla ice cream
1 (15-ounce) can unsweetened pumpkin purée (see Note)
1 cup packed brown sugar (without any lumps)
½ teaspoon salt
½ teaspoon cinnamon
½ teaspoon ginger
¼ teaspoon nutmeg
3 (9-inch) graham-cracker crumb crusts
Whipped cream, for garnish
Cinnamon sticks, for garnish

Let ice cream soften. Meanwhile, in a large bowl, thoroughly mix pumpkin purée, brown sugar, salt, cinnamon, ginger, and nutmeg, removing and discarding any lumps of brown sugar. Add softened ice cream and blend thoroughly.

Pour ice cream into prepared crusts, allowing some crust to show for a pretty presentation. Freeze until ready to use, covering with plastic wrap once the pie is frozen throughout.

If desired, garnish with whipped cream and broken pieces of cinnamon sticks.

Note: *If you have only sweetened pumpkin purée on hand, omit the sugar and spices.*

Maple Pumpkin Pie

SERVES 8 TO 10

From Ken Goff, instructor at Le Cordon Bleu and former chef of Dakota Bar and Grill in Minneapolis, Minnesota, who was one of the first local chefs to emphasize regional ingredients. His pie keeps a flaky and crisp crust because the cooked filling is added after the pie shell is baked. Goff prepares his own purée, but the canned variety will work just fine. For a lot of company, either make 2 pies or prepare a second favorite of a different flavor.

1 baked (10-inch) pie shell (or a 9½-inch deep-dish shell)
2½ cups pumpkin purée, homemade or canned (see Notes)
1 cup heavy cream
3 whole eggs, beaten slightly
1 cup pure maple syrup
1 teaspoon vanilla extract
⅛ teaspoon nutmeg
1 teaspoon allspice
1 tablespoon ground ginger
2 tablespoons ground cinnamon
2 pinches ground cloves
1 tablespoon potato starch (see Notes)
Whipped cream or ice cream, for garnish

To make homemade pumpkin purée: Cut up cooking pumpkin and remove seeds and peel. Lightly spray or butter a baking pan and put pumpkin in it. Cover pan with aluminum foil. Bake pumpkin at 325° F for about 10 minutes; then prick holes in the aluminum foil. Continue baking for 30 minutes or until tender. Process pumpkin flesh in a blender or food processor to make a purée.

To make pie: In a large, deep saucepan, whisk together pumpkin purée and cream. Over low heat, slowly bring to a boil, stirring occasionally (cover to keep mixture from sputtering all over).

Meanwhile, in a medium bowl whisk together eggs, maple syrup, vanilla extract, nutmeg, allspice, ginger, cinnamon, cloves, and potato starch.

When pumpkin mixture has come to a boil, ladle a small amount (about 1 cup) of pumpkin into egg mixture while stirring to prevent scrambling the egg. Whisk all of egg mixture into pumpkin mixture. Continue to cook, stirring often, until mixture boils thoroughly and thickens. Remove from heat and pour into pie shell. Chill. Bring to room temperature before serving. If desired, serve with lightly whipped cream or ice cream.

Notes:
- *If you are buying canned pumpkin, be sure to get pumpkin purée and not pumpkin pie filling, which already has spices in it. They usually are stocked together in the baking section of the supermarket, and it's easy to confuse the two.*
- *Potato starch is stocked with flour or with kosher foods in the supermarket.*

HOW THANKSGIVING BECAME OFFICIAL

It may not have mattered to our forecooks in 1863 which day of the week Abraham Lincoln set aside as Thanksgiving. Maybe Mary Todd Lincoln didn't mind a midweek celebration, though it's safe to assume she wasn't poised in front of the wood stove on that last Thursday of November almost 150 years ago. But here's betting a shiny penny, of the Lincoln variety, that if today's president were to announce a special holiday geared toward eating, it wouldn't be midweek.

Some fourscore and six decades ago, Thursday won the designation partly by default. Though it had taken almost 250 years for the holiday to become official, days of thanksgiving were sporadically held in America since the Puritans' first harvest in 1621. Lincoln's proclamation took heed of those early celebrations, often held on Thursdays because of conflicts with other days of the week.

Sunday was the Sabbath, a day the Puritans didn't associate with celebrations, and Saturday was spent in preparation for the holy day. Monday, the day after the Sabbath, didn't leave enough time for cooking. Friday, a day of fasting for Catholics, was ruled out to avoid any overtone of religious conflict. That left Thursday, when midweek religious services traditionally were held with afternoon sermons for those with the leisure to attend. Not so incidentally, though historians overlook this obvious point, a holiday on Thursday meant the cooks had three days to prepare for the big meal. Wise move for the time.

WINTER

MENUS

Holiday Cocktail Party   226
Pomegranate Punch
Shrimp Salad in Radicchio Cups
French Twists
Phyllo Bundles
Crostini with White Bean and Sun-Dried Tomato Purée
Crostini with Roast Beef and Roasted Red Peppers
Edamame Spread
Merlot Roasted Mushrooms
Mini-Tarts
Homemade Mint Candies
Spicy Almonds

Crown Roast Dinner   240
French Onion Soup
Roasted Root Vegetables with Sage
Crown Roast of Pork with Orzo Pilaf
Bostoni Cream Pies

Elegant Dinner Party   248
Cream of Celery Soup
Beef Burgundy with Hot Egg Noodles
Pear and Blue Cheese Salad
Apple Crumble Pie

Post-Holiday Winter Celebration   254
Cream of Carrot Soup
Rock Cornish Game Hens with Apple Cider Sauce
Roasted Potatoes with Sage and Garlic
Poached Pears with Caramel and Pistachios

Flavors of Spain   260
Mixed Greens with Blood Oranges
Flatbread with Fresh Thyme and Black Peppercorns
Mediterranean Seafood Stew
Pear Tart with Walnuts and Cheese

Pasta Party   270
Mixed Greens with Simple Vinaigrette
Pasta with Three Sauces
    Spaghetti with Ricotta Marinara and Meatballs
    Farfalle Provençal
    Penne with Caramelized Onions and Mushrooms
Rustic Bread with Roasted Garlic Butter
Chocolate-Espresso Bars

Last-Minute Party   280
Greens with Seared Scallops and
    Orange Vinaigrette
Mushroom Risotto
Steamed Broccolini
Popovers
Chocolate Cups with Ice Cream and Chocolate Sauce

Dinner à Deux   286
Kir Royale
Butterhead Lettuce with Pomegranates and
    Toasted Walnuts
Swiss Fondue or Châteaubriand with
    Wild Mushrooms and Madeira
Chocolate Soufflé for Two

WINTER

RECIPES BY COURSE

Make Ahead

WEEKS IN ADVANCE

Make ice ring for punch.

Prepare almonds and store in airtight container in the refrigerator.

Make French Twists; freeze and bake later.

Thaw phyllo overnight in refrigerator and prepare Phyllo Bundles; freeze and bake later.

Make and bake mini-tart shells; freeze and fill later.

Make candies.

UP TO 2 DAYS IN ADVANCE

Thaw puff pastry overnight for French Twists.

UP TO A DAY IN ADVANCE

Prepare shrimp salad.

Bake French Twists.

Make white bean purée for crostini.

Roast mushrooms.

UP TO 8 HOURS IN ADVANCE

Toast bread for crostini.

Prepare edamame spread.

UP TO 2 HOURS IN ADVANCE

Assemble radicchio cups with salad and refrigerate, covered.

Assemble mini-tarts.

Put almonds in a serving dish.

HOLIDAY COCKTAIL PARTY

For 20

Pomegranate Punch
Shrimp Salad in Radicchio Cups
French Twists
Phyllo Bundles
Crostini with White Bean and Sun-Dried Tomato Purée
Crostini with Roast Beef and Roasted Red Peppers
Edamame Spread
Merlot Roasted Mushrooms
Mini-Tarts
Homemade Mint Candies
Spicy Almonds

HOLIDAYS POSE A DILEMMA for many cooks. This is the time of year when we want to prepare the biggest, best celebrations ever. Yet it's also when we are the most strapped for time.

So how does a busy cook entertain?

Creatively. By leaning on the culinary expertise of others, you can put out a holiday spread that will make guests gasp, "How did you ever do that?"

The secret is to make use of good-quality prepared foods from bakeries, delis, restaurants—even foods right off the supermarket shelf—and mesh them with easy-to-make recipes that even a novice cook can prepare. In that spirit, we offer a holiday hors d'oeuvres party for twenty that can be adapted to accommodate any cook's timetable.

Let your holiday party ring with good cheer—and good taste—with a little bit of help from your culinary friends. Here's a party plan that's sure to please everyone.

First, you'll need to plan the number of hors d'oeuvres to serve for a large group. That will depend on your budget, on the amount of preparation time available and, certainly, on the amount of energy you have. As a rule of thumb, for a gathering of twenty in a cocktail environment, six to eight different hors d'oeuvres would be reasonable. You'll also need to calculate the amount of food necessary to keep all those folks content. Just how much to provide will depend on the time of day the party is held, as well as the guests who are invited. (As we all know, there are guests with dainty appetites and those prepared for a feeding frenzy.) For an approximate measure, plan on two or three of each hors d'oeuvres per person.

All that food calls for a lot of platters. If you need additional service pieces and don't want to buy new ones, head to a party store (which is sometimes also a paper warehouse), where there's often a selection of inexpensive plastic serving dishes (some silver colored) that look surprisingly presentable.

UP TO 1 HOUR IN ADVANCE

Assemble crostini.

Bring roasted mushrooms to room temperature.

Make pomegranate punch.

LAST-MINUTE PREP

Bake Phyllo Bundles.

Shortcut Savvy

Buy bakery-made puff pastry twists or breadsticks.

Buy ready-made pot stickers as a substitute for Phyllo Bundles.

Purchase Italian cured meats, thinly sliced and rolled up with mozzarella, to be sliced and served as pinwheels. They are found in the deli section.

Buy ready-made marinated feta or mozzarella in cubes, which are available in the refrigerated deli section in jars or tubs. Serve with toothpicks.

Buy bakery-made cookies or mini-tarts.

Beverage

Pomegranate punch is the right color (red) and the right flavor of the season (pomegranate). If preferred, offer an assortment of wines (red and white) or sparkling wine, in addition.

Just which recipes you'll prepare—and which foods you'll buy ready-made—are your prerogative. The guests won't care where their food comes from, as long as it tastes good. Accept their compliments with grace as they express their amazement at your culinary prowess. After all, the holidays are a time for secrets.

Keep thawing times in mind as you plan food preparation. Some items, such as phyllo dough, must be thawed overnight in a refrigerator.

And remember, when serving food at a buffet for an extended period, keep the platters small and replenish them often to keep the food looking—and tasting—fresh. For the sake of safety, no food should be sitting at room temperature for more than two hours.

Pomegranate Punch
MAKES 20 (½ CUP) OR 10 (1 CUP) SERVINGS

3½ cups pomegranate juice
2½ cups orange juice
2½ cups sparkling water
1½ cups vodka (optional, or use additional sparkling water)

In a punch bowl, mix together juices with sparkling water and vodka. Add ice ring made from water with the addition of pomegranate seeds or orange slices for decoration. (See page 215 for how to seed a pomegranate.)

Shrimp Salad in Radicchio Cups

MAKES 40 OR MORE HORS D'OEUVRES

Lettuce wraps have become popular—too popular if you're trying to provide something different at the table. But the concept is transferable: a spicy filling inside a green leaf. Well, this leaf is reddish purple, and the filling is a shrimp salad. It not only tastes good, but the colors also add some interest to your buffet. Radicchio (rah-DEE-kee-oh) is a red-leafed salad green with a slightly bitter flavor. It's purchased in a small head, like iceberg lettuce or cabbage. The firm, tender leaves make good cups for serving.

⅓ cup sour cream
⅓ cup plain nonfat yogurt (see Note)
2 teaspoons prepared horseradish (optional)
1 cup peeled, seeded, and chopped cucumber
3 chopped green onions with some tops included
2 heaping tablespoons chopped fresh dill, or 2 teaspoons dried dill, plus
    extra for garnish
1 pound cooked, shelled medium shrimp, cut into ½- to ¾-inch pieces
Salt and white pepper
2 heads radicchio

Stir the sour cream, yogurt, and horseradish together in a medium bowl. Stir in cucumber, green onions, dill, and shrimp. Season to taste with salt and pepper. Cover and chill several hours or overnight to blend flavors. (Can be made ahead to this point.)

    A few hours before serving, cut head of radicchio in half lengthwise and pull apart leaves. If leaves are still too big for finger food, cut (or pull) them apart again. Fill each leaf with 1 tablespoon or so of salad. Refrigerate, covered, until ready to serve.

Variation: Instead of radicchio leaves, use Belgian endive to hold the salad.

Note: *If you don't have both sour cream and plain yogurt, use just one of the two. The extra tang that the yogurt provides is nice, but not necessary. Or you could substitute mayonnaise.*

French Twists
MAKES 28 TWISTS
For 20 guests, double the recipe.

This recipe is a variation on a traditional breadstick-like appetizer.

1 sheet of frozen puff pastry, thawed
About 1 tablespoon tomato paste
A few drops olive oil
1 egg
1 tablespoon water
Freshly grated Parmesan
Freshly cracked black pepper (optional)

On lightly floured surface, roll out puff pastry sheet slightly to make a 14 x 10-inch rectangle. In a small dish, mix tomato paste with a little olive oil to make spreading easier. Brush tomato paste mixture along one of the long sides of the pastry sheet and spread out to cover half of the surface.

Fold dough in half to cover tomato paste. Roll gently with rolling pin to make the dough stick together. In a small dish, whisk egg with water and brush mixture on top of pastry dough. Sprinkle Parmesan and black pepper, if desired, on top.

Using a pizza cutter, cut ½-inch strips crosswise. Twist strips into corkscrew shapes. (Can be made ahead to this point; place the twists in a freezer bag and freeze until ready to use.)

Preheat oven to 400° F. Place strips on ungreased baking sheet and bake for about 10 minutes, or until nicely browned.

Variation: Sprinkle coarse salt instead of Parmesan and black pepper on top of the twists.

Phyllo Bundles

MAKES ABOUT 60 BUNDLES

Phyllo leaves make an elegant presentation, but they often require a lot of time for the folding and layering that's usually needed. These bundles, however, are almost effortless, and they can be made ahead and frozen. Keep in mind the phyllo needs to be defrosted in advance.

½ pound spicy bulk sausage, such as Italian
2 tablespoons chopped fresh sage
9 sheets frozen phyllo, thawed according to package directions
8 tablespoons (1 stick) butter, melted

Brown sausage and drain grease. Mix in sage.

Be sure to keep phyllo leaves covered with a clean cloth when not working with them, as they will dry out quickly. Place one sheet of phyllo dough on a clean counter and brush with melted butter. Add a second sheet and brush with melted butter. Add a third sheet, brush with melted butter, and cut the stack of sheets into 3-inch squares. (A pizza cutter works well.)

Place a teaspoon or so of cooked sausage in the center of each phyllo square. Pull up the four corners of each square and scrunch together at the top, twisting slightly to keep phyllo bundle closed. With the remaining phyllo leaves, repeat the process of buttering and stacking 3 leaves at a time, cutting into squares, filling, and closing the bundles. Freeze unbaked phyllo bundles on a flat surface and transfer to freezer bags until ready to use. (Can be made in advance to this point.)

Preheat oven to 375° F. Place frozen bundles on ungreased cookie sheet and bake for 10 minutes, or until lightly browned. Serve hot or warm.

Variation: Instead of sausage, stuff with cream cheese or feta cheese, or add chopped spinach to either.

Crostini with White Bean and Sun-Dried Tomato Purée

MAKES 20 CROSTINI

1 tablespoon minced garlic

1 tablespoon olive oil, plus more for bread

1 (15.8-ounce) can Great Northern beans, drained and rinsed

2 tablespoons white wine vinegar or lemon juice

2 tablespoons water

1 tablespoon chopped fresh sage or rosemary, plus more for garnish

4 oil-packed sun-dried tomato halves, cut up slightly

½ teaspoon (or more) salt

Freshly ground white pepper

1 baguette, sliced ½-inch thick, or 1 loaf thinly sliced (2½- x 2½-inch)
   cocktail bread (see Note)

In a small saucepan, sauté garlic in olive oil until fragrant (do not let brown).

In a blender or food processor, combine beans, garlic, and olive oil, vinegar, water, sage or rosemary, sun-dried tomatoes, salt, and pepper. Purée until almost smooth. Check seasonings and adjust to taste. (This topping can be made a day in advance and refrigerated.)

Preheat oven to 400° F. Place bread slices on a baking sheet and brush with oil. Toast for 5 minutes; then flip pieces over and toast for another 5 minutes. Cool. (This can be done up to 8 hours in advance; wrap cooled bread until use.)

To serve, top oiled side of each bread slice with about 2 teaspoons of white bean purée. Garnish with additional herbs.

Variation: Rinse and drain an additional can of white beans; garnish each crostini with a few whole white beans.

Note: *The topping is designed to cover about 20 slices of baguette. Depending on the size of the baguette, you may want to double this recipe.*

Crostini with Roast Beef and Roasted Red Peppers

MAKES 20 SERVINGS

1 baguette, sliced ½-inch thick, or 1 loaf thinly sliced (2½- x 2½-inch)
   cocktail bread (see Note)
Olive oil
8 ounces goat cheese (also called chèvre)
½ pound thinly sliced or shaved roast beef (from deli)
1 (about 7-ounce) jar roasted red peppers, cut into ¼-inch by 2-inch strips

Preheat oven to 400° F.

Place bread slices on a baking sheet and brush with oil. Toast for 5 minutes; then flip pieces over and toast for another 5 minutes. Cool. (This can be done up to 8 hours hours in advance; cool thoroughly and wrap until use.)

To serve, spread a thin coating of goat cheese on top of oiled side of bread slices Top with roast beef and a strip or two of roasted pepper.

Variation: Instead of meat, top the goat cheese with fig chutney. Or spread a thin coating of pomegranate molasses on top of the cheese, with thin slices of smoked duck breast on top of the molasses.

Note: *The topping is designed to cover about 20 slices of baguette. Depending on the size of the baguette, you may want to double this recipe.*

Edamame Spread

MAKES 1 CUP

Edamame (eh-dah-MAH-meh) is the Japanese word for green soybeans. They can be found packaged in the produce section or in the freezer section of the supermarket. For the latter, they simply need to be thawed and sprinkled with coarse salt—a practically instant appetizer. Or they can be puréed and used as a spread with crackers or slices of bread.

2 cups edamame without the shell (10-ounce package)
½ cup or more cream or milk
2 tablespoons lemon juice
Salt and white pepper

In a blender or food processor, combine the soybeans with cream. Purée until smooth (add additional cream to desired consistency). Remove purée to another container and add the lemon juice, and salt and pepper to taste. Serve with crackers or slices of bread.

Variation: Serve edamame in the shell for guests, who can shell them for the peas inside (and who will enjoy the taste of the salt on the exterior). Take a 1-pound package of frozen edamame in the shell. Drop the frozen pods into boiling water for a minute to defrost; drain and rinse in cold water to stop cooking. Drain again. Sprinkle pods with coarse salt and serve. Makes about 2 cups.

Merlot Roasted Mushrooms

MAKES 40 OR MORE MUSHROOMS

4 (8-ounce) packages (2 pounds) small whole mushrooms (such as baby
     bellas or button)
¼ cup merlot (or another light red wine)
¼ cup chicken stock
2 tablespoons olive oil
2 fresh thyme sprigs
Salt and freshly ground black pepper

Preheat oven to 375° F.

Clean mushrooms by wiping them off with a damp paper towel. In a
baking pan or dish, mix together wine, stock, olive oil, and thyme; season to
taste with salt and pepper. Add mushrooms and toss. Cover and roast for
30 minutes.

Remove cover and continue roasting for another 15 minutes. Remove
from oven and cool. (Can be made in advance to this point.)

If made ahead, bring mushrooms to room temperature before serving.
To serve, place in bowl with toothpicks either stuck in the mushrooms or
placed in a container at the side (for use in picking them up).

Mini-Tarts
MAKES 40 (2-INCH) TARTS

Multiple desserts are always a pleasure at a buffet. These bite-size tarts add lovely color to the table, as well.

2 (9-inch) unbaked prepared pie crusts (see Note)
Assorted ready-made fillings, preserves, puddings (such as lemon curd, fig, ginger, pomegranate, fruit pie filling, chocolate)
Crushed pistachios, for garnish
Lemon zest, for garnish

Preheat oven to 400° F.

If using frozen pie dough, thaw it out according to package directions. Roll out dough. Using a 2- to 3-inch round cookie cutter (or glass rim), cut out tart shells from the dough.

Place tart shells in ungreased mini-muffin pans and shape to fit like mini-pie crusts. Prick the bottom of the shells and bake for about 5 minutes. (The mini-muffin pans are necessary because the dough doesn't keep its shape otherwise.) Cool and keep covered until ready to serve. (Can be made in advance to this point.)

Shortly before serving, drop about 1 tablespoon of filling into each tart shell. Sprinkle with pistachios or lemon zest on top, if desired.

Variation: Add a dab of crème fraîche in the bottom of the crust before topping with filling. Or, with an electric mixer, beat together 1 (3-ounce) package softened cream cheese, 2 tablespoons powdered sugar, and 2 tablespoons milk until smooth. Add to bottom of tarts before topping with pie filling.

Note: *The pie dough can be homemade or purchased from the freezer or refrigerated section of the supermarket; it needs to be unbaked, so that it can be cut to size for mini-tarts.*

Homemade Mint Candies

MAKES ABOUT 4 DOZEN (¾-INCH) MINTS

This recipe calls for flavoring oil, which comes in many varieties, any of which can be used in these candies. For the old-fashioned dinner mints, I use wintergreen, clove, and cinnamon. Other oil flavors include licorice, crème de menthe, peppermint, spearmint, lemon, and butter rum—as well as the more modern flavors of watermelon, bubblegum, and piña colada. Give your guests a hint of what they'll be nibbling by using food coloring that matches the flavors. (I use green for wintergreen, white for clove, and red for cinnamon.)

This recipe won't work if your kitchen is extremely humid, for example if soup is simmering while you're making the candy.

1 egg white (see Notes)
1 tablespoon milk
2½ cups powdered sugar
Flavoring oil, such as oil of wintergreen, clove, or cinnamon (see Notes)
Food coloring, if desired

In a large bowl, beat together egg white, milk, and powdered sugar. Divide the mixture by the number of flavoring oils you will be using, placing each portion in a separate bowl. Add a drop of oil flavoring to each portion, mixing it in thoroughly with a spoon; taste and adjust with additional drops, if desired. Color each portion according to its flavor (such as green for wintergreen flavor, red for cinnamon). The mixture will be stiff.

Take about ½ teaspoon of the mixture and roll it in your hands to form a ½-inch ball. Place on wax paper and lightly flatten it with a fork. Repeat with remaining candy mixture. Candy is ready to eat immediately. To store, stack in a covered container in the refrigerator, separating candy layers with wax paper. Store different flavors in separate containers so the flavors don't mix. To serve, bring to room temperature.

Notes:
- *Be sure to use pasteurized egg white, because it will not be cooked.*
- *Flavoring oils can be found in cake- and candy-supply stores.*

Spicy Almonds

MAKES 3 CUPS

⅓ cup sugar

2 teaspoons cayenne pepper

3 cups (about 1 pound) whole almonds, with or without skins

Combine sugar, cayenne, and almonds in a frying pan and cook over medium heat until sugar dissolves and the almonds are fragrant, about 10 to 15 minutes. Pour out onto wax paper and cool. Separate almonds, and store in an airtight container in the refrigerator.

SIMPLE PLEASURES

For as far back as I can remember, the dinner table at family gatherings included mints made by Bertha, a gentle great-aunt with a perpetual smile and seemingly endless patience. Her small candies, tinted in pastels, weren't much bigger than my thumb. That daintiness may have been part of their charm. Tiny and pretty in holiday colors, the mints easily could be popped whole into an awaiting mouth, though I preferred to nibble mine slowly, savoring its intense flavors—especially the clove mints that could make me wince if a few too many drops of flavoring had ended up in the batch.

Back then, it didn't seem unusual that Bertha made mints for family gatherings. This was an era when everything at the table was homemade and, for the Christmas holidays, that meant it was a little more special than at other times. Every family member had a specialty.

Years later, once the mints recipe was passed along to me, I tackled the project one December afternoon after tracking down a store that sold oil of wintergreen and oil of clove. To my surprise and great pleasure, I discovered what Bertha must have known all along (perhaps that was why she was smiling): There is almost no effort required in making this recipe. It is simply powdered sugar with a little liquid and flavoring. The candies don't even have to cook.

Today when I'm short of time or energy and I know there is a table that needs something homemade, I pull out Bertha's recipe and set to work. Homemade couldn't be easier.

NEED MORE IDEAS?

Many other recipes in this book lend themselves equally well to a cocktail buffet. Some work well in the same form as the original recipe; others can be easily adapted for a cocktail buffet. If you're feeling ambitious and want to expand the menu offerings, or if you'd like to make substitutions for some items on this menu, check out these further possibilities:

SPREADS AND DIPS

Lentil and Black Olive Spread (page 24)

Carrot, Curry, and Cumin Spread (page 25)

Eggplant and Roasted Red Pepper Spread (page 26)

Smoked Salmon Spread with crackers or served in mini-phyllo tarts (page 34)

Blue Cheese Mousse with crackers or served in mini-phyllo tarts (page 35)

Sun-Dried Tomato Dip with assorted vegetables (page 53)

Nacho Cheese Sauce with tortilla chips (page 81)

Guacamole for a Crowd with tortilla chips (page 82)

Pico de Gallo with tortilla chips (page 83)

Curried Onion Chutney with roasted vegetables (page 104)

Green Olive Sauce and Black Olive Sauce with crackers (page 109)

Caramelized Onion Dip with any chips (page 132)

Raita (yogurt sauce) with lamb kebabs or with fresh vegetables (page 150)

Pineapple Salsa with tortilla chips (page 179)

BITE-SIZE

Chicken Salad Mini-Cups (page 32)

Roasted New Potatoes with Sweet Onions and Olives served on skewers (page 54)

Mushroom and Onion Quiche prepared in mini-muffin tins using a base of ready-made pie crust that you have prebaked (page 61)

Pesto-Stuffed Eggs (page 115)

Caramelized Leek, Goat Cheese, and Sun-Dried Tomato Triangles (page 172)

Quesadilla with Brie and Roasted Red Peppers cut into smaller portions (page 180)

Smoked Duck and Caramelized Onion Pizza cut into small pieces (page 191)

Shrimp, Avocado, and Tomato Pizza cut into small pieces (page 192)

Feta, Sun-Dried Tomato, and Artichoke Pizza cut into small pieces (page 193)

Flatbread with Fresh Thyme and Black Peppercorns (page 262)

NIBBLES

Marinated Olives (page 55)

Roasted Green Beans (page 201)

MEAT

Chicken Drumsticks with Ginger and Garlic (page 101)

Lamb Kebabs with Harissa (page 149)

UP TO A WEEK IN ADVANCE

Order the crown roast from
the butcher.

UP TO 2 DAYS IN ADVANCE

Make custard.

UP TO A DAY IN ADVANCE

Make the soup broth.

Toast bread and cut to fit bowls.

Roast the root vegetables.

Prepare pilaf.

UP TO 8 HOURS IN ADVANCE

Bake the cake portion of the
mini–Boston cream pies.

UP TO 3 TO 4 HOURS IN
ADVANCE

Prepare pork and roast.

LAST-MINUTE PREP

Reheat soup broth.

Butter bread and bake the
cheese toast in the soup bowls.

Reheat the vegetables.

Assemble dessert and melt
chocolate immediately before
serving.

CROWN ROAST DINNER

For 8

French Onion Soup
Roasted Root Vegetables with Sage
Crown Roast of Pork with Orzo Pilaf
Bostoni Cream Pies

WHEN IT COMES TO DINNER PARTIES, 'tis the season for the spectacular, as host tries to outshine host and guests reap the benefits at sumptuously laden tables. Never mind that there are parties galore. Here are flavors that won't be found on every dinner table and a menu to delight the most discriminating guests and the busiest cooks.

The meal begins with French onion soup, served with melted Swiss cheese over toasted bread. It's somewhat difficult to eat gracefully, but no matter. The flavors are worth the effort. Don't be put off by the length of the recipe. Although there are many steps to the dish, they are all simple.

It's followed by a crown roast of pork, which is rarely seen on dinner tables except for very special occasions. It's made of two pork loins tied together to create a "crown," with the tips of the rib bones sticking up in true crown-like fashion. The hollow spot inside the circle of meat is usually filled with rice or vegetables. For this menu, the interior filling is the small rice-shaped pasta called orzo. The crown roast is ideal for a dinner party because it involves very little work for the cook, who has time to concentrate on other dishes. Roasted root vegetables round out the hearty meal.

Dessert is as spectacular as the main dish, with mini–Boston cream pies for all.

Shortcut Savvy

Buy prepared soup.

Buy prepared rice (available in freezer section).

Modify the dessert concept with unfrosted cupcakes of yellow cake, placed on home-made custard or pudding. Or purchase bakery-made dessert.

Beverage

Start out with an amontillado sherry with the soup, followed by a Beaujolais with the crown roast. Finish up with coffee for dessert.

French Onion Soup

SERVES 8

4 tablespoons (½ stick) butter

2 pounds (about 8 to 10, depending on size) yellow onions, peeled and
thinly sliced

½ cup red wine (optional)

3 quarts (12 cups) beef stock (see Note)

3 fresh thyme sprigs or ¾ teaspoon dried thyme

2 bay leaves

Salt and freshly ground black pepper

8 (½-inch thick) slices of French bread, cut to fit into individual bowls

8 ounces Gruyère or Swiss cheese, grated

Heat butter in a large (4-quart) saucepan over medium heat. Cook onions
on medium for about an hour, stirring only occasionally, until they are
golden and begin to caramelize.

Add red wine, scraping up the brotwn particles on the bottom of the
pan. Add stock, thyme, and bay leaves. Partially cover and simmer over
medium-low heat for 45 to 50 minutes. Taste for seasoning and correct
with salt and pepper. Remove bay leaves. (Can be made in advance to this
point and refrigerated.)

To serve: Preheat oven to 350° F. Reheat soup if made earlier. Toast
bread until brown. (Can be done ahead to this point.)

Before serving, butter the bread. (If bread is not toasted and buttered,
it will soak up the soup like a sponge.)

Ladle hot soup into ovenproof bowls placed on a baking pan or tray.
Add toasted bread to each bowl; sprinkle with grated cheese. Bake for
10 to 15 minutes or until cheese has melted.

Note: *If you are using canned condensed beef broth, use 4 (10.5-ounce)
cans and add enough water to measure 12 cups. Stick with low-sodium
broth for the best flavor.*

Roasted Root Vegetables with Sage
SERVES 8

This recipe is adaptable; use whatever vegetables you prefer. Remember, you're the cook.

4 medium beets, peeled and quartered
2 large Yukon Gold potatoes, unpeeled and cut into chunks
2 parsnips, peeled and cut into cubes
2 carrots, peeled and sliced
1 sweet potato, peeled and cut into cubes
2 large onions, peeled and quartered
¼ cup olive oil
1 garlic clove, minced
8 fresh sage leaves
Coarse salt and freshly cracked pepper

Preheat oven to 375° F. In a large bowl, toss beets, potatoes, parsnips, carrots, sweet potato, and onion with olive oil, garlic, and sage. Spread the vegetables on a heavy rimmed baking sheet or pan. Sprinkle with salt and pepper to taste. Roast until tender, stirring occasionally, about 1 hour. (If prepared ahead and oven space is limited, reheat slowly, covered, on the stove with a little additional oil, or covered in a 350° F oven for about 20 minutes.)

Crown Roast of Pork with Orzo Pilaf
MAKES 8 TO 10 SERVINGS

This roast must be specially ordered from meat departments; some butchers require several days' notice. Slightly smaller versions can be ordered (though it can't be too small because it has to be formed into a circle). This roast is filled with a simple seasoned orzo, a small pasta shaped like rice; you could also substitute wild rice. There should be enough room in the oven for both the crown roast and the soup bowls, but check in advance, in case you need to remove the roast for 15 minutes while the soup takes its place.

CROWN ROAST
About 8 pounds crown roast (16 to 20 ribs to allow 2 per person)
¼ cup light corn syrup
1 teaspoon soy sauce

ORZO PILAF
1 medium onion, chopped (about ¾ cup)
½ green bell pepper, chopped (about ½ cup)
½ red bell pepper, chopped (about ½ cup)
2 garlic cloves, minced
2 tablespoons butter or margarine
2 cups chicken broth (or water)
4 cups water
3 cups uncooked orzo

FOR CROWN ROAST
Rinse crown roast and pat dry. If using a meat thermometer, insert so bulb reaches center of thickest part of meat, avoiding fat and bone. Place in shallow roasting pan. Roast, uncovered, at 350° F for 2½ to 3 hours. Mix together corn syrup and soy sauce; use to baste roast periodically.

Remove meat from the oven when the meat thermometer reaches 170° F, or when meat is no longer pink. Drain off fat; place meat on serving plate.

FOR ORZO PILAF

Prepare the pilaf about 45 minutes before roast is done (or pilaf can be made a day in advance and reheated in the oven with roast). In a large skillet, sauté the onion, green bell pepper, red bell pepper, and garlic in hot butter or margarine until tender, but not brown.

Add the onion mixture to the chicken broth, water, and orzo; bring to a boil, then reduce heat. Cover and simmer for 15 to 20 minutes or until pasta is done and liquid is absorbed, adding additional water while cooking if necessary (drain off any extra water). For a spectacular presentation, spoon orzo into the center of the crown roast and bring to the table.

TO SERVE

Cut the string around the roast and remove. Using a fork to steady the ribs, cut between the ribs. (Plan on two ribs per person.) For serving purposes, orzo can be transferred to a serving dish or left on the platter with the roast.

Bostoni Cream Pies

MAKES 8 CAKES

A variation on Boston Cream Pie, this remarkable dessert features individual cakes with custard at the bottom, topped with an orange chiffon cake and warm melted chocolate. It is adapted from pastry chef Kurtis L. Baguley of Bistro Don Giovanni in Napa, California, and Bistro Scala in San Francisco, and was served to gasps of pleasure at a food editors conference. Boston cream pie, of course, isn't an actual pie. It's made from chiffon or sponge cake, with a layer of custard and topping of chocolate.

CUSTARD
⅓ cup sugar
2 tablespoons flour
2 tablespoons cornstarch
4 egg yolks
1⅓ cup milk
¾ teaspoon vanilla

ORANGE CHIFFON CAKE
3 eggs, separated
½ teaspoon cream of tartar
¾ cup cake flour
⅓ cup sugar
¾ teaspoon baking powder
¼ teaspoon salt
2 tablespoons canola oil or other neutral oil
⅓ cup freshly squeezed orange juice
1 tablespoon grated orange zest
½ teaspoon vanilla extract

WARM CHOCOLATE GLAZE
8 ounces good quality semisweet chocolate, in any form

FOR CUSTARD
In a medium bowl, beat sugar, flour, cornstarch, and egg yolks on high speed until thick and pale yellow, about 2 minutes.

Meanwhile, bring milk to a simmer in a medium stainless-steel saucepan over low heat. Gradually pour about one-third of the hot milk into the egg mixture, stirring constantly. Pour the egg mixture back into the pan and cook, whisking constantly and scraping the bottom and corners of the pan to prevent scorching, over low to medium heat until the custard is thickened and begins to bubble. Continue to cook, whisking for 1 minute.

Pour the custard into a clean bowl, add the vanilla, and combine thoroughly. Cover the surface of the custard with a piece of wax or parchment paper to prevent a skin from forming. Let cool, then refrigerate. (Can be made up to 2 days in advance.)

FOR ORANGE CHIFFON CAKE

Preheat the oven to 325° F.

Grease regular size muffin tins with nonstick cooking spray.

In a small bowl, whip 3 egg whites until frothy. Add cream of tartar; continue beating until soft peaks form. Set aside.

Sift cake flour, sugar, baking powder, and salt into a large bowl. Add oil, 3 lightly beaten yolks, orange juice, zest, and vanilla extract. Beat until smooth.

Gently fold the beaten whites into the cake batter. Fill the greased molds nearly to the top with batter. (Any extra batter can be used to make cupcakes.) Bake about 15 minutes, until tops bounce back when lightly pressed with your fingertip. (Tops will be lightly colored.) Do not overbake. Remove from the oven and cool pan on a wire rack. Remove cakes from the pan. Cover cakes to keep them moist until ready to use.

FOR WARM CHOCOLATE GLAZE

If chocolate is in one piece, break into smaller pieces. Melt chocolate over low heat in small saucepan.

FINAL ASSEMBLY

Place about ¼ cup custard in bottom of each serving dish (such as dessert plates, decorative bowls, or ramekins). Top with a cake and drizzle warm chocolate over each. Serve immediately.

Variation: The serious cook might frown on this, but you could make cupcakes from a yellow cake mix to use in place of the chiffon cake. And you could make or buy vanilla pudding to use instead of the custard. Or buy some prepared chocolate sauce to warm, then drizzle, and your guests will be happy.

Note: *The cake batter fits in 8 or 9 regular-size muffin tins. If you have larger tins, or popover pans, you'll need to double the cake recipe. (The custard amount won't change.)*

UP TO SEVERAL DAYS IN
ADVANCE

Make Beef Burgundy.

UP TO A DAY IN ADVANCE

Make soup.

Make vinaigrette.

UP TO 8 HOURS IN ADVANCE

Make apple pie.

UP TO 1 HOUR IN ADVANCE

Assemble salad.

LAST-MINUTE PREP

Cook noodles.

Reheat Beef Burgundy

Reheat soup and add cream.

Shortcut Savvy

Buy prewashed salad greens.

Buy a pie from the bakery.

Beverage

Start out with vouvray with
the celery soup. A modestly
priced Burgundy is a natural
with beef Burgundy. For dessert a sweet ice wine or, for a
change of pace, an aged rum,
is a good finish.

ELEGANT DINNER PARTY

For 8

Cream of Celery Soup
Beef Burgundy with Hot Egg Noodles
Pear and Blue Cheese Salad
Apple Crumble Pie

THE HEART OF THE HOLIDAYS is in the kitchen. That's where they begin and end. Where the hustle and bustle—the magic of the holidays—mysteriously takes form amid the flour and butter, the roasting pan and the cookie sheet. That's where not only the cook can be found, but also the guests who are taking a peek—if not a nibble—at the upcoming meal.

Holidays and hospitality. They belong together as surely as a turkey and dressing. Long after the last dish has been put away, the swirl of dis-carded gift-wrapping bundled up, what remains of the holiday is the warm memory of the time around the table.

For the cook, that hustle and bustle before the meal requires some forethought. Energetic work should not be confused with chaos. What fol-lows is an elegant meal suited for the occasion that can be prepared much in advance. This is one of my favorite meals for company. Celery soup starts the dinner with simple, clean flavors and a hint of formality. A salad of pears and blue cheese is a pleasant change of taste from the usual green salad. Beef Burgundy serves as a robust entrée that almost melts in your mouth. And a variation of apple pie offers a rich ending to the perfect meal.

So let the festivities begin . . . in your kitchen.

Cream of Celery Soup
MAKES ABOUT 8 CUPS

3 tablespoons olive oil
1 package (1 large bunch) celery, trimmed of leaves, peeled, and coarsely
     cut (reserve celery leaves, if fresh, for garnish)
2 medium onions, chopped (about 1½ cups)
2 small potatoes, peeled and chopped (about 1½ cups)
6 cups chicken broth
Salt and freshly cracked pepper
½ cup cream
Sour cream, for garnish
Celery leaves or minced parsley, dill, or fresh chives, for garnish

In a large soup pot over medium heat, heat oil and cook celery and onions for about 15 minutes. Add potatoes and cook for another 5 minutes. Add broth and bring to a boil. Reduce heat and simmer, uncovered, for 25 to 30 minutes, or until vegetables are tender. Set aside to cool slightly before puréeing. (For information on puréeing hot liquids, see the Cook's Notes for Asparagus Soup on page 40.)

In a blender, purée the vegetables and broth and return to the pot. Season to taste with salt and pepper. (Can be made in advance to this point.)

To serve, add cream and heat through. Garnish with a dab of sour cream or sprinkle with celery leaves or herbs.

Beef Burgundy with Hot Egg Noodles
SERVES 6 TO 8

BEEF BURGUNDY

4 pounds boneless beef chuck, cut into 1½-inch pieces

¼ cup flour, divided

6 tablespoons vegetable oil, divided

4 large shallots, finely chopped

4 medium onions, halved lengthwise, then thinly sliced lengthwise

2 garlic cloves, chopped

2 carrots, thinly sliced

2 cups dry red wine, such as Burgundy

12 slices bacon

2 (10-ounce) packages pearl onions

2 teaspoons salt

2 teaspoons black pepper

Finely chopped parsley, for garnish

HOT BUTTERED NOODLES

16 ounces uncooked egg noodles

2 tablespoons butter

FOR BEEF BURGUNDY

Toss chunks of meat in flour, reserving any remaining flour.

Put about 1 tablespoon oil in a large frying pan over medium heat. Add enough meat to cover the bottom of pan and brown, turning occasionally. Remove meat from pan and put in a slow cooker (or a Dutch oven or a casserole dish with a cover). Repeat with remaining floured meat until all is browned, adding additional oil as needed.

In same frying pan over medium heat, add about 2 tablespoons oil. Add the shallots, onions, and garlic. Cook until shallots begin to brown. Add any remaining flour to onion mixture. Add mixture to meat, along with carrots and wine.

In the same frying pan, cook bacon until it begins to crisp. Remove and drain on paper toweling (reserve bacon grease in pan). Cut up bacon coarsely and add to meat.

Meanwhile, blanch pearl onions in boiling water for 1 minute. Drain and peel. Cook pearl onions, uncovered, in bacon grease over medium heat for about 5 minutes; add to meat mixture with salt and pepper (if cooking the meat in the oven, add pearl onions later).

Set the slow cooker at low heat for about 6 hours or at high for 3 hours.

If using a Dutch oven, cook on the stovetop over low heat for about 3 hours. Check periodically to make sure liquid hasn't evaporated. Add water, if necessary.

If using a casserole dish, place covered dish in a 350° F oven and cook for about 3 hours. Add pearl onions about midway through cooking time.

This can be made several days in advance. It should be reheated slowly over medium-low heat, with additional water added if needed.

FOR HOT BUTTERED NOODLES
Cook noodles according to package directions. Drain and toss with butter.

FOR SERVING
Serve Beef Burgundy on a bed of buttered egg noodles; garnish with finely chopped parsley.

Pear and Blue Cheese Salad

SERVES 8

VINAIGRETTE
3 tablespoons pear-infused vinegar, or white wine vinegar (see Note)
1 shallot, minced
½ cup extra-virgin olive oil
Salt and freshly cracked pepper

SALAD
4 ripe pears, peeled and sliced
2 teaspoons lemon juice
6 to 8 cups mixed greens (about 8 ounces)
2 ounces blue cheese crumbles

FOR VINAIGRETTE
In a small bowl, mix together vinegar and shallot. Whisk olive oil into vinegar. Season to taste with salt and pepper. (Can be made a day ahead and refrigerated.)

FOR SALAD ASSEMBLY
Dip pear slices in lemon juice and set aside.

Place mixed greens on individual plates. Top with pear slices. Drizzle with vinaigrette and sprinkle with blue cheese.

Note: *Pear-infused vinegar offers a wonderful boost of pear flavor to this salad. It can be found in many supermarkets where gourmet vinegars are sold.*

Apple Crumble Pie
SERVES 8

I like to serve this with an aged cheddar at the table to nibble.

APPLE FILLING

3¼ pounds tart apples (such as Granny Smith), peeled and sliced
    ¼-inch thick
⅔ cup sugar
2 tablespoons flour
2 teaspoons cinnamon
2 tablespoons butter, melted
9- or 10-inch unbaked pie crust

TOPPING

1 cup flour
½ cup sugar
¼ cup packed brown sugar
1½ teaspoons cinnamon
½ teaspoon salt
6 tablespoons (¾ stick) chilled butter, cut into ½-inch cubes

FOR APPLE FILLING

Preheat oven to 400° F.

In a large bowl, toss together apple slices, sugar, flour, cinnamon, and melted butter. Place in pie crust, mounding in center.

FOR TOPPING AND BAKING PIE

In a medium bowl, stir together flour, sugar, brown sugar, cinnamon, and salt. Cut in chilled butter until mixture resembles small peas. Sprinkle over top of apple filling.

Place pie on baking sheet (to catch any drippings) and bake until top is golden, about 30 minutes. Cover edges or top with aluminum foil if either browns too quickly.

Reduce heat to 350° F and continue baking until apples are tender, about 20 to 30 minutes more.

POST-HOLIDAY WINTER CELEBRATION

For 6

Cream of Carrot Soup
Rock Cornish Game Hens with Apple Cider Sauce
Roasted Potatoes with Sage and Garlic
Poached Pears with Caramel and Pistachios

NOW THAT THE HOLIDAY BUSTLE has faded, and meals for twenty are memories, it's time to enjoy the remaining weeks of winter with a menu that warms the spirit and pleases the palate. You don't need a crowd to celebrate. Or, for that matter, a reason. You've made it through the holidays and that's cause enough. When the wind is howling and the snowflakes are piling up, it's comforting to reach for hearty fare and share a meal with guests.

This menu begins with a lovely, fragrant carrot soup. With this small, manageable guest list, Rock Cornish game hens are the main course, nature's own single servings. These are topped with an apple cider sauce served with sage-flavored roasted potatoes. A simple but rich dessert of pears with caramel finishes off this meal with style.

Cream of Carrot Soup

MAKES 6 CUPS

5 to 6 medium carrots (about 1 pound), peeled and sliced
1 large onion, sliced (about 1 cup)
1 leek, diced (see Note)
2 ribs celery, sliced (about 1 cup)
2 medium russet potatoes, peeled and cubed (about 2 cups)
5 cups chicken broth
1 teaspoon salt
Freshly cracked pepper
¾ cup half-and-half
Sour cream, for garnish
Snipped fresh dill or chives, for garnish

Combine the carrots, onion, leek, celery, potatoes, and chicken broth in a large saucepan. Bring to a boil, and reduce to a simmer; cook uncovered for about 20 minutes or until the vegetables are tender.

Set aside to cool slightly before puréeing. (For information on puréeing hot liquids, see the Note for Asparagus Soup on page 40.) Purée the soup in small batches in a food processor or blender. Return to saucepan and season to taste with salt and pepper. (Can be made ahead to this point.) Add half-and-half and heat through. Serve with a dollop of sour cream and fresh dill or chives.

Variation: Make a ginger carrot soup by adding 1 tablespoon minced, peeled fresh ginger root to the vegetable mixture as it simmers.

Variation: Make a curried carrot soup by adding 2 teaspoons curry powder to the vegetable mixture as it simmers.

Note: *Leeks need to be carefully cleaned because dirt gets in between the many layers. To clean a leek, slit the white portion from top to bottom and separate the layers to rinse them. Discard the green portion.*

Rock Cornish Game Hens with Apple Cider Sauce
SERVES 6

Rock Cornish game hens are hybrids of Cornish and White Rock chickens. These small chickens can weigh up to 2½ pounds apiece. With relatively little meat in proportion to the bones, they generally are prepared as single servings.

For this recipe, unfiltered apple cider (usually found in the supermarket produce section) is used to baste the hens and make the thin sauce that bears little resemblance to traditional gravy. Unfiltered cider has a more intense, tart flavor than does filtered cider, which tends to look and taste more like thin apple juice. If filtered cider is used, add a tablespoon of lemon juice to the sauce to give it some tang.

6 Rock Cornish game hens (about 18 to 24 ounces each)
Salt and white pepper
3 unpeeled, cored apples, chopped (about 3 cups)
2 medium onions, chopped (about 1½ cups)
2 cups apple cider, preferably unfiltered, divided
1 tablespoon or more cornstarch
1 tablespoon butter (optional)
Pickled crab apples, for garnish (found with pickles in the supermarket)

Preheat oven to 375° F.

Rinse hens thoroughly inside and out, and dry. Salt and pepper inside of hens. Set aside hens, breast-side up, in baking pan with at least 2-inch sides. The pan should be large enough to hold all hens without crowding—or use two pans.

In a bowl, mix together apples and onions and stuff an equal portion into each of the 6 hens' cavities. Pour 1 cup of cider over top of hens.

Roast hens in the oven for 1 hour, basting occasionally with pan juices. Hens should be golden in color when done. Remove hens to a serving platter and cover to keep them warm.

On the stovetop, in a saucepan or in the game-hen baking pan if it is stovetop safe, add remaining 1 cup apple cider and loosen browned bits from the bottom of the pan while cooking on low heat—a process called deglazing. Simmer until liquid has been reduced slightly (which intensifies the flavors), 5 to 10 minutes. Strain off any excess fat with a baster, if you have one, or carefully pour off any fat.

Mix cornstarch with enough water to make a smooth, thin paste; gradually add it to cider mixture, stirring continuously. Simmer for a few minutes until the sauce thickens slightly. Season to taste with salt and pepper. Strain sauce and add butter, if desired, for a more complex flavor.

Serve the game hens family-style on a large platter surrounded by Roasted Potatoes with Sage and Garlic and garnished with pickled crab apples. Drizzle the Apple Cider Sauce on top of the roasted game hens or serve it in a side dish.

Roasted Potatoes with Sage and Garlic
SERVES 6

Red potatoes or Yukon Golds are particularly well suited to roasting. Both have a firm texture (the trade calls it "waxy") that roasts well. Their color also looks attractive on a platter. The yellow interior of a Yukon Gold looks especially pretty here.

7 or 8 medium potatoes, scrubbed and cut into thick slices (do not peel)
2 tablespoons or more olive oil
2 to 4 tablespoons fresh sage, minced
2 to 4 large garlic cloves, minced
Salt and white pepper

Toss potatoes with olive oil, sage, and garlic; season to taste with salt and pepper. Place in a baking pan and roast at 375° F for 1 hour, turning occasionally. (The potatoes can be roasted at the same time as the game hens, but use a different pan.)

Poached Pears with Caramel and Pistachios
SERVES 6

Caramel and apples are the traditional fall medley, but pears can be matched with this sweet, rich sauce just as tastefully for a light dessert. Here they are poached first in a sugar syrup, then served with caramel sauce and crushed pistachios. Be sure to buy the pears at least a few days in advance to give them time to ripen before they are poached. To speed up the process, place them in a ripening bowl or in a closed paper bag.

POACHED PEARS
1 vanilla bean (see Note)
6 cups water
⅔ cup sugar
2 tablespoons lemon juice
6 pears

CARAMEL SAUCE
About 40 caramels (to make ¾ cup sauce)
2 to 3 tablespoons milk or cream
1 cup uncolored pistachios, shelled and crushed, for garnish (uncolored because red or green won't do for this dessert)

FOR POACHED PEARS
Cut the vanilla bean in half lengthwise and scrape the seeds into a large saucepan with the bean, 6 cups water, sugar, and lemon juice.

Simmer over medium heat until the sugar is completely dissolved and a syrup is formed, about 5 minutes. Meanwhile, prepare the pears by peeling them and cutting them in half lengthwise. Use a melon baller or spoon to scrape out the interior core.

Add the pears to the hot liquid and return to a low simmer. Continue to simmer, covered, over low heat until the pears are tender when pierced with a knife, about 5 minutes, depending on ripeness of pear. Do not overcook the pears or they will fall apart.

Remove from heat and let the pears cool in the syrup. Drain well and set aside, or refrigerate if using later. (Can be made in advance to this point; cover when refrigerated. Bring to room temperature before serving.)

FOR CARAMEL SAUCE

Melt caramels slowly, adding a few tablespoons of milk or cream as needed to make a sauce thin enough drizzle.

To serve, present 2 pear halves on each individual plate. The caramel sauce can either be pooled underneath the pears or drizzled on top—or both. Garnish with crushed pistachios.

Note: *Vanilla beans are sold in the spice section of the supermarket.*

Make Ahead

UP TO A WEEK IN ADVANCE

Buy pears to assure that they are ripe in time.

UP TO 2 DAYS IN ADVANCE

Make flatbread dough to bake the next day.

UP TO A DAY IN ADVANCE

Make vinaigrette.

Prepare fish stock, if making your own (or make earlier and freeze).

Bake flatbread.

Make dough for tart.

UP TO 8 HOURS IN ADVANCE

Make orange supremes.

Clean seafood.

Prepare vegetable base for stew.

Make pear tart.

UP TO 1 HOUR IN ADVANCE

If you want flatbread freshly baked and hot from the oven, bake it now.

LAST-MINUTE PREP

Assemble the salad.

Reheat stew and add seafood.

Reheat pear tart if desired.

FLAVORS OF SPAIN

For 6

Mixed Greens with Blood Oranges
Flatbread with Fresh Thyme and Black Peppercorns
Mediterranean Seafood Stew
Pear Tart with Walnuts and Cheese

IT'S MIDWINTER. We've shoveled enough of the white stuff for a while. We need adventure. Think sun-dappled sea, bite-size tapas nibbled with a glass of sherry. If that doesn't melt your mood, concentrate on grapevines and flamenco dancers. Think Spain. (Never mind that it's winter there, too. This is your daydream.)

Head to the kitchen where you can indulge in Spanish flavors with a winter menu dripping with olive oil, fragrant with pungent garlic and manchego cheese, brought to life with foods from the sea.

Snow? What snow?

This menu is for those with a sense of adventure, for cooks who don't mind dinner staring back at them (read on about the fish stock). Half the intrigue of cooking is creating a new dish for the first time, experimenting with an unfamiliar technique, or sampling a new flavor.

Many travelers and restaurant-goers already are familiar with some foods of Spain: tapas, paellas, flans, and garlic soups. These foods are nourishing and robust, made simply with down-to-earth ingredients.

Take advantage of those post-skating or skiing outings or even a Super Bowl gathering to find your sense of adventure with Spanish flavors in the following menu.

Good eating! *Que aproveche!*

Mixed Greens with Blood Oranges
SERVES 6

This simple green salad is heavy with garlic. As the defining characteristic, the garlic used for the vinaigrette is best fresh, since commercially prepared minced garlic loses its pungency in the jar. Blood oranges are small with a vivid red interior; they are available in the winter. Other oranges could be substituted.

VINAIGRETTE
¼ cup olive oil
4 garlic cloves, finely minced
1 tablespoon sherry vinegar or white wine vinegar
Salt

SALAD
1 small bunch red leaf lettuce, leaves pulled apart
1 small bunch green leaf lettuce, leaves pulled apart
2 or 3 blood oranges (or clementines or navel oranges; see Note)

Continued on page 262.

Beverage

For starters, try the traditional Spanish aperitif, fino sherry, delicate and very dry, noted for its fragrance and pale color. Some prefer their dry sherry cool; others prefer it with ice. For the stew, try a Rioja, a dry Spanish wine similar to a French Bordeaux, or a rosado (a Spanish rosé) made of garanacha or tempranillo.

For dessert, serve Harveys Bristol Cream Sherry, a sweetened sherry that can be drunk at room temperature or chilled. Despite its name, this beverage is from Spain, as are all true sherries.

FOR VINAIGRETTE

Warm oil in skillet over low heat and add garlic. Cook until garlic begins to turn color. Remove from heat and let cool.

In a small bowl, mix together vinegar and garlic oil. Season to taste with salt. (Can be made a day ahead; store in a glass jar in the refrigerator.)

FOR SALAD ASSEMBLY

Prepare oranges: Cut off top and bottom of orange, slicing through the white pulp. Using a sharp knife, cut off the remaining peel all the way to the actual fruit, removing all the white pulp and outside membrane of the orange. To remove the orange pieces, use a sharp knife to cut out the individual segments. Store in the refrigerator, covered, until ready to use.

Just before serving, toss greens with vinaigrette in a large bowl; divide among 6 individual salad plates. Garnish each plate with three segments of orange.

Note: *The salad is garnished with what chefs call a "supreme" (pronounced su-PREHM, and not su-PREME) of orange segments, which are simply orange sections taken out of the tough white membranes that encase them. The same procedure can be used on grapefruit. For both, the fruit is prettier, as well as easier and more pleasant to eat in salads, when the membranes are removed. If you're trying this for the first time, you may want to experiment on an extra piece of fruit. (There is some waste of fruit, too, with this.)*

Flatbread with Fresh Thyme and Black Peppercorns
MAKES 4 FLATBREADS

This bread is a keeper, whether or not the meal is Spanish in flavor. Simple to make, it's a cross between Italian focaccia and a pizza crust (for which it could be used at another meal). The bread can be made in advance, then served at room temperature or heated slightly. Or it could be rolled out an hour before mealtime and served hot out of the oven. Though the bread is almost effortless to make, some cooks still won't have time to prepare it.

In that case, the seasonings can be added to dress up commercially prepared focaccia, which is readily available at supermarket bakeries. Or simply substitute a hard, crusty French loaf. This flatbread is adapted slightly from *Season in Spain* by Ann and Larry Walker.

1½ cups warm water (105° to 115° F)
1 tablespoon yeast (slightly less than 1½ packages)
2 tablespoons olive oil
1½ teaspoons salt
4 cups flour, divided
Cornmeal
Olive oil
Fresh thyme, chopped
Black peppercorns, freshly ground

In the bowl of an electric mixer, stir together 1½ cups warm water and yeast and let sit for about about 5 minutes while the yeast dissolves. Using the mixer, combine the oil, salt, and 1 cup of the flour. Mix in the remaining flour. Do not add more flour, even if the dough is sticky.

Oil a bowl and roll dough in the bowl to coat the dough with oil. Cover the bowl and let dough rise, in a warm place, to double its size, about 45 minutes. Punch dough down and divide into quarters. (Can be done a day ahead up to this point. You also can bake the bread a day ahead, or, if you want to bake it immediately before serving, refrigerate the dough until ready to use. If it has risen, punch it down again, and let it warm up slightly before rolling it out.)

Preheat oven to 450° F. Lightly sprinkle 2 ungreased baking sheets with cornmeal.

Roll the dough out into long oval shapes (you won't need to flour the rolling surface for this), about 11 x 6 inches. Place dough on the baking sheets and brush with a little olive oil. Sprinkle fresh thyme and freshly ground black pepper on top.

Cover dough with a clean cloth and let rest for about 10 minutes, then bake for about 15 minutes, or until the flatbread is golden underneath and cooked through. Serve immediately warm, or at room temperature.

Mediterranean Seafood Stew

SERVES 6

8 cups fish stock (see recipe)

12 clams

12 mussels

12 sea scallops

12 medium-size shrimp

2 tablespoons olive oil

6 garlic cloves, peeled and minced

1 large onion, chopped (about 1 cup)

3 slices lemon

A few strands saffron, crushed (optional, see Note)

2 sprigs fresh thyme, chopped

2 sprigs parsley

Salt and freshly ground pepper

1 (16-ounce) can whole Italian plum tomatoes, chopped

Prepare fish stock as directed (preferably a day or more ahead), or use commercially made fish broth. When you are ready to make the stew, bring fish stock to a simmer in a 3-quart stockpot while cleaning the seafood.

Be sure both the clam and mussel shells are tightly closed before cooking them. If the mussel shells are slightly open, poke a knife inside and touch the mussel. If the mussel is still alive, as it should be, it will slowly close its shell; if not, discard opened shells. The same is true for the clam shells.

Scrub exterior of clam and mussel shells with a vegetable brush to remove sand, and rinse under cold water. Barnacles and the fuzz on the mussel shell that is called a "beard" can be cut off with a sharp knife. Peel and devein shrimp; scallops don't need to be rinsed unless their juices smell slightly off.

Heat olive oil in a skillet and sauté garlic and onion until soft. Add to simmering stock, along with lemon, saffron, thyme, and parsley. Season to taste with salt and pepper. (Can be made in advance to this point.)

Immediately before serving, add clams and mussels first to the broth; cook until shells are just barely beginning to open, about 5 minutes. Add tomatoes with juice, scallops, and shrimp; cook until done (scallops will turn opaque; shrimp will be pink), about 5 minutes. Serve immediately.

COOK'S NOTES

The French prepare bouillabaisse; Italian-Americans in San Francisco make cioppino. Both are hearty stews made of fish, shellfish, herbs, and tomatoes. Spain has its own version, though the name for it varies from region to region. What all these stews have in common is that they're made from whatever seafood is fresh and available at the moment the cook is ready. In a similar spirit, this Spanish stew gets a midwestern twang with elements that are easy to obtain in this area. Perhaps not authentic in Spanish cuisine, this version is true to the spirit of using whatever seafood is available.

In the Midwest that includes mussels, clams, sea scallops, and shrimp, which can be purchased at most fish counters. The traditional Spanish components of octopus and squid are omitted on the basis that the novelty might push some cooks right over the snowbank. But if either has a spot on your list of favorites, by all means add one or both.

The stew begins with a fish stock base that can be made from scratch or purchased from some seafood purveyors and restaurants. Some upscale supermarkets sell seafood stock in waxed boxes (similar to the containers for juice drinks), called aseptic packaging, in the soup section. If you're making it yourself, the stock can be made easily at home, though the shopping effort takes some tenacity, so plan ahead (see Cook's Notes on page 267).

For the stew, figure about two per person of the clams, mussels, scallops, and shrimp. If you're squeamish about clams or mussels, use more of the others, or add some chunks of other white fish, such as halibut or cod. And don't be surprised by the smaller than usual amount of broth. The servings may have less liquid but the seafood itself is quite filling.

Fish Stock

MAKES ABOUT 8 CUPS

2 tablespoons olive oil
1 large onion, sliced
1 small carrot, sliced
1 small celery rib with leaves, sliced
8 cups cold water
About 5 to 6 pounds fish bones (heads, frames, trimmings)
    or shellfish trimmings, rinsed
6 parsley sprigs with stems
6 fresh thyme sprigs
1 bay leaf
8 peppercorns
2 slices of lemon
1½ cups dry white wine

Heat olive oil in 10-quart pot and add onion, carrot, and celery. Cook, stirring occasionally, until the vegetables are soft, about 10 minutes. Add 8 cups cold water and fish parts to pot and bring mixture slowly to a simmer. (Do not boil or the stock will get cloudy.)

Add parsley, thyme, bay leaf, peppercorns, lemon slices, and white wine. Cover the pan partially and simmer slowly for about 40 minutes. Skim off any foam that forms on the top.

Strain stock and cool. Refrigerate; then discard any fat that has risen to the surface. Refrigerate and use within a few days or freeze.

COOK'S NOTES

Fish bones are not as easy to find in the Midwest as on the coasts, because much of the fish sold locally is processed (cut up and filleted) before it arrives in the heartland. Ask at your supermarket for fish bones to be ordered. Some larger grocery stores also sell fish parts. Salmon heads and bones are often available locally, though they are not traditionally used because they give the stock a distinctly salmon flavor. The bones and trimmings from white fish, such as cod or halibut, are preferred. But with our spirit of adventure, use whatever you can find. Whole trout is readily available and will suffice, though it's not as flavorful as saltwater fish. Fish fillets aren't an option; they won't impart as much flavor as the bones.

To make the broth as flavorful as possible, gather whatever fish you can find from the local resources you have at hand, then add an assortment of other seafood tastes: a few mussels or clams, a couple of crab legs. Even shells from the shrimp you'll later use in the stew make a good addition. (If you happen to indulge in lobster tails occasionally, freeze the shell until you're ready to make a stock. The same is true of walleye caught in the summer; save the trimmings in the freezer.) All this will give the broth an added dimension. Makes the stock at least a day in advance as it's not particularly fragrant when cooking.

Pear Tart with Walnuts and Cheese
MAKES 6 TO 8 SERVINGS

Winter pears, manchego cheese, and walnuts make up this tart, which in the Spanish tradition is simple and not overly sweet. (A slice of fruit and a wedge of cheese are perfectly acceptable to end a Spanish meal.) Even dessert fanciers will give this tart a favorable nod despite its homespun flavors. What sets it apart from the usual fruit tart is the addition of manchego (mahn-CHAY-goh), Spain's most famous cheese. Made from sheep's milk, manchego is similar in flavor and texture to Italy's Parmesan or Asiago cheese, either of which can be substituted. Manchego is available at specialty cheese shops. To keep a thread of the Spanish tradition, serve the tart with slices of manchego. This recipe has been adapted from *Season in Spain* by Ann and Larry Walker.

CRUST
1½ cups flour
Pinch salt
1 teaspoon sugar
8 tablespoons (1 stick) cold butter, cut into small pieces
3 tablespoons ice water

FILLING
¼ cup flour
1½ cups grated sharp cheese (manchego, Asiago, or Parmesan)
5 large pears (about 3 pounds), peeled, cored, and cut into small chunks
    (see Notes)
2 (2-ounce) packages walnut pieces, coarsely chopped
½ cup sugar
Grated zest of 1 lemon

FOR CRUST
With a fork or a food processor, mix together 1½ cups flour, salt, and 1 teaspoon sugar. Cut in (or pulse) butter into flour until particles are the size of small peas. Add the cold water a tablespoon at a time, until the flour is thoroughly moistened and the pastry can be easily gathered into a ball. Flatten the pastry and wrap it in plastic wrap; refrigerate for at least

30 minutes. (Can be made a day ahead; then warm up slightly to make it pliable enough to be rolled out.)

Preheat oven to 350° F.

Roll out dough into an 11- or 12-inch circle on a floured surface. Transfer the dough to a 9- or 10-inch pan, preferably a tart pan with a removable rim. (The crimped edges of the tart pan make it look pretty, but a regular pie pan could also be used.) Parbake tart shell in the oven for 5 to 8 minutes to prevent crust from getting soggy.

FOR FILLING

Increase oven temperature to 400° F. Mix ¼ cup flour with cheese, and toss with pear chunks, walnuts, ½ cup sugar, and lemon zest. Place in crust. Bake for 15 minutes. Lower oven temperature to 350° F and bake until tart is golden and fruit is tender, about 45 to 55 minutes more. The tart is best served warm. If made in advance, reheat, covered, at 350° F.

Notes:

- *Since ripe pears are about as likely in midwestern markets as Maine lobsters in Lake Superior, the key to making this dessert is to buy the pears a few days in advance of when needed. The pears will ripen faster if stored in a closed paper bag or fruit-ripening bowl.*

- *If you prefer to make the tart the same day, but are pressed for time, one easy shortcut is to use a commercial pie crust, which will speed up the effort considerably. The filling itself takes only a few minutes to assemble.*

UP TO A WEEK IN ADVANCE

Prepare meatballs and freeze.

UP TO A DAY IN ADVANCE

Partially cook the three pastas
(see Cooking Pasta in Advance
on page 273).

Caramelize onions and cook
mushrooms for sauce.

Make roasted garlic butter.

Make vinaigrette.

Prepare Provençal mixture.

Make Chocolate Espresso Bars.

LAST-MINUTE PREP

Assemble salad.

Reheat meatballs in the oven.

Make Ricotta Marinara.

Reheat Caramelized Onions
and Mushrooms.

Finish cooking the three pastas.

Toss each pasta with its respec-
tive sauce.

| Shortcut Savvy |

Use commercially prepared
marinara sauce.

Buy premade frozen meatballs.

Use packaged lettuce.

Buy prepared roasted garlic
butter.

Buy bread from bakery.

Buy prepared bar cookies.

PASTA PARTY

For 8

Mixed Greens with Simple Vinaigrette
Pasta with Three Sauces
    Spaghetti with Ricotta Marinara and Meatballs
    Farfalle Provençal
    Penne with Caramelized Onions and Mushrooms
Rustic Bread with Roasted Garlic Butter
Chocolate-Espresso Bars

WHEN I WAS A KID, we referred to pasta as noodles and smothered it with American cheese. When we were trying to be fashionable, we bought extra-long spaghetti (we called it spaghetti noodles to differentiate it from macaroni noodles, which most others called elbow macaroni) and topped it with our version of the traditional long-simmered sauce.

An Italian—even an Italian-American—probably would have shuddered at such midwestern atrocities to an old cuisine. We wouldn't have cared. Who wanted authentic? We just wanted a meal that tasted good and that, frankly, seemed a bit exotic.

In that spirit, here are midwestern versions of pasta favorites. These won't be mistaken for authentic Italian cuisine. But we don't care. It tastes good—really good—and that's all that matters. In fact, it's good enough for company this winter, whether it's a gathering around the TV during Sunday football, an impromptu after-sledding party, or the neighbors stopping by after a date with the snowblower.

The recipes that follow are adaptable in quantity and ingredients. You can feed many or few, depending on who is visiting. That is why many of the ingredients are listed as approximations. (With hearty eaters, cook more pasta; if they eat like birds, make less. And if you don't like capers, don't use them. No one will notice.)

Three pastas serve as the basis for this menu. With different shapes and different sauces, they offer plenty of variety in flavor (as well as provoke the eternal question of why, given the same ingredients, do noodles of different shapes seem to taste different?).

For the hard-to-please diner who gets nervous when anything out of the ordinary is placed on a plate—there's one in every crowd and you know who they are—we offer a familiar sauce. That is, familiar but not predictable. Ricotta marinara sauce is simply a little ricotta cheese added to a bottled marinara sauce (and there are plenty of good ones out there), or to your own favorite homemade version. The ricotta makes a big flavor difference, giving the sauce a lasagna-like flavor.

Add meatballs, either from the market or the make-your-own, Swedish-influenced ones included here (this is a global culinary world). Toss

Beverage

Start out with vermouth bianco (a sweet white wine with an orange twist). Turn to a rustic Italian, such as primitivo or corvo rosso (Sicilian) for the pasta. To pair with the chocolate espresso bars, offer a cordial of Chambord, the raspberry liqueur.

with familiar strands of spaghetti, and you've got a dish with enough interest for the gourmet as well as for the pasta-phobic.

For the more adventurous, a Provençal sauce offers an incredibly easy, uncooked sauce with the sun-baked flavors of the French countryside. (We can use all the sun-baking we can get this time of year.) In this case, the sauce is tossed with farfalle (fahr-FAH-lay), a pasta shaped like a butterfly or bowtie.

You could, of course, spend more time on the sauce by roasting your own out-of-season red sweet peppers, marinating your own artichoke hearts, and pitting deli-bought kalamata olives. But that's unnecessary, unless you have an incredible amount of time on your hands. All the ingredients are readily available in jars on many grocery shelves (often along the aisle with the olives). That includes capers, the tiny, pickled flower buds that come in a range of sizes, from the petite variety (remarkably similar in appearance to rabbit pellets) to ones as large as your thumb.

Though the Provençal sauce traces its roots to France, its practical nature makes it fit for the Midwest. This is a dish many of our grandmothers would have loved, made from preserved vegetables, ready to use when pulled from the cellar or pantry. For a more plebian name, you could just as well call the dish Pantry Pasta.

The only sauce that requires a little time—but hardly any more effort—is one with caramelized onions and mushrooms.

Buon appetito. Or as we say in the Midwest, "Please pass the noodles."

Mixed Greens with Simple Vinaigrette
SERVES 8

Whether or not this salad is interesting will depend on your choice of greens. Unless you have guests who demand iceberg (it is winter, after all), try some more unusual and colorful combinations, such as the blends of baby greens that include radicchio, frisée, and red oak.

⅓ cup white wine vinegar
1 teaspoon Dijon mustard
⅓ cup extra-virgin olive oil
Salt and freshly ground black pepper
8 cups mixed greens
Chopped green onions (optional)

Whisk together vinegar and mustard. Gradually whisk in olive oil. Season to taste with salt and pepper. Toss with greens and onions.

COOKING PASTA IN ADVANCE

Preparing three pastas for a crowd usually would require three sets of pans, or much time repeating the process. But it can be simplified. Many restaurants prepare pasta in advance by cooking it almost to al dente (firm to the bite, chewy but neither hard nor soft). *Almost* is the crucial word. The pasta is still firm, and it's definitely not done, but it's almost done. Then it's quickly rinsed in cold water, drained thoroughly, and tossed with a little olive oil to keep it from sticking together. The pasta is then covered and refrigerated. Immediately before serving, that same pasta is dipped into boiling water just for a moment to refresh and finish it off. Then it's drained (but not rinsed) and tossed with the sauce.

To simplify the process further, this all can be done with a pasta pot, a large stockpot-like pan with a sort of colander apparatus that holds the pasta. When the pasta is done, the colander with the pasta is lifted out and the boiling water is ready for the next batch. Kitchen shops and many department stores carry the pasta pots. Another option is to microwave the pasta to warm it up. (And, yes, restaurants do that, too.)

Spaghetti with Ricotta Marinara and Meatballs

SERVES 8 IN COMBINATION WITH OTHER PASTAS
OR 4 TO 6 AS A SINGLE ENTRÉE; MAKES 24 (1½-INCH) MEATBALLS

The ricotta in this recipe changes the color of the sauce from the deep red of a traditional marinara sauce to a salmon hue. If you've got a really hungry crowd, you may want to double the recipe. Adapted from a Swedish recipe from Louie Kahnk of Fridley, Minnesota.

RICOTTA MARINARA

1 jar commercial marinara sauce (about 26 ounces)

4 to 8 ounces ricotta cheese

16 ounces cooked spaghetti

20 or more cooked meatballs (recipe follows)

1 tablespoon chopped, fresh flat-leaf parsley

Freshly grated Parmesan or Romano cheese

MEATBALLS

1 cup (½-inch) bread cubes, cut from soft bread

¼ cup milk

1 small onion, finely chopped (about ½ cup)

2 tablespoons butter

1 pound ground beef

½ pound ground pork

1 tablespoon very fine bread crumbs

1 teaspoon paprika

½ teaspoon poultry seasoning

½ teaspoon salt

¼ teaspoon pepper

1 egg, beaten

FOR SAUCE

Heat marinara sauce gently. Break up ricotta cheese and add to marinara to heat slightly. (The ricotta does not have to be blended in thoroughly; in fact, it looks more interesting if it is not.)

Top cooked pasta with marinara sauce and meatballs. Garnish with parsley. Pass Parmesan or Romano cheese on the side, to add as desired.

FOR MEATBALLS

Preheat oven to 350° F.

In a large bowl, soak bread cubes in milk; squeeze cubes dry and discard remaining milk. Melt butter in skillet and sauté onion until translucent.

To the bowl with the bread cubes, add the ground beef, ground pork, sautéed onion, bread crumbs, paprika, poultry seasoning, salt, pepper, and egg. Mix well with your hands. Shape meat mixture into 24 (1½-inch) balls.

Cover a jelly roll pan in aluminum foil. Place meatballs on the aluminum foil and bake until cooked through, about 15 to 20 minutes. (Meatballs can be frozen at this point; then thawed and reheated before served on pasta.)

Farfalle Provençal

SERVES 8 IN COMBINATION WITH OTHER PASTAS;
OR 4 TO 6 AS A SINGLE ENTRÉE

Provençal (proh-vahn-SAHL) refers to the customs of the region of Provence in southeastern France, which borders the Mediterranean Sea, where the ingredients in this recipe are common. Farfalle (fahr-FAH-lay) is often called bow-tie pasta.

1 (12-ounce) jar roasted sweet red peppers, sliced
½ cup kalamata olives, pitted
1 (12-ounce) jar marinated artichoke hearts, cut into small chunks
1 to 2 tablespoons capers
12 to 16 ounces cooked farfalle (bow-tie pasta)
1 to 2 tablespoons julienned fresh basil

Drain peppers, olives, artichokes, and capers well. Toss together in a large bowl with cooked pasta. Garnish with basil and serve.

Penne with Caramelized Onions and Mushrooms

SERVES 8 IN COMBINATION WITH OTHER PASTAS;
OR 4 TO 6 AS A SINGLE ENTRÉE

Add whichever type of mushroom you prefer. To make it a little more interesting, use a mushroom other than the white button variety; cremini or shiitake work well. The quantity of mushrooms varies, as indicated, because the packages they come in range from 4 to 8 ounces; use up whatever is in the package.

4 tablespoons olive oil, divided
5 to 6 large onions, sliced (about 5 to 6 cups)
8 to 12 ounces fresh mushrooms, sliced; reserve several smaller ones
    whole, for garnish
Salt and freshly ground pepper
12 to 16 ounces cooked penne pasta
1 tablespoon chopped fresh thyme
Freshly grated or shaved Parmesan or Romano

Heat 3 tablespoons oil in large pan over low heat. Add onions, cover, and cook until the onions have turned golden brown, about 45 minutes to 1 hour, stirring occasionally.

In a separate pan, heat 1 tablespoon olive oil over medium heat. Add all of the mushrooms to the pan except for the ones being saved for the garnish. Sauté until slightly cooked, about 5 to 10 minutes (you don't want the mushrooms totally limp, but more tender than raw). Add sautéed mushrooms to caramelized onions. (Can be done a day in advance to this point.)

To serve, if sauce was prepared ahead, reheat over low heat, covered, with 2 tablespoons water added.

Toss cooked pasta with onion-mushroom mixture and place on a serving dish or on individual plates; sprinkle fresh thyme over pasta and garnish with the whole mushrooms. Pass Parmesan or Romano cheese on the side, to add as desired.

COOK'S NOTES

Penne (PEN-neh) is pasta shaped like a narrow tube (the word means "pen") with ends that are cut at an angle (like a quill pen). It comes in various diameters, and with either a smooth surface or a ribbed surface (which is called penne rigate).

Roasted Garlic Butter

MAKES ABOUT 1½ CUPS

Serve this butter with a loaf—or two or three—of rustic artisan bread purchased from a bakery or the bakery section of a supermarket. One head of garlic makes a mild-flavored spread; if you've got garlic enthusiasts, try two heads of garlic.

1 head garlic
Olive oil
Salt and pepper
8 ounces (2 sticks) butter, softened (do not use margarine or spreads)
1 to 2 teaspoons finely chopped fresh parsley (optional)

Preheat oven to 400° F.

Pull away most of the paperlike skin from the garlic bulb, but leave enough to hold the cloves together. Slice ¼- to ½-inch off the top to expose the cloves.

Place garlic head in a small pan or covered baking dish, drizzle with olive oil, and sprinkle with salt and pepper. Cover with aluminum foil or lid and bake for about 45 minutes to 1 hour, until cloves are tender when pierced with a toothpick or fork. Cool slightly.

With an electric mixer, whip butter until smooth. Gently squeeze garlic out of cloves and into the bowl with butter; add parsley, if desired. Beat together thoroughly. Place butter mixture in bowl and refrigerate, covered, until ready to use.

Chocolate-Espresso Bars
MAKES 18 TO 24 BARS

CRUST
8 tablespoons (1 stick) butter, melted
½ cup sugar
2 cups flour

FILLING
8 tablespoons (1 stick) butter
½ cup sugar
¼ cup unsweetened cocoa powder
2 cups heavy cream
2 teaspoons instant espresso powder (optional; see Note)
1 teaspoon vanilla
2 eggs

FOR CRUST
Preheat oven to 350° F.

Mix melted butter with ½ cup sugar and flour. Press into bottom and ¼ inch up sides of an ungreased 9 x 13-inch pan. Bake for 15 to 20 minutes, or until crust is lightly brown. Remove from oven and cool slightly.

FOR FILLING
Melt ½ cup butter in a medium saucepan over low heat. Add ½ cup sugar, cocoa powder, and cream. Increase heat to medium and cook, stirring frequently, until small bubbles appear at the edge of the pan. Remove from heat and add espresso powder and vanilla.

In a small bowl, lightly whisk eggs. Pour a little of the hot cream mixture into the eggs, whisking continuously. Add a little more cream mixture, whisking again. Then pour egg mixture into the remaining cream mixture in the saucepan. (This back-and-forth process prevents the eggs from starting to cook in the hot cream mixture.) Pour filling onto baked crust. Bake for another 10 minutes or until the filling is barely set. Cool. Cover and store in the refrigerator.

Note: *If you are using espresso flavor, be sure to use instant espresso powder (or a stronger-than-usual helping of instant coffee powder). Don't use ground espresso beans because they won't dissolve in the filling.*

LAST-MINUTE PARTY

For 6

Greens with Seared Scallops and Orange Vinaigrette
Mushroom Risotto
Steamed Broccolini
Popovers
Chocolate Cups with Ice Cream and Chocolate Sauce

NIGHT FALLS QUICKLY IN THE WINTER, and for some that means a time of hibernation. But not so for the cook, who sees the darkness as a challenge: it's time for a party, even a last-minute gathering of just-met friends.

Here's a menu you can throw together quickly, provided you make a quick stop at the store. Better yet, have your company help in the kitchen because this meal involves some frequent stirring. For dessert, if you're short of time, pick something up at the bakery or assemble an instant one with storebought chocolate dessert cups and whatever ice cream you prefer (or fresh fruit, lemon curd, or even pudding) for an instant—yet impressive—dessert.

Greens with Seared Scallops and Orange Vinaigrette
SERVES 6

Who says a salad is only green? For this, serve seared scallops atop greens for a show-stopper first course. Since the scallops are pricey, you could get away with a single plump scallop for the appetizer. Or splurge on two.

1 tablespoon frozen orange juice concentrate, thawed
1 tablespoon white wine vinegar
Salt and freshly ground black pepper
¼ cup extra-virgin olive oil, preferrably orange flavored (see Note)
12 sea scallops
1 to 2 tablespoons olive oil
3 cups mixed greens

Make vinaigrette by mixing orange juice concentrate and vinegar in a small bowl; season to taste with salt and pepper. Whisk in ¼ cup olive oil.

To prepare scallops, rinse them and pat dry. In a large frying pan over medium heat, add 1 to 2 tablespoons olive oil and, when it's hot, the scallops. Sear on both sides until light brown and cooked through, about 2 minutes per side, depending on thickness of scallop. (The scallops will turn opaque when done.)

To serve, portion greens among individual plates. Top each plate with 2 scallops and drizzle with vinaigrette.

Note: *To pump up the orange flavor in the vinaigrette, try using a blood-orange-flavored olive oil. To make your own, grate some orange zest into the olive oil you'll be using; store it in the refrigerator overnight and you'll have a fragrant oil. Discard any leftover oil because flavored oils, for food safety reasons, need to be pasteurized if stored for any length of time.*

Mushroom Risotto
SERVES 6

Choose a variety of mushrooms for the best flavor. The recipe calls for arborio or carnaroli rice, which are traditional risotto rices. Do not use regular long-grain rice. You'll need either a very large frying pan or two smaller ones to accommodate all the ingredients and be able to stir them easily. An extra pair of hands will be helpful for this dish; make this an interactive meal and ask for help. Note that the operational word in this recipe is "stir." The finished dish will be creamy.

About 1½ cups (1½ ounces) dried mushrooms, such as porcinis
4 cups boiling water
About 5 cups chicken stock
Salt
4 tablespoons extra-virgin olive oil, divided
½ cup finely chopped onions
1 pound fresh mushrooms, trimmed and cut into thick slices
3 large garlic cloves, minced
¾ to 1½ teaspoons fresh thyme (or ½ to ¾ teaspoon dried thyme)
2 cups arborio or carnaroli rice
¾ cup dry white wine (such as pinot grigio or sauvignon blanc), or water
½ cup freshly grated Parmesan, or more
⅓ cup chopped fresh flat-leaf parsley

Place dried mushrooms in a large bowl and pour 4 cups boiling water over them. Let sit for 30 minutes to reconstitute, then drain, reserving the liquid and squeezing the mushrooms to remove all the liquid. Coarsely chop the mushrooms and set aside.

Measure the mushroom liquid into a large saucepan and add enough chicken stock to equal 9 cups. If stock is unsalted, add about ½ teaspoon salt. Bring the liquid to a simmer in a covered saucepan and keep it at a low simmer.

Meanwhile, heat 2 tablespoons oil in a large heavy pan. Add the onion and cook, stirring, until soft and translucent. Add both reconstituted and fresh mushrooms. Cook, stirring occasionally, until mushrooms begin to release their liquid. Add garlic and thyme. Cook, stirring, until mushroom liquid has just about evaporated. Add the remaining 2 tablespoons oil and rice; stir to coat rice with oil.

Stir in wine or water and cook over medium heat, stirring constantly. When the wine has just about evaporated, stir in about ½ cup of simmering broth, or enough to just cover the rice. Cook, stirring often, until broth is just about absorbed, making sure to swipe the sides and bottom of the pan. Add another ½ cup of broth and continue to cook, slowly adding more broth when rice is almost dry. Continue this process for about 20 minutes or more, until most of broth has been used and rice is al dente (chewy but not hard in the middle). Check the seasoning and add more salt, if needed.

Add a final ½ cup of broth and stir in the Parmesan and parsley. You may have some leftover broth; save it for another use. The risotto consistency should be like a creamy porridge.

Variation: Make Mushroom-Spinach Risotto by adding ½ pound cooked chopped (and well-drained) spinach to the cooked risotto immediately before serving.

Steamed Broccolini
SERVES 6

Don't remember broccolini from your childhood? Not surprising because it's a trademarked hybrid, sometimes called baby broccoli. This is a cross between broccoli and Chinese kale, which gives it slender stalks with tiny buds at the top that look like the head of a broccoli stalk. The flavor is a bit peppery. It's usually sold packaged and in the refrigerated part of the produce section. Broccoli can be substituted.

3 bunches (about 2 pounds) broccolini or broccoli
Juice of ½ lemon
Salt

Steam broccolini over a pot of boiling water for about 5 minutes or until the stalks are tender but still have some bite. Sprinkle with lemon juice and a little salt.

Continued on page 284.

Variation: After steaming the broccolini, plunge it into cold water to stop the cooking; then drain. In a frying pan over medium heat, warm up 2 tablespoons olive oil and a garlic clove for a few minutes. Sprinkle with a little lemon juice, salt, and pepper, toss with broccolini, and serve.

Popovers
MAKES 6

My family visits restaurants that serve popovers solely because of these puffy delights. Hot and steamy, served straight from the oven, these are the gold standard for bread, especially on a chilly night. Popover pans or deep muffin tins will give you the biggest popovers. The batter can be made up to a day in advance and refrigerated. Remove it from the refrigerator about 20 minutes before baking the popovers.

Nonstick spray, for greasing
3 eggs
1 cup milk
4 tablespoons (½ stick) butter, melted
1 cup flour
¼ teaspoon salt

Preheat oven to 400° F. Grease a 12-count muffin pan with nonstick spray. Preheat the pan for at least 10 minutes.

In a large bowl, beat eggs until frothy. Add milk and butter, mixing well.

In a separate bowl, stir together flour and salt. Add flour mixture to milk mixture, stirring just enough to moisten dry ingredients (do not overmix).

When the batter is ready, take the hot muffin pan out of the oven and pour batter to fill cups half to two-thirds full. Bake for 30 to 40 minutes, or until puffy and well browned. Serve immediately.

Variation: Add a little grated Parmesan or fresh minced herbs to the batter. Or add ¼ cup crumbled blue cheese for a tangy popover.

Chocolate Cups with Ice Cream and Chocolate Sauce
SERVES 6

This is an instant dessert. Chocolate cups are available at upscale super-markets, usually in the baking department. Simply add a scoop of ice cream or sorbet and you're both set and elegant.

4 ounces semisweet chocolate
5 tablespoons milk
6 chocolate cups
1 pint ice cream, frozen yogurt, or sorbet (chocolate-cherry is
    particularly good)

Melt chocolate over low heat. Stir in milk gradually to make sauce. Place chocolate cups on individual plates. Fill with small scoop of ice cream. Drizzle with hot chocolate sauce, and serve immediately.

For 2

Kir Royale
Butterhead Lettuce with Pomegranates and Toasted Walnuts
Swiss Fondue, or
Châteaubriand with Wild Mushrooms and Madeira
Chocolate Soufflé for Two

"I'M HUNGRY," SHE WHISPERED, and brushed aside the loose tendrils of auburn hair that fell across her heart-shaped face.

"Hungry for what?" he asked, with a hopeful glint in the eye, his broad shoulders crowding the two cooks in the kitchen.

"Hungry for fondue," she said, reaching for the grater. Her hazel eyes gazed longingly into his, then at the Swiss cheese in her hand.

"My burners are hot," she said, "and so am I." She reached for the controls and turned down the heat on the stovetop.

"I'm hot, too," he said feverishly. "I'm on fire." His billowy sleeve smoked as the gas flame caressed the fabric. He moaned as the flame kissed his arm.

In an instant, she rescued him, a damp towel in one hand, a glass of champagne in the other.

"Let me cool you off," she said, and smiled.

This is how your Valentine's Day dinner starts, right? Well, maybe only in movies—or romance novels.

There's a classic love scene on film that takes place outside an Italian restaurant. Two young sweethearts share a plate of spaghetti only to find that they are nibbling on the same strand. It's from Disney's "Lady and the Tramp"—and the sweethearts are two dogs.

Other than loved ones, few people share food off the same plate (except for kids—and we know how often they get sick).

Oh, there's the occasional bowl of dip with chips (from which we hope the others aren't double-dipping). The oversized container of popcorn (let's hope no one licks any fingers). A whole pizza with slices (don't grab the pepperoni off another's portion). A taste of someone's ice cream (germs don't grow in the cold, do they?). But, generally, sharing food is akin to using another's toothbrush—too close for comfort.

Consider, however, the power of sharing a meal with a loved one, especially your valentine. Not a dinner with separate place settings, but a meal in which lovers indulge together, dipping into the same fare, bonding, if you will, forkful by forkful.

A meal such as this has the potential to be the most powerful aphrodisiac of all. Who needs oysters? Artichokes? Truffles?

As Omar Khayyan wrote, "A jug of wine, a loaf of bread and thou." He wasn't planning to dine alone.

Need help with your meal of seduction? The following recipes will set you on the path. The rest of the journey is up to you.

To begin your meal, pop open a bottle of bubbly. True, you're likely to have separate glasses, but sparkling wine signifies something special to share. Better yet, intertwine arms with your loved one as you toast the evening—just like in the movies.

For the main course, there are two options, so as to offer a light or heavy alternative, or a choice if there are vegetarians in the mix. Fondue-for-two is one option to set the right tone for a valentine dinner. Dust off the fondue pot in the attic, or plan ahead and buy one. Unlike usual fondue etiquette, there's no need to worry about eating off the fondue forks in this meal for two. Another option is to indulge in a slab of Châteaubriand together, just like at the upscale restaurants. Carve it fireside and savor the flavor—and each other.

Dessert is also a joint affair. Scoop up a spoonful of rich chocolate in a warm soufflé for two. Whether or not it's an aphrodisiac, chocolate offers the sense of indulgence and decadence expected for a valentine dinner.

Kir Royale
SERVES 2

4 teaspoons crème de cassis (black-currant liqueur), divided
1 cup sparkling wine, divided

Pour 2 teaspoons crème de cassis in each of two glasses. Add ½ cup sparkling wine to each glass and serve immediately.

Butterhead Lettuce with Pomegranates and Toasted Walnuts

SERVES 2

Why pomegranates for this meal? Scholars think that Eve used a pomegranate—not an apple—in that famous scene in the Garden of Eden. Need I say more? You'll have leftover seeds and vinaigrette. Pomegranates are at the end of their season in early February, so you really need to plan ahead and buy one as early as possible. They keep well in the refrigerator for weeks. If you can't find one, substitute slices of fresh pear that have been dipped in lemon juice to prevent browning.

2 tablespoons to ¼ cup chopped walnuts
2 tablespoons (or more) pomegranate seeds (from 1 pomegranate)
1½ teaspoons red wine vinegar
4½ teaspoons balsamic vinegar
Salt and freshly cracked pepper
6 tablespoons extra-virgin olive oil
2 handfuls (about 2 cups) torn leaves of butterhead lettuce (such as butter or Boston)

Place walnuts in a dry saucepan to toast over low heat for 5 to 10 minutes, or until nuts become fragrant. Remove from heat and set aside to cool.

To seed pomegranate, make a slit in the center of the fruit big enough to insert both your thumbs. Then submerge fruit in a bowl of water, pulling fruit apart into two pieces. Still underwater, loosen seeds and pick off and discard the white pith. Drain seeds and pat dry. (Working under water prevents juice from squirting and staining anything it touches.)

To make vinaigrette, whisk both vinegars together; season to taste with salt and pepper. Whisk in olive oil.

To assemble salad, divide lettuce among two plates. Sprinkle walnuts and pomegranate seeds on top. Drizzle with vinaigrette.

Swiss Fondue
SERVES 2 OR MORE

You will need to make the fondue on the stovetop, where there is sufficient heat to melt the cheese. Then transfer the fondue pot to the warming stand, where it will be served. What to dip? Let your own food preferences guide you, whether it's a variety of vegetables (some precooked, some raw), bread, or sausage.

1¾ cups dry white wine
1 tablespoon lemon juice
1 pound Swiss cheese, finely diced
3 tablespoons flour
¼ teaspoon white pepper
¼ teaspoon nutmeg or paprika
Salt

FOR DIPPING
Cubed bread (from French or Italian loaves, bagels, or focaccia)
Mushroom caps
Boiled new potatoes
Grilled mini-sausages
Cherry tomatoes

Pour wine into a pot on the stovetop over low heat until bubbles start to rise to the surface; do not boil. Add lemon juice.

Meanwhile, place diced cheese in a bowl, sprinkle with flour, and mix lightly. Add cheese mixture a handful at a time to the wine, stirring constantly and making sure each handful is melted before the next is added.

Once all the cheese has melted, add pepper and either nutmeg or paprika, stirring until blended. Season to taste with salt.

To serve, arrange foods for dipping on a platter. Transfer the cheese mixture to a fondue pot over a warming stand.

Variation: Use half Swiss and half Gruyère cheese.

Variation: Use equal amounts Swiss cheese and caraway-seed-flavored cheese.

Variation: Sauté 1 cup chopped mushrooms in a little butter with a little minced onion. Cook the mushrooms until the vegetable liquid has evaporated. When the cheese fondue is ready to serve, stir in the mushroom mixture.

Variation: Peel and seed 2 tomatoes; chop very fine. When the cheese fondue is ready to serve, stir in the tomatoes.

Variation: This one includes no alcohol. Over low heat, melt 2 tablespoons butter in the fondue pot. Add flour and stir until smooth. Gradually add 2 cups milk, stirring to prevent lumps. Season to taste with salt, paprika, and nutmeg. Heat throughout; then gradually add 1 pound of finely diced white cheddar, handful by handful, making sure each addition has melted before adding more cheese to the pot.

You could substitute Brie or Camembert for the cheddar. (White cheddar is used, rather than the traditional orange, because its color is more appealing in this fondue.)

Châteaubriand with Wild Mushrooms and Madeira

SERVES 2 OR MORE

Châteaubriand is not a cut of beef, but a recipe named after a nineteenth-century French statesman, François Châteaubriand. The meat is simply a center cut from beef tenderloin, usually served with a flavorful sauce and vegetables. Adapted from *How to Cook Meat* by Christopher Schlesinger and John Willoughby.

CHÂTEAUBRIAND

1 (1 pound) beef tenderloin
Kosher salt
Freshly cracked black pepper
1 small onion, sliced (about ½ cup)
1 carrot, peeled and diced (about ½ cup)
1 rib celery, diced (about ¼ cup)
8 to 12 ounces wild mushrooms (porcini, portobellos, chanterelles, shiitakes), stems removed and reserved, thinly sliced (the quantity of mushrooms varies, as indicated, because the packages range in size from 4 to 8 ounces; use up whatever is in the package)
1 plum tomato, cored and diced
3 tablespoons olive oil

SAUCE

1 cup beef stock
2 tablespoons unsalted butter
¼ cup diced red onion
Mushroom slices (see above)
⅓ cup Madeira wine
1 cup beef broth
Kosher salt and freshly cracked black pepper

FOR CHÂTEAUBRIAND

Preheat oven to 500° F.

Pat meat dry with paper towels, then rub it all over with salt and pepper.

Place roast on a sturdy rack in a medium roasting pan. Scatter the onion, carrot, celery, mushroom stems (the slices will be used in the sauce) and tomato around the meat and drizzle olive oil over the vegetables. Place in the oven and roast until meat is well browned, about 20 minutes.

Reduce the oven temperature to 300° F, stir the vegetables around, and roast until the meat is done to your liking, 20 to 25 minutes more for rare.

To check for doneness, insert a meat thermometer into the center of the roast (see sidebar). Remove the meat from the oven 5 degrees before it reaches your preferred temperature. Transfer it to a serving plate and cover it loosely with aluminum foil. Allow it to rest for 10 to 20 minutes while you prepare the sauce (the temperature will rise during this time as the meat continues to cook).

FOR SAUCE

Melt the butter over medium heat in a large frying pan. Add the red onion and cook, stirring occasionally, until translucent, 7 to 9 minutes. Add the mushroom slices and cook, stirring occasionally, until they are cooked but not mushy, 5 to 7 minutes more. Add the Madeira and simmer until slightly reduced, 3 to 5 minutes. Add beef broth and simmer for 5 minutes more. Season to taste with salt and pepper.

To serve, cut the beef into slices about 1 inch thick and serve with the sauce.

Notes:

- *This recipe is versatile: If you are really pressed for time, you could skip making the sauce entirely and the meat would still be wonderful on its own.*
- *Want a potato with your meal? Bake two russets while the meat is roasting. Wash and poke with the tines of a fork a few times, and then place in oven. Bake until tender when pressed, about 1 hour.*

TEMPERATURES AND DONENESS

125° F	rare
135° F	medium rare
140° F	medium
150° F	medium well
160° F	well done

Chocolate Soufflé for Two
SERVES 2

This requires a 5-inch round baking dish, which holds about 2 cups.

SOUFFLÉ
2 (1-ounce) squares semisweet chocolate
2 eggs, separated
¼ cup sugar
½ teaspoon vanilla extract

CHOCOLATE SAUCE
2 (1-ounce) squares semisweet chocolate
3 tablespoons heavy cream
¼ to ½ teaspoon orange extract (optional)

FOR SOUFFLÉ
Preheat oven to 400° F, with the oven rack in the middle position.

Melt 2 squares of chocolate in microwave or over low heat in sauce-pan. Set aside to cool.

Separate egg whites from yolks and place them in separate bowls. Beat egg whites with an electric mixer until they form stiff peaks. Set aside.

Add sugar and vanilla to yolks and beat with an electric mixer or whisk for 1 minute, or until thick and light yellow. Add melted chocolate to yolk mixture a little bit at a time, and mix thoroughly. Fold in egg whites until no white is showing.

Pour the mixture into a 5-inch round (2-cup) ungreased baking dish. Bake for about 20 minutes, or until the soufflé has risen and the top is firm. Remove from oven.

FOR CHOCOLATE SAUCE
While the soufflé is baking, melt two squares of chocolate. Gradually add cream, mixing thoroughly; then mix in orange extract. If you want a thinner sauce, add a teaspoon or more cream.

Immediately after removing soufflé from the oven, pour chocolate sauce over it and serve with two spoons.

Acknowledgments

N
O WRITER WORKS ALONE. And that's true for cooks, too. Oh, we might think we do, isolated as we are in front of the computer—or at the stove. But at every stroke of the key or stir of the whisk are all those who have shown us the way in the past.

For me that means a long line of cooks who have shared the communion of both kitchen and table, from my grandmother Martha Nelson, whose holiday dinners included a raucous kids' corner, to my maternal aunts Joan Odden and Clarice Granz, who knew how to entertain. For as long as I remember, my mother and her sisters have traded recipes and talked about food with me. Their unflagging support and unexpected emails ("I loved that recipe!" and "What a great article in Taste!") helped me meet another day and another deadline. Everyone should have family like that.

My thanks go to Carmen Bonilla, who worked as food stylist on many of these menus as I developed them for the *Star Tribune*. She served a much broader role for me then and now, however, as she patiently answered my questions and offered a culinary tutorial on why recipes work and how to make them better. Both she and Ken Goff provided many of the wine recommendations.

The *Star Tribune* gave me the greatest gift over the years: a blank sheet. I could be as creative as I wanted, a generous benefit I eagerly grabbed. The newspaper has graciously allowed me to compile here many of the menus that ran earlier in newsprint. My

thanks also extend to the readers of the Taste section, whose stories, encouragement, and suggestions have inspired me for almost three decades.

Pamela McClanahan and the Minnesota Historical Society Press took a chance at a novice author and showed me the way of book publication. Michael Hanson finessed the copy to make it fit. Gretchen Bratvold asked all the right questions as copyeditor extraordinaire. Terri Hudoba assured that the index was as usable as the text. I greatly appreciate all of their skill and collaboration in bringing this book to fruition.

My children and their father were forced, by virtue of the absence of any other food, to eat sample menu after sample menu until I got the recipes just right. I like to think that the palates of Jenny, Elizabeth, and Eric have grown because of this—and that their psyches have not been damaged by too many variations on a theme. I seem to recall a particular phrase, "I will not eat any more pasta," after a particularly long stretch of sauce preparations that exasperated Michael Dean. Ten years later, I think he's finally recovered and will sample a noodle or two.

And, finally, for my mother and father, Laverne and Don Svitak, who babysat over the years while I was preparing dinner parties for others, a simple thank-you does not seem adequate. My parents showed me the importance of gathering friends and family around the dinner table. They started me on the path that I have so enthusiastically embraced. For this, and so much more, I am forever grateful.

Index

B

P

S

....

Come One, Come All was designed and set in type
by BRIAN DONAHUE in Minneapolis, Minnesota.
The typefaces are Requiem and Whitney.
Printed at Maple Press, York, Pennsylvania.

....